Widnall

Widnall

A CAPITAL CONTRIVER

*The story of a Victorian household
in the village of Grantchester*

CHRISTINE JENNINGS

Christine Jennings

FOLLY PRESS

Published by Folly Press
c/o Carol Green Publishing,
2 Station Road, Swavesey,
Cambridge CB4 5QJ, United Kingdom

First published in 2003

Printed in the United Kingdom at
the University Press, Cambridge

Design/typography by Dale Tomlinson
using Founder's Caslon™ type

*A catalogue record for this book is available
from the British Library*

ISBN 0 9544818 0 1 paperback

This book is dedicated to

PETER DUDLEY WARD

who, like

SAMUEL PAGE WIDNALL,

*has been a preserver of memories
and a capital contriver.*

*

The Parish Church, Grantchester – lithograph by William Fleetwood Varley c. 1820

Contents

Acknowledgements

SAMUEL PAGE WIDNALL would scarcely be remembered at all if Peter Ward had not, in the nick of time, collected all the volumes, photographs and models which provide the essential material for this account. I can only thank him for entrusting me with the task of attempting to tell the story of those Victorians whose lives left such an impression upon the Old Vicarage, Peter's own home for the greater part of his life, which he still loves deeply. Throughout, Peter has provided wonderful encouragement and – since it has taken so long – patience.

The present owners of the Old Vicarage love it too; and Mary Archer has been generous in her support for this enterprise, giving me access to her own collection of Widnalliana and the opportunity to wander in the garden and take my own photographs. In this book my final chapter tells just a little about the years following Aunt Lally's death. This period is described more fully in Mary Archer's own book, *Rupert Brooke and the Old Vicarage, Grantchester*.

No Widnall relatives have been traced; but I have received great kindness from descendants of the nieces and nephews on the Smith side: Wing-Cdr John Smith-Carington of Ashby Folville, Harry Smith-Carington and Peter Giles. Kevin Armstrong, formerly of Harston House, was also helpful, contributing a good deal about the Greene family.

Imperfect as it is, my text would have been even less coherent without the good advice given by David Wootton. Others who read and made valuable comments upon draft versions were Betty Bury, Joyce Baird and my daughter Pippa Goodhart.

The local history was derived from many sources. First of all I must acknowledge the flying start provided by the notes already compiled by Bill Clamp, a knowledgeable Old Inhabitant of the village. Archivists and librarians at the Shire Hall Record Office, the Cambridgeshire Collection, the University Library and the libraries of King's, St John's and Downing Colleges have all been helpful.

It is impossible to mention every individual from whom I have gleaned information. But the list must include George Bolton, Caroline Burkitt, Robin Callan of The Orchard, Monty Chisholm, Richenda Huxley, John Lester, Anthony Pemberton, Amanda Scrase, Ian Steen and Ann Stow. The Widnall model of Grantchester Church has just been expertly restored by Hugh Salt, and is now on public view.

Like so many women pursuing a private obsession and demanding time on the family computer, I owe endless thanks for the tolerance and support of my husband.

Introduction

SAMUEL PAGE WIDNALL, the subject of this book, was a village worthy. All his life was rooted in Grantchester, a village some three miles from Cambridge. He moved house only once, leaving his original home for a more romantic, venerable house about a hundred yards down the road. This was the Old Vicarage, a place which still bears his imprint.

Grantchester has changed a good deal since his time. Once secluded and self-sufficient, concerned with farming and its great watermill, it has become more suburban: from its tidy houses there is now a daily exodus by car to jobs in Cambridge or industrial enterprises nearby. But much remains, and a walk through the water-meadows, with a distant view of the roof of King's College Chapel caught in the light against a dark sky, still emphasizes the sense of its being a place apart. And it is thanks to S. P. Widnall, variously described as farmer, nurseryman, photographer, author, inventor and model-maker, that a pretty strong impression of the village as it used to be may be recovered. That 'child-man' could not resist using his many talents to record in photographs the appearance of his surroundings and its more notable inhabitants, and to make for posterity exact models of its notable buildings.

Almost all the source-material for my book, the collection of 'Widnalliana', is contained in one large cardboard box. It was gathered half a century ago by Peter Ward, then living at the Old Vicarage. His father, Dudley Ward, had been a steadfast friend of Rupert Brooke, that dazzling young scholar-poet who had gathered his friends (the 'Neo-Pagans' later known as the Bloomsbury Group) to share his delight in the corner of Grantchester where he had taken lodgings. A poem, written in a fit of homesickness when he was away in Berlin, expresses his affection for the place: *The Old Vicarage, Grantchester* is widely known and draws visitors to the village still. Brooke died early in the Great War. When the house was offered for sale some years later, his mother felt that Dudley Ward should have it; and that is how it came into the possession of his son, Peter. At that time a few old people in the village could still recall 'Uncle Page' Widnall, and rather more 'Aunt Lally'

Smith, his sister-in-law. They were legendary figures. A great-nephew described the ageing Widnall – 'Page looked like a Parson at first sight. But NOT <u>quite</u> on inspection! ... Always a round semi-clerical Hat (with a cabbage leaf inside in Summer)'. And memories of Aunt Lally would set off a twiddling of fingers beside the face, evoking the long ringlets which dangled beneath her lace cap – a fashion adopted in the 1840s and continued until her death.

*

It was in 1996 that I was assembling a small exhibition concerning the village's history. On show were a scale model of Grantchester Church, c1875, and another of the Manor House, both made by S. P. Widnall. But Peter Ward and his box of treasures had by then moved to Norfolk. I asked if I might see it, and drove over to Cley-next-the-Sea. There, I was not only allowed to look at the contents of his box, but – an even greater privilege – to take it away with me to enjoy and study more closely. In it I found several heavy leather-bound volumes: *Uncle Page's Book*, compiled from diaries kept throughout their lives by S. P. Widnall and Lally (Sarah) Smith; photograph albums; a holiday journal; some small books written and printed by S.P.W. himself; and recollections of the

Uncle Page's Book, combining the diaries of S. P. Widnall '(P)' and Lally Smith '(SS)'

Widnall household written by friends and a great-nephew. The diary provides the essential narrative, though in tantalisingly scrappy form; the photographs, despite their unsympathetic format, bring a sense of immediacy; Lally Smith's holiday journal, and her pupil Polly Greene's memoirs in prose and rhyme, are a delight.

From this material I intended to compile an article, or a short booklet. Yet, searching in libraries and public archives, the whole project widened and grew. 'WIDNALL' extends backwards to Page Widnall's parents and their once-famous Flower Gardens in Grantchester. It spreads sideways to include his wife's family and a great nursery business at Worcester; and on to a further generation involved in engineering projects and enhanced social status. Nor can one ignore the family's contacts with the increasingly lively university nearby. Page Widnall was a farmer, and his sister-in-law ran a little school in the house, yet their interests were never confined to those occupations.

The Old Vicarage trio, Mr & Mrs Widnall & Miss Smith, were total Victorians. Their dates actually correspond closely to those of the Queen (1819–1901) – Lally Smith, the eldest, living from 1822–1908. And their activities, for those who suppose middle-class Victorians to have been hidebound and repressed, are unexpectedly lively and joyful. Even their more curious pursuits – walking the hills to gather rare ferns, dressing-up and spouting comic verse, bizarre experiments with luminous paint – turn out to have been popular ones in their time. Throughout their lives ran that eager awareness of new developments in technology, exploration, the arts, antiquarian studies and natural history … for the Victorians were great self-educators, absorbing all that was offered in the publication of encyclopaedias and monthly journals, in sermons and public meetings.

*

Names: I refer to my central character as 'Page' or 'S.P.W.', as he does himself. Similarly, his wife Elizabeth is called 'Lilly' and her sister Sarah Smith is 'Lally'. (Polly and Dolly, Libby and Patty … nicknames were customary, but identities should become clear by consulting the family tree.)

'The diary': a less cumbersome way of referring to *Uncle Page's Book*, which combines two diaries. In quoting from it, I do so as written. The flavour of the original seems worth preserving, with its abrupt leaps from one topic to the next, its breathless lack of punctuation and occasional oddity of spelling. As presented, the diary gives entries day by day which may be from widely separated years. So, just as in the children's puzzle where a sequence of dots needs to be connected before a shape appears, these entries had to be transcribed in chronological order before the narrative emerged. There were lots of names; but who were these people? In searching for answers I made some fascinating discoveries and some new friends.

*

'The history of the Victorian Age will never be written; we know too much about it.' So begins Lytton Strachey's preface to his *Eminent Victorians*. In the quest for insight he felt it best to 'row out over that great ocean of material, and lower down into it, here and there, a little bucket, which will bring up to the light of day some characteristic specimen … to be examined with a careful curiosity.' The contents of my small bucket have, as it happens, concerned a place well known to Lytton Strachey; although he and the group of friends who wandered, talking and laughing, under the Old Vicarage chestnuts by the river seem to have been quite unaware of that Victorian household (not at all eminent) whose own energy and hilarity had given the place much of its peculiar enchantment.

Prologue

SACRED

TO THE MEMORY OF

SAMUEL WIDNALL

WHO DIED FEBRUARY 20, 1848, AGED 58 YEARS

ALSO OF ELIZABETH HIS WIFE

WHO DIED OCTR 2ND 1863

ALSO OF HANNAH WIDNALL

WHO DIED JAN. 12, 1866, AGED 73 YEARS

AND OF ELIZABETH

THE BELOVED WIFE OF SAMUEL PAGE WIDNALL

WHO DIED JAN 2 1886 AGED 59

ALSO OF SAMUEL PAGE WIDNALL

WHO DIED DEC 16, 1894 AGED 67

BORN JUNE 20, 1821 LALLY SMITH DIED FEB 26, 1908

The grey slate memorials set under the east window of Grantchester Church are easily overlooked. One is filled with the names of the Widnall family; and another, beside it, commemorates Mrs Sarah Page, who died February 25th 1827, aged 73 years. These people, once of some significance in the village, are the principal characters in my narrative.

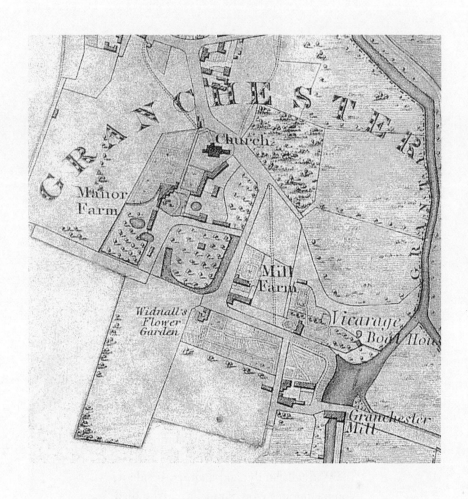

From a map prepared for Col. Pemberton of Trumpington Hall in 1847. Widnall's Flower Garden, with its Nursery House, is shown beneath Manor Farm and Mill Farm. The Vicarage (later Old Vicarage) appears to the right.

[6]

CHAPTER I

Background – Widnalls & Freemans

*The Old Vicarage ... A magician lived in that house and ruled the village
with gentle, unquestioned power. His name was Mr Widnall.*

POLLY GREENE*

———— ◆ ————

THE FUTURE MAGICIAN – farmer, photographer, actor-manager, author,
printer, local historian, model-maker, botanist, inventor – was Samuel
Page Widnall.

He was born on Christmas Day, 1825. His parents, Samuel and Elizabeth, had been married for eleven years. An earlier child, named after his
maternal grandfather John Freeman, had been born in 1818 but must
have died soon after. Page Widnall was to be brought up as an only
child, in secure and happy surroundings.

The Widnall parents had arrived in the village of Grantchester, just
south of Cambridge, in about 1815 and were by now well established.
Their home, newly built, was known as the Nursery House. Its front

The Nursery House – later called Vine Cottage.

*The Joy of Remembering, by Mary C. Greene, from the opening recollections of childhood.

presented a picture-book appearance: plain yellow brick, a shallow-pitched slate roof, and matching bay windows flanking a pretty porch. It had two parlours, five bedrooms and all the necessary offices, besides 'Stable, Harness-room, Gig-house, &c.' and a summer-house. And in late summer its gardens were ablaze with every possible variety of dahlias.

It stood beside one of the many bends of the road which ran down from Trumpington and over the river Cam and, crossing a millstream, rose and twisted through the village. Across the road, slightly uphill, was an older and larger house known as Yew Garth. There, at the time of Page's birth, lived an old widow, Mrs Sarah Page, his great-aunt, and her sister-in-law Mrs Elizabeth Freeman, his grandmother. Sarah Page died when he was in his second year, and after that Grandmother Freeman joined them in the Nursery House. Yet although Page would have little memory of that great-aunt, she was an important figure in their family history.

*

Page's father, Samuel Widnall, was himself a remarkable man, a nursery-man-florist already building up a reputation for exceptional skill in developing hybrid varieties of a quite recently introduced flower, the dahlia.

The known facts of his origin are sparse. His parents, William and Elizabeth Widnall, lived in Lincolnshire; his father's dates are 1755–1843. Samuel Widnall himself (1790–1848) was born at Wellingore, the eldest of seven or more children. It seems that the family later moved to Bingham, Notts (and the younger children were baptised at Lowdham, a few miles further north). In these largely rural places the father's occupation was likely to have been that of a skilled country tradesman – farmer? market gardener? blacksmith?* – respectable, hardworking, prudent and fairly well-read.

At some time young Samuel Widnall came south. There may have been useful introductions, for, unusual as the name is, there were one or two 'Widnells' [sic] in Cambridge early in the nineteenth century. Ezekiel Widnell (died 1763) and his son Richard Widnell (died 1803) were King's College cooks, at that time an occupation not under regulation by the college but independent, allowing them to sell their services and hire out crockery and silver at a good profit.

Whatever his early life may have been, the young man from the Lincs/Notts border country seems to have had sufficient education,

---

*Widnall is a rare name, and a known family of blacksmith Widnalls in that area at the beginning of the 20th century may be of significance.

native intelligence and a willingness to work hard to ensure rapid success in any undertaking. He was soon farming, raising crops on fields on the then southern edge of Cambridge owned by Trinity Hall, later built upon as 'New Town' (Norwich Street, Bateman Street); but at the same time he must have been acquiring his exceptional skill as a nurseryman. How this came about is again unknown, yet a warm and trusting friendship with the Curator of the University Botanic Garden is almost certain to have had something to do with it.

*

In 1814, when he was twenty-four, Samuel Widnall married Elizabeth Freeman, three years older than himself. She was a farmer's daughter, from Little Abington; and it was a family connection of hers which was probably of prime importance in Samuel Widnall's business arrangements, enabling the fortunate couple to set up a nursery garden on a fine site in the village of Grantchester.

This was Elizabeth's aunt who, born Sarah Freeman, had made a late marriage to a wealthy farmer, Thomas Page. And even if little Samuel Page Widnall was to have no clear memory of his formidable great-aunt Sarah, there would be no escaping her influence. For in the family his first Christian name, easily confused with his father, was never used. He was 'Page' – not a true family name, just the surname acquired through Sarah Freeman's marriage, at the age of forty and by special licence, to a man of substance.

As he grew up, Page Widnall must have gathered some impression of Aunt Sarah's importance in bringing his parents to Grantchester and helping them to set up their business. It had been long ago, probably in 1779, that Sarah had herself moved the seven or eight miles from her native village to serve as housekeeper to the Rev. Dr Samuel Peck, who, no longer Vicar of Trumpington, had moved to Yewgarth in Grantchester. He – Fellow of Trinity College and also Deputy Chancellor of the Diocese of Ely – had accumulated parcels of land and other property, much of which was to come to Sarah at his death, in 1791. She then, having no doubt learnt a good deal about property transactions from the old clergyman-don, had made some bold purchases of land and copyhold tenancies for herself, assisted by one of Grantchester's principal farmers, Benjamin Howard.*

*See Appendix I for more concerning the relationship between the Rev. Sam. Peck and the Widnalls' acquisition of property in Grantchester.

It was a time when impending enclosure meant that the whole pattern of farming in the parish was about to change. Grantchester, which for centuries had been laid out in three large, and three lesser, fields divided into furlong strips for cultivation by many farmers* and with areas of common land to be grazed by all, would henceforth be redivided into more coherent sections enclosed by hedges, in which a few farmers – the bigger, more successful farmers – could raise better crops by more advanced methods. Each farmer got, in acreage, the equivalent of the area he had owned or leased under the old system; so it is not surprising to find some urgent bargaining in the last years before Grantchester's Inclosure Award [sic] was granted in 1802. It was during this preparatory period, in December 1794, that Sarah married Thomas Page and added her farmland to his.

Thomas Page was a good man, greatly respected, and their combined holding of eighty-one acres in Grantchester was not all. His will decreed that after his death the property he owned in Harlton should be offered for sale to its tenant for the sum of £100,000. In due course his widow would have a substantial inheritance, most of which would pass to her brother's family, but some to the Widnalls.

*

The Freeman family of Little Abington seem to have been enterprising people. John Freeman was a farmer; his son Robert was a wheelwright; and the marriage of his daughter Elizabeth to the energetic young Samuel Widnall was, it seems, approved. Robert Freeman and his wife Joanna were raising a large family – ten children, of whom two died in infancy. After their little daughter Maria had died at nine months they called their next baby, another girl, 'Maria Widnal' [sic]. And although *Uncle Page's Book* makes no mention of Robert Freeman, his daughters Sarah (who married a prosperous farmer, Charles Tofts) and Elizabeth (Mrs Clark) would keep up close relations with their cousin Page Widnall into old age.

So, within a year or two of their own marriage the young Widnalls were setting up home in Grantchester. Aunt Sarah Page's property included a freehold close, a fertile area sloping south and eastwards, ready to be laid out as a nursery garden. At the upper end, by the road, the Nursery House was built. The layout is shown in *Baker's New Map*

---

*Tenants, mostly, of Cambridge colleges whose endowments had included these lands. King's, Corpus Christi, St Catharine's and St John's all owned sections; also Merton College, Oxford.

of 1830 ('delineated from actual survey'). From the wording of the will
made by Sarah Page in 1819 it is clear that already by that date 'Samuel
Widnall of Grantchester gardener' was established with 2 acres 7 perch-
es of nursery garden; and by 1830 he was prospering and the garden had
been extended to 6? acres. A visit to Widnall's Flower Gardens had
become a pleasant extension to the customary 'Grantchester Grind' – the
short excursion taken on foot, horseback or carriage by the leisured people of Cambridge. Here, boasted his advertisement, in late summer they
would find 'upwards of 160 varieties of DOUBLE DAHLIAS...
not surpassed by any other collection in the kingdom'.

Samuel Widnall had chosen a most profitable flower as his speciality.
The dahlia had been introduced to this country only in 1789. It was native
to Mexico, and is said to have been brought to Europe as a possible substitute for the potato rather than for its bloom, originally rather unimpres-
sive, so that at first little notice was taken of it in this country. Then, after
the Napoleonic wars, the first cultivars arrived from France and Germany,
and interest in England began to quicken. By careful propagation from
seed, exciting new varieties were produced and attracted high prices.
The dahlia craze was beginning, and the competition to raise spectacular
novelties intensified. Horticultural society shows and illustrated maga-
zines encouraged growers to vie with each other to achieve perfection. In
this rivalry, Widnall perhaps had a certain advantage. He seems to have
had a connection with the Botanic Garden of the University of Cambridge.

This was through his friendship with Arthur Biggs, fourteen years
his senior (whose confidence in him is proved by his appointment of
Widnall as executor of his will). Biggs had been appointed Curator of
the Old or Walkerian Botanic Garden in 1813 and remained in charge for
32 years. (Unlike the present-day Director, who is a qualified botanist,
the post at that time was a strictly practical one, simply taking charge of
the garden and its plants.) A house was provided for the Curator overlooking the four-acre garden near the centre of Cambridge* and he
received a stipend of £80 p.a. with extras such as £5 for journeys to London and £5.4s allowance for beer. He was also free to

> ... exchange seeds and duplicate with other Gardeners for the benefit of
> ... the Collection but ... the ... Garden was not to be considered a
> Nursery Garden to raise Plants for his own profit, or to keep them for
> himself or other persons ...

*The Botanic Garden removed to its present much larger site in 1846–52

Both Samuel Widnall and Arthur Biggs must surely have found they could assist each other very usefully, for the Garden would receive samples of the newest horticultural discoveries, and gifts of seeds and cuttings were enough for further propagation.

*

Samuel's small son Page was growing up amidst all this activity, watching the yearly rotation of jobs as seeds were sown, thinned, weeded; tubers were sprouted, planted out, mulched, staked; blooms were culled, bunched, packed into wicker baskets; the finest selected for harvesting seeds; the frost-touched withering plants lifted and dried; and then tubers and seeds labelled and stored, ready for the cycle to begin again. Perhaps father and son together pored over the illustrations in the local newspaper and the *Gardeners' Chronicle* advertising marvellous new machines and gadgets for farmers and horticulturalists. And in addition to the nursery, with its glasshouses and all the devices used for raising a whole range of flowers and shrubs as well as dahlias, there was the small Mill Farm* with its own routine of cultivation and tending of livestock, all a part of his daily life.

Down the slope from his home was an old redbrick house with steeply-pitched roof and massive chimneys, the Vicarage, at that time occupied by lay tenants.

It stood in a large, leafy garden and had its own boathouse by the river. Further on was Grantchester Mill, a high building astride the millstream – its swirling pool a magical though dangerous place for boys' games. In the millstream they would find fish and wildfowl in abundance; on the bridge above they could watch carts and wagons unloading grain and collecting flour; and, half-deafened with the rush of water, hear the rumble of turning cog-wheels and the rattle of chains from the pulley high above the road. The boy Page must have become familiar with the mill and pondered the fascinating connections of paddlewheel, cogs and millstones driven by the force of the stream flowing to join the river Granta towards Cambridge and beyond. His understanding of natural history and of mechanics was absorbed from early days in such surroundings.

Similarly, a walk uphill from his home would have stirred thoughts of antiquity. On the slope stood the village church, and beside it the

*Mill Farm was where the present Orchard Tea Garden buildings stand.

ancient Manor House, both offering, in inconsistencies of roof and windows, puzzles for the observant and curious to consider. Below the church on the north side of the winding road was a sloping area of woodland with two ponds and, down by the meadows, remains of mysterious earthworks. This was 'Ball's Grove', an adventure-playground with strong suggestions of legend.

On into the centre of the village the boy would pass huddled cottages, old public houses – the Green Man, the Red Lion and the Blue Ball – and the various small shops. In his early days a small Toll House projected into the road at the junction with the Coton Road, the 'New Road' which had been created in 1800. Also new was the National School, a little thatched building with a bell-tower on top. It was built in 1830, when Page was four years old, and to it came the 'children of the labouring poor', some tramping all the way from neighbouring villages. In the few larger houses lived the village's principal farmers, but Grantchester was a place with no grand family as 'squire'.

In the daytime there were likely to be people – familiar people – about most of the time, servants on errands, children playing, housewives emerging from their cramped homes to draw water from one of the communal pumps or to shake out a mat; or perhaps, in summer, sitting outside with their sewing. There would be farm labourers leading horses, gentry passing by in their light carriages, the pedlar with a pony-drawn cart laden with candles, crockery, soap, baskets … all the wares which the village could not itself supply. Most of the business of everyday life was visible: the blacksmith in his forge, the carpenter at his lathe, the milking of cows, the stitching of clothes.

Father & Son

———•◦•———

GRANTCHESTER WAS SELF-CONTAINED. But the place which became familiar to Page during his schooldays was altogether more exciting. Up at
Trumpington, where he went to school, the main road carried traffic on
its way to London, with sights and sounds – stagecoaches with coach-
horns, teams of horses clattering and whinnying – bound to lead to
thoughts of the world beyond his birthplace.

In the summer of 1834 the eight-year-old was taken for a long journey
by his father, and made his first few diary entries:

16 *July* Set out to drive to Nottingham with Father dined at
Peterborough. Slept at Bourne & fell out of bed

22 *July* Went to the ruins of Nocton Hall burnt down on the 16th.
Saw the large chestnut tree said to be the largest in England

25 *July* I weighed 4 stone 3 lbs

26 *July* I went into Mortimers Hole at Nottingham Castle

The entries are intriguing. This was a great adventure, riding in the family chaise up the Great North Road. They did not go straight to Nottingham, for Nocton is in Lincolnshire, a few miles from his father's
birthplace, Wellingore. And the choice of experiences recorded is
already characteristic – the great 200-year-old Hall gutted by fire; the
breathtaking spread of a tree; the romantic castle. But, apart from these
excitements, it seems to have been an adventure with a purpose. Old
William Widnall was near the end of his life, and Samuel must have
wanted to introduce his own son to his Widnall relatives and to places
with family associations.

Page was a lively boy, and it was at about this age that he tried an
experiment. He had heard that a bad-tempered old Cambridge don was
particularly enraged by the sound of whistling. So, seeing this famous
character walking through Grantchester, he whistled. The result was a
gratifying display of rage. It is recorded in *A Gossiping Stroll Through the
Streets of Cambridge* (1892) in the rather ponderous style of his old age:

Some sixty years ago there was a fellow of [Queens'] college ... he never heard a person whistle but he thought it was done to insult him. The writer well remembers hearing this when a child, and one day seeing him pass his house at Grantchester, he contrived to utter the obnoxious sound as an experiment; it succeeded only too well, for the old gentleman turned back towards the spot from whence it came, but the culprit had fled into the house, and taken refuge, if we remember rightly in a bedroom, for a knock was heard at the front door and a stern voice demanding if there were any boys in the garden, as one had insulted him. My mother who knew nothing of the matter, said she thought there were none about, but he could search in the garden if he wished. He did so, but the quest being fruitless he at length departed and the culprit crept out from his hiding place.

It is a minor incident, yet characteristic, for experiments – many of the early ones perhaps mischievous – were to be a part of his life.

*

Some idea of the places he knew as a boy – both in Trumpington and Grantchester itself, then very much a backwater – can be recovered from the reminiscences he set down in later life. In a sixpenny pamphlet of 1889, *Reminiscences of Trumpington Fifty Years Ago*, he described scenes of his childhood. The traffic through Trumpington – the main route to London – now so changed:

We often remark, what would our Grandfathers say to this or that modern invention, for instance, what would they think could they stand now on the Trumpington road, and see the telegraph wires, or the puffing trains in the distance!

And then he compared with this 'the number of FOUR HORSE COACHES' which kept up a regular service to London, – the *Lynn Mail*, the *Times*, the *Star*, the *Beehive*, the *Telegraph*, the *Fly*, the *Rapid* and so on, some coming from Kings Lynn or Wisbech. In addition there were the WAGONS [his caps], which he called the 'goods trains' of the period.

These were of an enormous size, drawn by eight horses, and at the back was a projection shaded by an awning, or tilt, for the accommodation of travellers who were too poor to journey by coach. I well remember seeing them looking very comfortable sitting in the straw...

There were also those who drove to London in their private carriages.

> I remember driving more than once with my father, when we stayed at the 'Four Swans' in Bishops-gate street, a curious old inn since pulled down; two tiers of galleries ran round the yard, giving access to long rows of bedrooms.

He recalled the herds of oxen and flocks of sheep passing along – oxen sometimes falling lame from a long journey and having to be shod by the blacksmith; and the geese and turkeys driven along to supply Londoners with Christmas dinners, too. He mentioned the stocks and the whipping-post, the weighbridge and other things since fallen out of use.

This little booklet also tells the reason why he knew that traffic so well; for here he describes his time at Mr Cumming's.* For several years he went daily from Grantchester as a day boarder. 'I must have been a very little fellow when I first went, I forget the exact time.' In his final year he was a full boarder; but it was before then that he was allowed a special thrill one day, when the coachman of the *Fly* stopped and lifted him up so that he rode into Cambridge on the lofty seat beside him. He was then given tea at the man's home in a stable-yard, and driven home to Grantchester by pony and trap. The school was well-placed for watching those stagecoaches, since it stood opposite the Coach & Horses inn. Further along the Trumpington Road towards Cambridge was the junction with Long Road, where on one side there was a weighbridge and near the other a windmill – both sure to prompt questions from the small boy about their mechanism.

Mr Cumming's School took in a few poorer boys, 'children of the hardy sons of toil', paid for by some charity. A distinction was made in the seating arrangements, but perhaps the pupils mixed fairly freely at playtimes. The school was conducted in one large room, with the master sitting at his desk on a dais. For mealtimes the boys had to eat standing up: bread and milk for breakfast, pudding followed by meat for dinner. They had textbooks for geography and history, but all learning tended to be by rote. Reading practice was from the New Testament; arithmetic was severely practical.

> I have still one of our class books, Pinnock's First Catechism, it is certainly very varied in its instruction, we had a certain number of these questions and answers to learn, some of them left an impression, for instance the chapter on bread –
> *Question* What is Bread?
> *Answer* Bread is the chief support of man, is a baked mass of dough &c.

*SPW's spelling: in his boyhood the school was under the direction of James Cuming, whose son Charles did the teaching. In 1833 there were 32 fee-paying boys, the fee being 2 guineas. *(Victoria County History)*

Question What is French Bread?
Answer It is a kind of fancy bread, prepared with warm milk, instead of
       water, and having the addition of eggs and fresh butter &c.
This I thought must be very nice and when I went home tried to instruct
my mother in that matter, and urged her to make some for me.
… I do not remember any examinations but we used to have prizes
awarded, these consisted sometimes of books. I still possess one,
White's Natural History of Selborne, but I also remember having a
small pestle and mortar, and a Parian bust of George IV.

The regime was a benevolent one for its time, and the boys had a good
deal of freedom to explore the country around or swim in the river. And
they were enterprising in their games together – conducting a funeral for
a dead canary ('I believe I was the undertaker, as I was always fond of
carpentering'), or elaborate mock elections.

*

All through these years Samuel Widnall's nursery business thrived.
Enthusiasm for the dahlia – almost comparable to the 'tulip mania' of 17th
century Holland (though not quite reaching its excesses) – was raging, for
the plant supplied gaudy colour throughout those difficult months of late
summer; just at a period, too, when so many new middle-class villas were
being built with gardens laid out with flowerbeds. Some idea of Widnall's
growing fame is displayed in a publication of 1835, *A History of the different
varieties of the Georgiana or Dahlia* by James Sinclair. This consists of

PARAGON.

*A History of the different varieties of the Georgiana
or Dahlia* by James Sinclair

17

paper-bound monthly issues[*] of fine lithographs with a short text, select-
ing several of Widnall's own dahlias as prime examples of 'the form of the
flower and the brilliancy of the colours' achieved by rigorous selection.

It may be proper to state that such has been the increase in Mr Widnall's
collection of the Georgiana within these last three years, that he has
discarded 200 varieties of named Dahlias which had previously been
considered fine flowers...

He was now able to charge half a guinea or more for each plant.

When the Cambridge Florists' Society held its 1838 Dahlia Shew [*sic*]
'open to all England', it was thought only fair to separate the exhibits of
the amateurs from those of the professionals, and Mr Widnall provided
three prizes to encourage their efforts. When it came to the professionals'
own stand, it was found that Widnall had won comprehensively, getting
top marks in almost every category. The *Cambridge Chronicle* reported
that 'The tables were literally crowded with blooms, positively dazzling
from their infinite variety of colours, and all repaying a close inspection
by their perfect symmetry of shape...'; and it was less admiring of only
one item of the display:

Were we inclined to be captious, we might take an exception to an
angular and very grotesque figure at the further end of the room,
intended to represent our gracious Queen; though we question
whether it could have been better executed with dahlia blooms.
Then why make the attempt?[†]

That same October the village of Grantchester held its own show, a
great publicity stunt for the nursery gardens. It was to become an annual
event; and on this first occasion 'upwards of fifty gentlemen' gathered for
dinner in a large booth set in the garden of the Red Lion. Mr Widnall
had, of course, decorated the booth and rooms of the house with 'devices
formed with dahlias'; and 'a pole (upwards of 35 feet in height) ornamented with thousands of dahlias, was erected in front of the house'.

By 1839, when *Robson's Directory* came out, Samuel Widnall, 'florist
and nurseryman', had become famous:

At Grantchester two miles south west from Cambridge are the Dahlia
Grounds of Mr Widnall the florist: they are the most extensive of any in
England occupying about six acres. Every year thousands of dahlias of

---

[*]Three are known to have survived, but the series was probably continued.
[†]One is tempted to suspect that this may have been produced by a 12-year-old boy

fresh variety are produced from seed; from which the choicest are sent to beautify the gardens of Great Britain, the Royal Gardens of France and Russia, and also exported in great quantities from this little village to Germany and to all parts of the United States of America.

It was already evident that Widnall had a flair for showmanship. An event on 10th January 1840 gave him a wonderful opportunity. As his son noted in his diary: 'Father posted 193 letters first day of Penny Post' – which must surely have been a mass-mailing of advertisements.

That same energy led to an original enterprise later in the year. It happened that the Royal Agricultural Society, which had been formed the year before with an inaugural show at Oxford, was to hold its 1840 show in the heart of Cambridge. The great area of Parker's Piece was fenced with enclosures for livestock; and the grounds of Downing College, opposite, provided ample space for a huge pavilion, since at that time the site extended from Lensfield Road to Downing Street.

Mr Widnall seized this opportunity. The Agricultural Show was held on 15th July; and a day later, before the pavilion and tents were dismantled, he mounted his own Horticultural Show. Tickets cost 5/- and sold well – after all, the town was still full of fine visitors, and local nurserymen were eager to show off their produce.

The *Cambridge Chronicle* afterwards listed the awards. Mr Widnall had done well with his raspberries and redcurrants, but excelled with his flowers, winning with 'Best 12 Dahlias (distinct varieties)', 'Best collection of Plants (in pots)' and 'Best six Plants (hardy, &c., in pots)'. The newspaper listed (surely with pride and amazement) the eminent visitors assembled: 'Dukes (6), Marquisses (3), Earls (6), M. le Comte de Guizet, Lords (19), 2 Right Hons', and so on down the ranks. The paper also printed an Abstract of the Accounts. Expenses had amounted to £271. 11s, and profits to £448. 18s 6d. Mr Widnall presented £450 to Addenbrookes Hospital, and was later made a Life Governor.

Another view of that momentous year was set down by the fourteen-year-old Page:

1840   1 *Jan*   Present of Writing Desk from my Cousin GFW
       7 *Jan*   Father bought a dog, Nel
    10 *Jan*   Father posted 193 letters first day of Penny Post
    10 *Feb*   A Holiday the Queen Married
    9 *April*   Father sowed the Dahlia seed. 12 lights –
   23 *May*   Left off my large Collars

28 *May*   Amelia our servant married to J. Benton – I went to tea
Father. Mr Press & Mr Payne came after stopped till 11 o'clock

30 *June*   Fired a gun for the 1st time

7 *July*   Nearly all day sealing admission tickets (Horticultural Fete)

15 *July*   Went to the Great Agricultural Show Cambridge

17 *July*   Father presented the proceeds of Horticultural Fete to
Hospital £450

12 *Oct*   Father began to work the Farm [– this was perhaps
Grandmother Freeman's farm]

16 *Oct*   Mr Wing gave me 12 Canaries for my Aviary

17 *Dec*   Memorial from Addenbrookes Hospital presented & Father
made Life Gov.

29 *Dec*   Recd. Box of Evening Amusements from my Cousin G.F.
Widnall

His kind cousin G.F. Widnall may have been one of the people met during
that trip to Nottingham. It sounds as though he had been taken with this
young visitor and could afford to choose generous Christmas-and-birth-
day presents suitable for one so wideawake. The first of these recorded
presents had been a Cabinet Shakespeare when Page turned thirteen.

Generosity was perhaps a Widnall characteristic. Samuel Widnall followed his great donation to Addenbrookes Hospital with other efforts,
one of which is mentioned by the Rev. Joseph Romilly in his diary[*]. This
was a Grand Ball held in the Fitzwilliam Museum on 6th July, 1842,
when Widnall decorated the ballroom and 'sold elegant little bouquets
(1d each) for the ball: he sold 1000 and gave the £50 to the hospital'.

Romilly had also noted a less successful enterprise which had taken
place in September 1840. 'Flower-show in St John's Private Walks....
The profits of the show were to have been given to the Almshouses, but
profits, alas! there were none... Widnall for the 1st time in his life was
defeated in Dahlias...'

Samuel Widnall found other outlets for his generosity. In Grantchester
he gave an annual fête for all the schoolchildren, as reported in the newspaper:

> fitting up most tastefully a shed in a close of pasture opposite his
> nursery [the present Orchard], lining the inside with canvas, and
> elegantly festooning it with evergreens and flowers.

[*] *Romilly's Cambridge Diary*, the diary of the Rev. Joseph Romilly, Registary of the University
of Cambridge, [ed. M.E. Bury & J.D. Pickles]

The children were 'regaled with tea and plum-cake, and bread and butter' and prizes were distributed, some receiving 'a bible, and an order for clothes to the amount of six shillings' and none less than a shilling and a book. After wine and cake, there were three cheers for Mr and Mrs Widnall and the Curate. The *Cambridge Chronicle* concluded by adding:

> ... we would exhort all, who like Mr Widnall have been blessed by Providence with the good things of the world, to imitate his benevolent example, and we doubt not in the end they will feel as he does, that the more he exerts himself to do good the more blessings Providence seems to shower upon him.

It was an example which must throughout his childhood have impressed young Page.

By 1841 Widnall was able to issue a 24-page catalogue of dahlias and other plants. But in August 1843 there was a calamitous storm. Romilly noted that 'The Town presents a very curious & distressing spectacle from the shattered windows & desolated gardens...'; and out in Grantchester, Widnall's nursery gardens were ruined. A printed pamphlet* describes the devastation in some detail: 'upwards of 5,000 square feet of glass were shivered to atoms', and the farm crops were laid flat. His loss from all this was estimated to be at least £1,000; and earlier in the year another £150-worth of damage had occurred from floods.

Mercifully, plants have a way of recovering. Mr Widnall's nursery seems not to have been entirely destroyed, as in 1845 he was responsible for the splendid display of flowers at the opening ceremony of Cambridge Railway Station. The coming of the railway was to make a great change to the town. It brought the end of those old coaches plying down the road to London. There were a few accidents and inefficiencies at first; but soon the convenience and speed of travel by rail was welcomed, and the many different companies built their lines to every corner of the land. For Cambridge, it meant the arrival of the dreaded trippers. Romilly confided to his diary that:

> 1 *Sept* 1845... Today an Excursion train from London to Cambridge & back for 5s enlivened the Town by an importation of about 400 cockneys.

*

*Sent, perhaps, to his customers as an excuse for shortcomings in that year's deliveries. See Appendix II.

When Page's real schooldays ended one cannot tell. But it was only a beginning, for self-education continued throughout his life. His prize on leaving Mr Cumming's school had been the Rev. Gilbert White's *Natural History of Selborne*; and a more receptive mind for this particular book would be hard to find. It is likely to have been the 1833 edition, published by the Society for Promoting Christian Knowledge and 'arranged for young persons', in which the opening summary of White's life remarks that:

> Being of an unambitious temper, and strongly attached to the charms of rural scenery, he early fixed his residence in his native village, where he spent the greater part of his life in literary occupations, and especially the study of Nature...

This was surely a model for the Grantchester boy, who must have been fascinated by the book. It is illustrated with fine engravings, and the varieties of plants and wildlife are distinguished with Linnaean precision: with this book and his father's expertise, Page can never have had any difficulty in using correct botanic or zoological terms.

Gilbert White's learned observations are interspersed with homely wisdom; and in those days an author – even a clergyman – could without any thought of improper prejudice toss out the comment – 'the poor, who are always the worst economists, and therefore must continue very poor...', or tell of 'the idiot boy...[who] exerted all his few faculties on the pursuit ... of honey-bees, humble-bees and wasps'. The behaviour of birds and animals is described both with vivid accuracy and tender sympathy – as with White's illustration of how

> ...even great disparity of kind and size does not always prevent social advances and mutual fellowship [e.g. in the case of a horse and a hen kept together in an orchard] – The fowl would approach the quadruped with notes of complacency, rubbing herself gently against his legs; while the horse would look down with satisfaction, and move with the greatest caution and circumspection, lest he should trample his diminutive companion.

Something of that style rubbed off on Page; and the habit of noting and marvelling at curiosities of weather or appearances of strange birds was to remain till his last days.

More indications of what went on in that busy young mind appear in the stories written many years later – a medieval romance, a schoolboy adventure, a fiction of travel and scientific fantasy. For Page never entirely grew up: he cherished romantic notions of ruined castles and a passion for gadgets and inventions, especially ones to astonish or amuse, to the end of his days.

*

The years following school must have been spent time at his father's side, learning about the practicalities of farming and horticulture. Although Samuel Widnall was not one of the village's major farmers, he grew crops and raised livestock on several fields in the parish and had raised wheat and potatoes on land just south of Cambridge; and in addition to his show-garden there was a small field by the Coton Road reserved for growing the great quantities of dahlias. All these enterprises called for a wide range of expertise. The knowledge of crops and the management of livestock was duly absorbed by his son, together with competence in keeping records and business accounts. Something more was developing, too: an eye for craftsmanship, and those sorts of skill which might give a tradesman an advantage over his rivals, the ability to invent – to form a concept of some ingenious variation on an accepted design and either make it himself or get a carpenter or blacksmith to do the task. He read, he observed; and practice in the fiddly work with cuttings and seedlings must have cultivated the fine dexterity which would be valuable in his later activities. This ingenuity would become one of his special characteristics.

*

Father and son were mentioned together in the *Cambridge Chronicle's* report in 1847 of the visit of Queen Victoria and the Prince Consort to Cambridge. The occasion was the installation of Prince Albert as Chancellor of the University (an energetic Chancellor who would stir up that lethargic institution). Cambridge can scarcely have experienced such excitement before or since. It surpassed even the visit of October 1843, when the royal couple had arrived by coach. This time they travelled by rail. For the whole journey from London the royal train was greeted by cheering crowds at every station and along its route; the town was a-flutter with flags and bunting; thousands pressed into Trinity College and around the Senate House. The visit lasted from the 5th to the 8th July, marked by a succession of special events and commemorative Installation Medallions 'executed in the First Style of Art'. At Trinity College 3,558 tickets were sold, allowing the public to congregate on the far side of the river and gaze across to where 'On the lovely lawns of the college grounds were blended the attractions of intellect, of rank, of beauty...' It was reckoned that about 30,000 strangers had been attracted to the town.

The Installation Ceremony itself, held on the second day, in the insufferable heat of the crowded Senate House, was both a triumph and an ordeal. But the congratulatory outpourings and an almost inter-minable Choral Ode did end at last, and the royal couple proceeded to Downing College*. There they took their luncheon in a marquee set up in the garden of the recently-built Master's Lodge. And then, on this crowded day, the royal party paused to inspect the Horticultural Fête which once more filled the college grounds. This, said the *Illustrated London News*, 'was a delightful relief to the in-door ceremonies'. 5,000 tickets had been distributed. There were

> about 9 spacious tents ... military bands ... seats for those disposed to seek temporary repose or shelter from the scorching rays of the sun; and many who could not obtain seats stretched themselves on the grass, forming ... Watteau-like groups.

Royal visit to Downing College, 1847, HRH Prince Albert,
Chancellor of the University

Romilly attended the event, and noticed that 'Lord Hardwicke clumsily tore the Q's dress with his spurs, & a Farmer touched her gown & went about boasting "I've touched her"'. Exhibits had come from all parts of the country, a huge display in which Mr Widnall of Grantchester's contri-butions won many prizes. Amidst all this, reported the *Cambridge Chronicle*,

---

*which at that time was entered from Downing Street, where the gates opened to a long tree-lined vista leading all the way to Lensfield Road

An excellent model of the Grantchester Nursery was forwarded by Mr S. P. Widnall, jun., which displayed great taste and untiring perseverance, and was most minutely examined by her Majesty.

At the end of this memorable day, while the Queen and Prince moved on to inspect the newly-completed Fitzwilliam Museum building and the crowds were gasping at the ascent of a hot-air balloon from Parker's Piece, the Widnalls must have felt well pleased. Sam Widnall was to excel once more at another show later that year. And his son, now aged twenty-one, had shown an original creative talent* which might lead him away from a life devoted to the propagation of shrubs and flowers.

Then, on 20th February 1848, Page's beloved father died. He seems to have made a heroic journey to London just two days earlier, for he and his co-executor had presented themselves and made their oaths to prove the will of Arthur Biggs (who had died the previous month) on the 18th. The *Cambridge Chronicle* of the 26th February, whose main headline was 'Revolution in France – Abdication of the King', reported Samuel Widnall's death

> On the 20th inst., at Grantchester, in this country, after a long and painful illness, borne with christian resignation, in the 58th year of his age… His generous and liberal disposition endeared him to a large circle of friends and acquaintances, who deeply mourn his loss.

---

*– a talent which may already have shown itself; for in June 1845 Romilly had noted 'an imitation of the Round Church, [and] a Lilliputian garden & fountain' among the attractions at a show at Downing.

CHAPTER 3

Lilly & Lally

———•·•———

WHILE PAGE WIDNALL was growing up, another family was making a success of their own gardening business close to Worcester. This was Richard Smith's St John's Nursery. Although more than a hundred miles apart, the Widnalls and the Smiths must have already made contact by the late 1840s, and the link is likely to have been either through their trade or through relatives of both families in the Nottingham area.

However originated, the link was an important one; for two of the Smiths, Lilly and Lally, were to spend most of their lives in Grantchester. The whole Smith family, and some of their distant cousins, would come frequently to the village and intertwine their lives with those of the Widnall household. Their activities often appear in *Uncle Page's Book*, the combined diaries of Page Widnall and Lally Smith; and so they deserve inclusion in this account.

*

Sarah Smith, known to her family as Lally, was more regular with entries in her diary than Page Widnall had been in his early years. Her family history was more fully recorded, too; for when in later years her brother Richard became prosperous, he would establish his social credentials with a pedigree tracing the family line (Caringtons in earlier generations) back to the time of William the Conqueror, and adopt the name of Smith-Carington. That record traces the shifts of fortune as generations, rooted in Ashby Folville, Leicestershire, had later moved about the Midlands. In recent times the family had been living in the Nottingham area.

At the beginning of the 19th century a Richard Smith left Nottingham for Worcester. His father, also Richard, having 'little or no inheritance', had been 'engaged in the manufacture of the fine net lace then in vogue, and had machines of his own doing a good business', but in 1793 had lost all his property. And so in 1804 this Richard, then twenty-four, moved away to start a quite different enterprise. He developed nursery gardens at St John's, on the southern edge of Worcester, and succeeded

Lally, Anne (*top left & right*), Mrs Smith (*centre*), Richard and Lilly (*lower left & right*)

there in much the same way that Samuel Widnall was making a success of his own gardens at Grantchester. As with Widnall, marriage may have helped. Richard Smith first married Mary Dunn of Worcester, who died in 1819 without issue. After her death his second marriage at the age of forty, in 1820, to Ann Hanbury helped to restore the family fortunes. She, being an 'heiress', is honoured with her own family tree included in the great pedigree book.

Ann is described as 'coheir' of her father, Benjamin Hanbury of Bridgenorth. (She had a brother and three younger sisters, so it may be that three of her siblings had died by 1820.) Her family are very likely to have been connected with the wealthy Hanburys well-known among horticulturalists. (Her grandfather was a Daniel Hanbury, and so the naturalist-pharmacist of the same name, part-founder of the firm Allen & Hanbury, may have been a cousin.) As the ageing Mrs Smith, Ann was to be photographed holding a flower in her hand. A passion for botany was certainly passed on to the next generation.

Richard and Ann Smith had four children: Sarah, Anne, Richard and Elizabeth. The family, like Page Widnall's, seems to have combined hard work with contentment. Fond diminutives were used for all the children's names – Lally (from Sally), Annie, Dick and Lizzie or Lilly. They and the network of cousins and friends would remain close throughout their lives. And although the grand pedigree record does not reveal his trade, Richard Smith had been elected a member of the Royal Horticultural Society and his nursery business was steadily growing.

Lally, the eldest, stayed at school until past sixteen, although it cannot have been the regular school which we nowadays might expect. From at least the age of fourteen she went to Bridgenorth each year, staying with her Hanbury relations for a month or six weeks at a time. In 1839, at seventeen, she and her sister Anne attended the Worcester Musical Festival for three days; and the following year they had their first visit to London, accompanied by their father and some friends.

In 1844 Lally paid a long visit to her mother's cousins in London, the Robinsons, who lived in Belgrave Place. They were a good deal younger than her own parents, and they entertained her well.

16 *May* Lally saw the Duke of Wellington
18 *May* Lally went to the Italian opera, saw "Zampa" & an exquisite dance called "La Gitano" by M. Cerito. This was followed by the garden scene from Don Pasquale in which Grisi & Mario sang delightfully

21 *May* Saw Byron's very particular friend 'Hobhouse' now Sir John Hobhouse*. He is not tall, rather stout, & has a remarkable sort of aquiline nose.

29 *May* Went to the meeting of the Anti Corn Law League in Covent Garden theatre, heard Lord Dacie, Col. Thompson, Mr Holland of Dumbleton, Mr Cobden & Mr Bright

20 *June* Mr & Mrs H. Shelton came to see me [this being her birthday] at Mr Robinson's Belgrave Place

22 *June* Saw the Duke of Wellington again, he had on a blue coat white waistcoat & trowsers, & was leisurely walking his horse

28 *June* My first sight of the Sea. Mr Robinson took me to Ramsgate, stayed till Tuesday July 2nd

Visits to London were always lively, and this first one, including glimpses of the 'Iron Duke', Hérold's now-forgotten *Zampa*, the early stirrings of the Anti-Corn-Law League and a first visit to the seaside, was one to remember. It was Anne & Richard who, later that year, went to see the midget Tom Thumb (described scornfully by the *Illustrated London News* as 'a biped whose name was *Tom Thumb*, with the military prefix of "General", who strutted about like a miniature Napoleon'); but in 1846 Lally herself heard another phenomenon, the 'Infant Sappho'; and two years later she was back again, going to the opera.

Another young woman sharing the excitement over these same celebrities at that time was Queen Victoria, just two years older than Lally. Lally shared also her short stature, being only 4ft 10ins high (149cm) – measured on 6 Jan. 1848, when her brother Richard was 5ft 5ins and her father 5ft 8ins.

In common with the Queen and most young ladies, Lally was accomplished in piano-playing, in French and in watercolours. But for her there was to be no husband and brood of children. In health, despite one startling diary entry (30 Aug. 1844: 'Lally had a fit'), she had no major troubles and was to outlive the rest of her generation.

She was both earnest and lively, eager for new experiences and deeply moved by them. In the New Year of 1846 she was visiting Birmingham, where on 16th January she 'saw Cardinal Manning' and probably heard his charismatic preaching. On the 20th 'Sarah (Sally) Smith embraced the Roman Catholic faith while with Mrs Sheaths at Birmingham. A great grief to her family'. But on 12th February 'Sarah (Sally) Smith renounced

*Later Lord Broughton. It was Hobhouse who, out of loyalty to the poet, caused Byron's *Memoirs* to be destroyed.

the Roman Catholic religion'. And she returned to Worcester and Anglicanism.

Lally's first trip abroad was to Belgium, in June 1846, taking in Antwerp, Brussels, Waterloo,* a call on a friend at the Chateau de Cockilberg, Ghent and Ostend. The boat crossed back to Ramsgate, and from there, next day, they took another to London. Finally, on 19 June, 'Father Mother & I retd to Dulcie Domum after our pleasant foreign trip'.

Early next year, now aged twenty-five, Lally started to teach. 'Mrs Shelton introduced me to the Misses Collison, Baskerville House School. I have 10 pupils.' Two years later she was to be given a ring in remembrance of her first pupil by the grateful mother.

While Lally continued her fairly tranquil life of visits to friends and cousins, with in 1850 another teaching appointment (8 April 'My first day at Mrs Bayliss's 8 Pupils for Music & 6 for French'), one senses that the rest of her family were turning their attention to marriage: a well-considered business.

*

Lally's diary first mentions her brother Richard's future bride in September 1847. 'First evening with E. Stroud (Libby) at her Aunt's Bath Road.' (Three days later there is 'First meeting with Mr Strickland'; but that meeting was to lead to trouble.) Libby, perhaps known to Richard from earlier encounters, was aged twenty. She is described in the family pedigree as 'Elizabeth, 2nd daughter & coheir of Thomas Stroud, of Clewer, co. Bucks' and was born in Jermyn Street, London. Her brother and sisters would all become and remain close friends of the Smith family. Richard himself was just twenty-three. Their marriage took place next month, at St Peter's, Eaton Square, and was followed by a six-day 'wedding trip'. A few days later, 'Father, Richd, Lib, Liz & I went to the Southams [family friends] at Thorneloe'.

In January 1848 Lally notes, 'Moving Furniture into Shrubbery Cottage', the house which was to be home to the Smith family for many years. On 4 March: 'Terrible accident. Dear Mother almost killed by a runaway horse in a cart by the Nursery gates', and on the 22nd 'Mother came down 1st time after her accident'.

And then on 5th April 1848 another young man at last appears in Lally's

---

*W. M. Thackeray wrote a description of an almost identical tour at that time, taken by 'many hundreds of thousands of English.' At Waterloo, looking at the memorial tablets, he 'felt very much disappointed at not seeing the names of the *men* as well as the officers. Are they to be counted for nought? ... the men of that day were the winners of the battle...'

diary: 'SPW came to Shrubbery Cottage'. By this date, soon after his father's death, Page Widnall is likely to have made the cross-country journey through Oxford by rail. It may be that he wished to consult Mr Smith about matters concerning the Grantchester nursery, and also to meet the younger members of that family. He would certainly have found his surroundings there, the Vale of Evesham rich in orchards and the old city with its gothic cathedral overlooking the Severn, very much to his liking.

It may have been only a very brief visit. Next month, on 19 May, Lally noted, 'I went to London with Dick, Libby & Jane Stroud'. Next day, 'Went to Chiswick Fete met P. Widnall & Tom'. There is no telling how far Page Widnall and Tom Davis's acquaintance with the Smith family had already progressed or, indeed, whether Page and Tom were known to each other. Nor is anything recorded about the whereabouts of her sisters Annie and Lizzie at this time – simply the wonderful time she, Lally, had during her three and a half weeks' stay in London.

And, once again, it *was* a wonderful time: the diary records –

1848 20 *May* Went to the Opera at night, Lucretia Borgia, heard the famed Alboni. Grisi magnificent!

   27 *May* Went to the Opera Cov. Gar. La Favorita Grisi & Mario as usual splendid the whole Choir sang God save the Queen

   2 *May* Jas. Williams took us to Blackwall to see the Chinese Junk – we had whitebait at the "Artichoke"

   3 *June* Went to St James' Theatre to see the celebrated conjuror Robt. Houdin [Printed announcement of Houdini's performance pasted, as souvenir, into back of book]

   6 *June* Went to the Colosseum

   10 *June* Went to the Opera House Haymarket. Heard Jenny Lind

[The Donizetti operas, *Lucretia Borgia* and *La Favorita*, were all the rage; and Guilia Grisi, soprano, and the contralto Alboni were so famous that at the Academy of Music boxes would be named after them. Jenny Lind, 'the Swedish nightingale', had made her sensational debut in England not long before – and was, indeed, to be 'lionized' when she visited Cambridge the following March 'and with her accustomed generosity sent £100 to the Hospital'. (Romilly)]

*

Other matters were progressing. Both P. Widnall and Tom (Davis)* were suitors. On 17th July 'Dear Father, Mother, Anne & Lizzie set out for Grantchester, London & Yarmouth'. And on the 29th 'S. P. W. & E. S.

*whose father is referred to as 'Mr Davis (of Whitehall)'

became engaged'. It had been a rapid courtship, and quite possibly an arranged one. Yet it would not have been difficult for these two young people to find each other attractive. She would see a stocky, curly-haired fellow, bouncing with energy; and he a tall girl with a sweet smile. From the first they shared an interest in botany, in historical curiosities and in design.

So now Richard was safely married, and Lizzie's future arranged. Anne, however, seems to have got herself into an unwelcome tangle; and her sisters had to go to the rescue.

> 29 *July* Lally went to London on business connected with Stickland
> 31 *July* Lally & Liz called on Mr Stickland refusing him on the part
> of Anne, & Lally returned to Worcester

That settled, the Smith family holiday should have continued smoothly. But it came to an abrupt and shocking end.

> 5 *Aug* S.P.W. & Tom D. went to Yarmouth to join the Smiths
> [Page's entry]
> 8 *Aug* My dearly beloved Father died at Yarmouth at 8.40 p.m.
> [Lally's entry]

Richard Smith the elder had collapsed and died of a heart attack, and was buried in the alien churchyard at Great Yarmouth. Lally and her brother Richard travelled there but arrived just too late for the funeral. Next day it was Page who took the sisters, Lally and Liz (Lilly), to see the grave.

The whole network of activities concerning his children's marriages must have been stressful for Mr Smith. It was not until 9th May 1849 that Lally could write: 'Received the joyfull news that Stickland had withdrawn the action – Thanks be to God'. It seems that Stickland/Strickland, claiming to have been jilted, was making a Breach of Promise claim. Once that was cleared away, Anne was free to marry Tom Davis, the man whom, one suspects, her father had planned for her.

It must surely have been the wish of Mr Smith (and possibly of Samuel Widnall, or at least his widow) that the two great nursery enterprises, one at Grantchester and the other at Worcester, be linked. Richard Smith jnr should stay and build up the Worcester business, something he was to do to a quite staggering extent. The two younger daughters, Anne and Elizabeth, could by marriage bring the resources of both nurseries to an important new business, at Cambridge. For on 19th March 1849 Page notes: 'Opened Seed Shop at 21 King's Parade C'. This was *Widnall & Davis*, advertised as 'seedsmen, nurserymen and florists'. Probably Tom Davis was expected to provide the shrewd business sense, while Page Widnall supplied expertise in horticulture. Page's grandmother had recently died, leaving him her farm in Grantchester; and in addition to her land there was another legacy.

It was in May 1849 that Page and his mother travelled to London 'to receive the Biggs legacy'. This cryptic entry is the only mention in the diary of that name; but it suggests an important influence and a valuable bequest. As already related, Arthur Biggs, Curator of the University Botanic Garden, had died in January 1848 aged 82. In his Will he had named 'Samuel Widnall [Snr] of Grantchester ... Nurseryman, and William Key Ridgway, Curator of the Fitzwilliam Museum', as Executors. There were detailed instructions for bequests to his brother, nephews, nieces and servants; and Ridgway was to receive £10 for his trouble in executing the will and share with Widnall some residual lands and investments. When all expenses had been cleared, Samuel Widnall should have 'all my household goods and furniture the residue of my plate linen and china ready money [&c]'. Samuel Widnall had carried out his duties in proving the will just before his own death, and now all these chattels came to Page.

It is from this bequest that one deduces that long and close friendship which must have contributed so much horticultural lore and the useful connection with the Botanic Garden. Although his own home was evidently in the parish of St Andrew the Less in Cambridge, it may be that Arthur Biggs was nursed during his last months in Grantchester; for he is buried, with a fitting tombstone, in Grantchester churchyard. And those chattels? – the origin, perhaps, of the noble four-poster bed and other antique pieces with which Page was to furnish his home.

Very soon after this, Page and his mother made another journey together, to stay for a fortnight with the Smith family at Shrubbery Cottage. There, they paid calls on the Smiths' friends and went to see the 'China Works' at Worcester. During this time, Page noted: 'Began to make my tent'. Twelve days later he made seats for his tent ... and forty years after that proudly noted that it was still in use.

So at this early stage Elizabeth Smith encountered characteristic behaviour in her future husband. Not quite the diligent tradesman his father had been, Page was an irrepressibly creative dreamer. Here he was, with an idea which could not be delayed – constructing a framework, attaching cords, and quite possibly stitching the canvas himself.

After that visit, the couple must have built up their relationship mostly by correspondence. In November 'Liz, Page & Jane [Stroud] went to London'. In June 1850 Page went again to Worcester, when 'SPW & Liz drove to Kidderminster in Dogcart'; and three days later 'SPW took Liz, Lib, Lou & Lally on the River Severn'.

On 3 September 1850 there was a double wedding. Lally wrote:
My two dear sisters Anne & Lizzie married the former to Tom Davis the latter to S. P. Widnall who went to Clifton & Tom & Anne to Leamington

Page and his bride took their 'wedding trip' to South Wales, and then, via Worcester, to London.

CHAPTER 4

Young Mr & Mrs Widnall

THE SHORT HONEYMOON in Wales had been partly a botanic expedition. Page and his bride returned to Grantchester bearing specimens of ferns and flowers, to live at the Nursery House.

Their daily life is likely to have been modest, with the regular observance of family prayers and churchgoing established from the first. They had one servant, Maria Rayner, aged eighteen; and across the road – probably in Mill Farm (now Orchard House) – lived Page's mother and his aunt Hannah Widnall, with their own seventeen-year-old servant, Susan Laws. Page had the responsibilities of farming, maintaining the nursery gardens and taking his share in running the new shop.

Lizzie, as Page first called his wife, never appears as a forceful character. Yet she was a sustaining presence in the background: appearing, in every photograph he was to take of her, to be a sweet and tranquil person. When there were adventures, Lizzie/Lilly, if she was well enough, was always ready to join in. She had genuine artistic gifts, designing and executing embroidery, tending the garden and choosing decorations for the house.

So Lizzie was important in that household. But, while life with the energetic Page must have been full of fun, her share was always to be limited by that phrase 'if she was well enough'. And that perhaps was why, while her brother Richard and sister Anne had children, she had none. It was little Lally who was the more sparky one, who could record that in May 1849 she had gone 'with a large party to Malvern saw the Abbey Church & got locked in but escaped by the Vestry window'. Perhaps Lizzie would have had the spirit to do so too, but one wonders. Their mother (seen in Page's photographs) has an appearance of comfortable placidity and was said to carry herself 'in a stately way', a temperament and carriage seemingly inherited by her youngest daughter. In their marriage this was perhaps the ideal disposition; for Page was to have enough bright ideas for both of them.

In settling in, it was essential for Lilly to be introduced to her new neighbours in Grantchester.

Lilly Widnall

Page Widnall

Mrs Elizabeth Widnall (SPW's mother)

First, she needed to meet the Howards. Their family had for generations been prominent in the village. Benjamin Howard had assisted
Great-Aunt Sarah, when she was still Miss Freeman, in enlarging the
holdings of land she had inherited from Samuel Peck; and he had acted
as a witness to her marriage, in 1794, to Thomas Page. Benjamin's sons,
Thomas and Page Gregory, had shared the Howard family resources by
each becoming responsible for a part – Thomas as farmer, and Page as
miller.

Thomas Howard, gentleman farmer, had died in 1843, leaving his
widow Ellen with two small sons and a third to be born posthumously.
She was an accomplished person, and had already been taking in 'young
ladies' at Merton House, her large and pleasant home. Mrs Ellen
Howard, aged forty-four, was to become a particular friend; and her
boys – Thomas Frederick (Fred), William and Francis George (known
by his second name) – would be grateful for the guidance and companionship of a young uncle-figure, Page Widnall.

Page Gregory Howard (who shared that curious first name, in his
case derived from his grandmother, Ann Page of Barton) described
himself for the 1851 census as 'Landed Proprietor'. The family had
become gentry, and James Nutter was now in charge of Grantchester
Mill. The younger generation of these Howards – Charles, Page, Eliza
and Anne – were of much the same age as young Widnall. They lived
close to their cousins, in Wright's Farm*.

The other farming family particularly well known to the Widnalls
were the Lilleys of Manor Farm. Edward Lilley, from Bourn, had
towards the end of the 18th century taken the tenancy of 'Lordship Farm'
– just over 300 acres, owned by King's College. (Other tenants of the
college early in the century were Uriah Matthews of Lacies Farm, 236
acres; Benjamin Howard, of Scales and Audlies, 167 acres; and Angier,
with 124 acres.) But Edward Lilley, either by misfortune or mismanage-
ment, had fallen badly into debt and so passed the tenancy to his son
Frederick, now aged about fifty. (The rest of Edward's nine children
had gone their separate ways, one – David – marrying Elizabeth Eaden,
daughter of a successful business man. And, combining their two surnames, that enterprise was to become Eaden Lilley, the big Cambridge
department store.) At the time of Lilly Widnall's arrival in the village,
much of the Manor Farm must have looked new-built, for there had
been a calamitous fire in 1844 which destroyed all its outbuildings.†

*later to be known as Cedar House, or Cedar Lodge   †See Appendix III

[37]

It was at the end of December 1850 that Lally paid her first visit to the household. Having set out on the 28th she 'arrived at Granta from Worcester at 2 o'clock in the morning having missed the train'. She stayed for nearly three weeks and met a number of Page's friends.

Travel by rail seems to have been adopted eagerly by both the Smith and Widnall families. It was still quite new, and people accustomed to horse-drawn carriages had to adapt to the new form of transport; and Page later (in his *Gossiping Stroll* of 1892) described the early days:

> Travellers by train in those days [i.e. 1845–50] had not the comforts they now possess. The company seems to have tried to imitate the accommodation of the stage coach, where the outside passengers sat on benches in the open air; so, on the railways an open truck was provided with hard cross benches. The inside passengers by coach had cushioned seats and glass windows, so had those by train. But by coach there were only two classes, inside and out; by train an intermediate one was contrived, so carriages were made with uncushioned seats, a roof, and partially closed sides, but having large oval unglazed openings through which the wind passed freely. [He remembered] travelling from London in one of these second class carriages and having to put up an umbrella to keep off the rain which was driving in at the side...

The young Widnalls, the Smiths and Tom & Anne Davis would almost certainly have travelled in decent comfort on their journeys between Cambridge and Worcester (by London & North Western to Oxford via Bletchley*; and by the Great Western Railway to Worcester).

Now came 1851; and that summer there was an event not to be missed. The Great Exhibition opened on 1st May, and on 2nd June Page went to see it. Next day he was there again, together with Liz, his mother and Jane (Stroud, probably). A fortnight later Lally arrived. (Three years earlier, on a similar visit, she had been taken to the Chinese junk, a strange spectacle moored on the Thames which could be examined on payment of 1/-. One of the many good stories about the Exhibition's opening ceremony described the bringing forward of the hesitant 'Chinese Commissioner', who prostrated himself before the Queen during the singing of the Hallelujah Chorus. It turned out that this splendidly-robed gentleman was the proprietor of that same junk.) She went again to

---

*A line whose route was decided only after much controversy. One tentative suggestion had been to take the line through the centre of Grantchester.

the opera (Mozart's *Don Giovanni*, Meyerbeer's *Le Prophète*); but for her, too, the Exhibition was the great thrill. By 2nd July she could record, 'Fourth and last visit to the Great Exhibition went with Mr Hislop & spent nine hours there'.

The place itself was a wonder – the vast Crystal Palace, put up with such speed, all with the latest technology of cast iron and sheet glass, so light, so crammed with displays. The motto was 'The earth is the Lord's and all that therein is', and the exhibition's aim was to be all-encompassing. There were five main classes, sub-divided into thirty categories: Raw Materials; Machinery; Manufactures (Textile Fabrics, Metallic, Vitreous and Ceramic); Fine Arts; and Miscellaneous.

Page must have been fascinated by it all. Prince Albert was such an example! What intricate craftsmanship was displayed everywhere! What invention! What scope! Curiosities and fine artefacts had been brought from every continent, and Lilly and Lally shared his admiration – although perhaps with reservations about the zealous but indiscriminate use of ornament. Their own taste was far more restrained than that of the high fashion of that time.

*

Lally Smith returned to Worcester, where Richard's family and business were both developing. Shrubbery Cottage, home to an increasingly large and prosperous family, can have been no mere 'cottage', since so many people seem to have been accommodated there. (A photograph in one of the family albums of a large cottage-style house with thatched roof and slightly 'gothick' windows, resembling no known house in the Cambridge area, may possibly be of Shrubbery Cottage in the 1860s.)

Richard and Libby's first child, Alice (Elizabeth Alice), was born in October 1848, a year after their marriage and three months after her grandfather's sudden death at Great Yarmouth. There followed, at intervals of just over a year, Amy (Emily Stroud), Bertie (Herbert Hanbury) and Car (Richard Carington). The widowed Ann Smith lived there, and so did Lally. One or two domestic servants and a nurse are likely to have been part of the household, too.

In the summer of 1851 Tom and Anne Davis, though by now supposedly established in the Cambridge area, came home to Shrubbery Cottage for the birth of their own first child, Laura, and remained for another two months before returning to Grantchester. Lally, perhaps continuing to teach a few pupils, took a short trip with 'Dick, Lib and Matty

Stroud [a sister, Matilda, of Libby, Louise and Jane] in the dogcart to Stratford on Avon; stayed a night at Leamington, then on to Kenilworth and Warwick and back'. In October she had her 'first lesson at the School of Design', something which was to occupy her for three years.

The previous December Lally had made her first visit to Grantchester. This Christmas it was the turn of Page and Lilly to join the throng at Worcester.

1851 24 *Dec* Page & Lizzie arrived at 10 o'clock at night at Shrubbery
        Cottage
1852 5 *Jan*   SPW, Liz & Lally went to Little Malvern Priory Church
        most of which is in ruins
      7 *Jan*   Page & Lizzy went to Freame's Worcester and chose a
        Walnut table for their drawing room a present from Mr
        Cocks

Next month another present was noted: '14 Feb Lizzie's Valentine the Buhl* clock' – a token of devotion which would always be treasured.

*Usually spelt 'Boulle' – a richly ornamented style, with tortoiseshell inlay and gilt.

CHAPTER 5

The Old Vicarage

———•·•———

IT HAD BEEN ON 20 MARCH 1850, before Page Widnall's marriage, that 'Mr Martin called about exchanging the Vicarage'. The Rev. William Martin was the newly-appointed Vicar of Grantchester, who found that the old house did not suit him. Several of his predecessors had preferred to reside at their other living at Little Wilbraham, and Grantchester's Vicarage had been used by curates or tenants; and even back in 1800 the Master and Fellows of Corpus Christi College had agreed that a new vicarage was needed. In keeping with a tendency in many parishes at this period, Mr Martin wished to build something larger, more convenient, and with more ample provision for his carriage and horses.

The site he had in mind was in the centre of the village, land belonging to King's College but with a copyhold tenancy in the ownership of Page Widnall (who had recently inherited it from his grandmother). The conveyance documents survive, and show how ownership had been transferred from Samuel Peck to Sarah Freeman, then from her (as Sarah Page) to her brother John, and at his death to his sister Elizabeth (Page's grandmother). William Martin paid £100 and, with assistance from Queen Anne's Bounty, built his large yellow-brick residence.* Page, in turn, must have bought the freehold of the old Vicarage House from the diocesan authorities, who may have been glad to be rid of it. The 17th-century house was in a neglected state and suffered badly from damp; and only a romantic like Page Widnall would have found it attractive.

It was a place he had known from his boyhood, probably inside as well as out. After all, the Widnalls were sure to have known Edward Lilley, who at the beginning of the century had been one of the village's foremost farmers. When he was obliged to retire from the Manor Farm in favour of his son Frederick, he had lived economically with his daughters in the vicarage house. Later, in the 1840s, the Palmer family were there; and it must have been while they were such close neighbours that young Page first got to know Jonathan Palmer, one of Cambridge's principal printers.

*at the end of what is now known as Vicarage Drive

Making that arrangement, to exchange a plot of land which he had recently acquired through the death of his grandmother for the decrepit vicarage house, Page must already have started to dream a little. His father had become immensely successful and had left behind a well-appointed house and premises designed for the purpose of good business organization. Page himself was an admiring and dutiful son; and yet ... that other house steeped in history, that other garden with its great trees and river frontage, called to his imagination.

*

Widnall & Davis, the shop in King's Parade, Cambridge, part of the nursery enterprise at Grantchester, had been established by Page Widnall and Tom Davis in March 1849, and in the 1851 census SPW is duly set down as 'nurseryman'. But during that family visit to Worcester at the turn of the years 1851–52 there must have been some earnest discussion between the brothers-in-law. Richard, having succeeded his father as head of the St John's Nursery at Worcester, was doing well. It is probable that some of his own capital was invested in the Cambridge venture and that he took part in its business decisions. At the end of February, 1852, he travelled across to Grantchester; and six days later he returned, the *Widnall & Davis* partnership having been dissolved. It may be that stock and equipment could be transferred to the St John's Nursery. In any case Tom, Anne and the baby would go back to Worcestershire. And if there was any ill-feeling it was quickly soothed, for the families continued to exchange visits.

In September, indeed, Lally brought baby Laura to Grantchester for a few days, probably to keep her safely out of the way while her parents settled into their permanent home, at Malvern. This little niece became especially beloved, and would always feel at home at Grantchester.

The Widnalls, that September, gave one of their characteristic parties:

9 *Sept* Took Mrs Howard's young ladies up the river to tea had
fireworks on the river and supper on our return

And Lally, in Worcester, noted:

30 *Oct* Richd Lib & Anne thrown out of the dog cart coming from
Malvern Anne had her collar-bone broken

*

Page still had a farm to run, but, relieved of the business to which he had felt unsuited, he was able to indulge his own pursuits a little. Abandoning those vast beds of dahlias, he could frolic on the river with Ellen Howard's young ladies; and more importantly, he was now able to throw himself into the restoration of what would henceforward be called the Old Vicarage.

Although already his, it is clear that no improvements to the house had been undertaken by the end of 1851. On 12th October Joseph Romilly and his sister took a long walk out from Cambridge, first to Trumpington Church (where 'Lucy found the sermon very dry & the church damp & cold'), and they

> ... then walked to Grantchester & examined the tombstones & walked round the lovely church. We here met Mr Deighton who has been living during the summer in the tumbledown vicarage where I had Pupils in 1813: he told us that these last 2 nights thieves had tried to get in ...

But now, a year later, repairs were under way. It may be that the long French windows of the dining and drawing rooms were installed at this time, and also the verandah shading them. Other alterations would be made over the years; but the house's character was and remains comfortably old-fashioned. The old walnut table and the four-poster beds would settle in happily, as would the Chippendale chairs bought at a bargain price later on. One part of the furnishing, remembered with amusement, was a cupboard disguised as a bookcase filled with false spines bearing comic titles. And this was in keeping with the mood of the place: its charm seems to induce an impulse to playfulness. The Widnalls always enjoyed tinkering with the house and filling its garden with surprises, and their 20th-century successors continued to do so.

That garden lies quietly encircled – almost – by great trees. Below a line of chestnuts flows the millstream on its way to join the Granta (and then on, winding, towards Cambridge, where it becomes the Cam). The rushing sound of water coming down the mill-race could be heard, and the working of the mill; swans and lesser waterfowl cruised past reeds and willows. Green and moist, the garden used sometimes to flood in winter. But even in its neglected state its charms must have been evident, for, as Romilly had noted in 1837, the grounds were 'very prettily laid out'.

It was in the garden that Page indulged in his greatest project: a 'folly' known as the Castle Ruin. It stands beside the end of the main lawn, close to the river. A large structure, it is mainly built of the old-fash-

The Castle Ruin today

ioned (and locally made) 'clay bats', big bricks formed from clay mixed with straw and dried by sun and wind. The 'ruined' curved wall and carved archways are of clunch – local soft limestone. In less visible parts the normal East Anglian yellow brick is used as well. It is said that the young Widnall employed just one labourer to help in its construction. This seems scarcely credible, yet he certainly did the major part with his own hands, and the whole conception, with oriel window, carved heads, crenellated tower – a medieval fantasy – was his.

Lilly had seen, before her marriage, the restless young man with the urge to make things. She would scarcely be surprised now to find him drawing plans, stripping off his coat, sawing, chiselling and hammering. The Castle Ruin was both a folly and practical accommodation for all the activities he proposed. It looked – it looks still – wonderful silhouetted amidst early morning mists, and it takes on a sort of stagey glory with the evening glow upon it. The rooms inside became, upstairs, a long room which was to be used, in turns, as a small theatre, a photographic studio, and the 'tapestry room' (one cannot tell now quite what happened where). Downstairs the greater space must have been given to the workshop, for it was here that later a boat was built, and it would be here that he did his other carpentry, metalwork and carving.

It was not just the young man who was busy shaping his dreams in tangible form, but his wife as well. Their home was a shared enterprise, and one which bound them together throughout their years together.

Sadly, Lilly's contributions have mostly perished: moths and damp and sunlight destroy textiles, and so her embroideries are now all lost. But in the Ruin can be found, set in its 'gothic' window-frames, panes of painted glass which are surely hers – two birds (inexact likenesses of a thrush and a yellowhammer). The careful calligraphy which she added to the sundial has long washed away. But her plantings in this garden aspiring to become an Earthly Paradise may, here and there, be surviving still.

*

All the preparatory work took a long time; but on 7th June 1853 they 'began to move the furniture from the Nursery house to the Old Vicarage', and on the 8th they spent their first night there.

When Joseph Romilly passed through the village the following April he noticed the change:

> I went through Grantchester & Trumpington. I have learnt that the Vicarage ... is occupied by Mr Widnall (only child of the great Florist): the large house built by his Father is unoccupied – (it was lately occupied by a Mr Fowler who died there) ... [14 April 1854]

In taking his momentous change of direction, Page had had to find a way of using the former Nursery House and land which would continue to yield some income. His chosen solution was to let that house, now to be called 'Vine Cottage', with a much-reduced garden. On the piece of former nursery garden down the road he built a big square house, yellow brick with slate roof, resembling the Rev. William Martin's vicarage. This was later described as 'a detached Villa Residence, placed on an eminence, and having a raised Terrace round', with 'five airy bedrooms' and all the latest conveniences. He called it 'Riversdale'*. The property yielded £50 a year in rent; and as it turned out, it was to bring some rewarding friendships with its successive tenants.

*

The Widnall household was of its time, Victorian in its habits and conventional in its piety. Later on there were two living-in servants, and other help may have been employed in the house and garden. The seeming miracle of running a farm while going off for visits and pursuing so many unrelated activities was achieved by employing a bailiff; for there is

---

*which is still there, but now looks quite different, encased in the Edwardian red-brick enlargement made by a later owner, Richard Assheton, F.R.S.

no sign of Page – far less of his mother, though both were listed in the directories as 'farmers' – ploughing the fields or milking the cows.

The aspect of farming which Page did find fascinating and worth recording among his brief diary entries was innovation. Disasters (fire in the stackyard, damage from a gale) are mentioned; but also, eagerly, the wonders of the new incubator – the numbers of chicks hatched in brood after brood. As with all his activities, there was an readiness to try out the new possibilities suggested by articles read in periodicals. The inspiration of the Great Exhibition was to persist.

CHAPTER 6

Interim – Lally Smith

LALLY, while living at Worcester, led a gently busy life. She was teaching a few pupils music and French, painting flowers, and, like her brother-in-law Page, observing wildlife:

> *5 Aug* 1851 An Owl came and settled on the Cypress Arch (Shrubbery Cottage) at a little before 12 o'clock a very bright hot day its wings as it crouched on the Arch were at least a foot and a half wide, it was a buff colour with a pretty white face

She was a companion for her mother. There had been great concern three years before when a 'terrible accident' occurred – 'Dear Mother almost killed by a runaway horse in a cart by the Nursery gates'; but after her recovery Mrs Smith seems to have been in good health, and with Lally made journeys to Tenbury and to London. The two of them spent the New Year of 1853 at Bridgenorth, visiting Hanbury relatives and old friends. Then at the end of March they 'left Shrubbery Cottage for Pierpoint St'. Richard's family home must have become a tight fit for them all, since there were now four small children and attendant servants. It was time for withdrawal to quieter quarters.

In Worcester, Lally's love of music could flourish. A greatly-revered teacher, Mrs Shelton, had encouraged her interest: in May 1845 she 'gave Annie & me two pieces of Music dedicated to herself', and later Lally met Mr Havergal (a clergyman-composer of many psalm and hymn tunes) at her house. It was Mrs Shelton, too, who had introduced Lally to her first teaching post with the Misses Collison, Baskerville House School, where she had ten pupils. And there must have been plenty of concerts, both choral and instrumental, in that cathedral city.

Another of Lally's occupations during the years 1851–54 was to attend the School of Design; and when Lilly came for a visit in the summer of 1853 the two of them took a few lessons in 'Velvet painting', a curious variation on the usual painstaking watercolours (but then, Victorian ladies were apt to take up strange crafts: four years earlier 'Liz took 1st lesson on Wax flower making').

It must have been difficult to know whether to continue this pleasant life indefinitely, or to make a change. After all, sister Anne and her husband Tom Davis lived nearby at Malvern, and Lally had been watching the progress of their baby Laura closely. In January 1854 she noted proudly, 'Baby Laura two years and half old knows her letters can say "How doth the little busy Bee" "Jack & Jill" and can count up to 12.' But the course at the School of Design was coming to an end. She had a slight accident at the beginning of July – '2 July Lally had a fall from a rustic stump of wood in the Nursery at St John's and was insensible for some time' – but otherwise there was little drama.

A few days after the completion of Lally's art course, Richard, Libby, Alice and Amy made a visit to Grantchester. 'Alice photographed lying on the sofa', noted Page Widnall in his diary. And his next entry, on 24th July, was 'Lally came to live at Grantchester'.

CHAPTER 7

The Later 1850s

———•◦•———

LALLY CAME TO LIVE AT Grantchester. Rural life suited her – especially when it could be spent so close to Cambridge. There, the university's intellectual and social life was undergoing a renaissance: new disciplines were being introduced, student numbers were increasing, and music, drama and sport flourishing. Nor were Cambridge and Worcester, though 120 miles apart, impossibly far from each other. By now the railway network meant that ladies – even a single small lady like Lally – could safely travel in carriages reserved for their use, and their luggage – heavy leather trunks, basketwork hampers and hatboxes – all be taken care of by willing porters for a few small coins. Members of the family would make many journeys east and west.

At thirty-three years old, she was taking on the role of family support and maiden aunt. From now on, whenever visitors came to the Old Vicarage, members of the family had troubles, or Lilly and Page went on excursions, she would be ready to give a hand, rush to the rescue, or join in the fun. The household – Page, Lilly & Lally – would enjoy their shared enthusiasm for the arts, antiquities and the natural world.

Soon after Lally's arrival, Page and Lilly 'made a picture frame of fungus' – but it was a disastrous experiment. It 'made us very ill from breathing the dust which was poisonous'. So, while Lally went up to London to see the Crystal Palace on its new site at Sydenham, the Widnalls were slowly recovering from their arty-crafty folly. Lilly, especially, took a long time: the incident with the fungus spores led to weeks in bed and several more weeks' convalescence at Cromer.

In July 1855 Lilly found a lump in her right breast. Despite this, a fortnight later she was gallantly going with the others to London, where they as usual stayed with friends and went to the theatre. One day was spent at Hampstead with the Johnstons, when the trio 'had our portraits taken by them'; and finally they brought home their hostess Mrs Southam and her daughter Fanny for a spell in Grantchester.

Although the Old Vicarage itself was relatively humble, it was always welcoming, and greatly loved. Somehow the guests were accommodated and room was found for Lally's pupils too. For Lally had begun teaching again, and recorded in her diary that two little girls, Julia and Lizzie Lilley, started their lessons with her that summer (their brother Fred was to join later). These were the children of Frederick Lilley, the village's major farmer, and lived at the ancient Manor House.

The idea of running a small school in the Old Vicarage had been raised once before, when Page was a little boy. Indeed, it was when these same children's grandfather was in trouble that their aunts had wondered whether they might clear his debts by running one there. When Romilly had called at the house in November 1833 it was the unhappy Edward Lilley and his daughters, then in residence, whom he came to see and who sought his advice.

> ... it appears that Mr L. is 4 or 500£ in arrears with King's and they are importunate: the girls, poor things, are sadly in distress about it: they wished to consult with me about setting up a School in the Vicarage house: Kate seems to have all the energy: – I stated to them all the difficulties of their scheme, their youth, being unmarried, & not brought up to it, the necessity of having a middle aged woman long accustomed to school & to teaching children...

But now, more than 20 years later, Lally Smith, having been 'brought up to it', was the ideal schoolmistress.

Lally at the piano

Uncle Page's Book names many of her pupils. Over the course of more than 30 years many of them reappear as devoted friends. What did they learn? Their English was well attended to: for Lally, when writing her journal or a letter, was fluent and had a graceful hand. Her literary accomplishments would include writing at least one children's story, and compiling an original anthology of verse. She had sufficient French to enjoy travels on the Continent. She was a dedicated botanist, with a knowledge far beyond the ordinary amateur. She was skilled in water-colours. She could sing and play the piano. She had a good grasp of history. All these were usual ladylike accomplishments, developed in some branches to a greater than usual degree. In February 1859 is recorded 'Lally's first lesson in Geometry'; but whether she was receiving or imparting this lesson is not clear.

What is certain is that children at the Old Vicarage must have benefited from the whole ethos of the place. The minds of all three principal members of the household, Page, Lilly and Lally, were open to exploration and wonder; they themselves had never assumed that education ended when their schooldays finished. Uncle Page loved to show what specimens of plant, insect or rock he had discovered, what antiquarian curiosities had been unearthed, what device newly invented. Aunt Lilly was gifted in design and embroidery, and may well have been that very valuable grown-up, a 'good listener'. And there were, until their deaths, those formidable old widows Mrs Widnall and Mrs Smith (and the alarming-looking Miss Hannah Widnall) who had long experience of farm-management and horticulture.

(It is no wonder that the spirits said to haunt that house are not those of groaning old clerics but of children, eagerly tugging visitors with their little hands up to their attic schoolroom.)

*

The life they all three settled into during the late 1850s established a pattern continued through the following decades. *Uncle Page's Book* provides little snapshots of their activities, though a great deal must have been omitted; but fitful and scrappy as the entries are, they provide a fairly continuous record. There are the items of family news; visits; books read; plays, concerts, lectures attended; and occasional odd happenings in the garden or village. Though infuriatingly terse, the slightest-seeming entries often turn out to be significant. And the whole diary, steadily progressing through their lives, item by item, conveys that innocence and optimism shared by so many Victorians in similar circumstances.

They were all intensely family-minded; and 'family' extended to all those attachments by marriage, so that the story revealed in the diary jottings is of the flourishing or withering of various branches of the family tree. A major contrast which soon appears is of the diverging fortunes of those two nursery-gardeners, Page and Richard, reflecting the contrast in their characters.

Although the Widnall-Smith marriage had promised a strong dynasty, an ever-expanding business and further well-chosen connections, those expectations were not to be fulfilled. Page Widnall could not face a life dedicated to the narrow specialities of horticulture and meticulous book-keeping. Yet the business of raising and propagating the new plants coming from the Far East and the new World at that time might have produced a fortune, for the Victorians, in their increasing prosperity, were besotted with such things. It became the age of conservatories, jardinières, rockeries, shrubberies and gaudy bedding-plants. The Cambridge colleges were expanding; soon more of their dons would be permitted to marry and build their large houses and well laid-out gardens. But it was left to other local florists, seedsmen and plantsmen to make the most of these opportunities.

It was to be the end of the line, too, for the Widnall family. Page and Lilly, happily married, were to have no children. Richard Smith was taking his business seriously and successfully, and Libby bore him two daughters, to be followed by two sons. The Widnall and Smith careers had parted, yet family links would always remain strong.

While the railway enabled those links to be maintained with visits between Worcester and Cambridge, they were fortunate in having in London, too, several welcoming homes – old family friends, mostly related even if distantly. In a city which was undergoing huge changes – great engineering works to instal sewers and gas supplies, grandiose public buildings and new dwellings for workers – they could be sure of comfort.

Mozart's *Don Giovanni* (1851), Byron's *Sardanapalus* (1853), and *Henry VIII* (1855) are among the theatrical experiences. A book which Page thought worth mentioning is *The Caxtons*, by Bulwer Lytton – a historical novel set in the 15th century. And in that same year, 1854, Lally records the borrowing of a book which gave her great delight, the *Life of Mrs Sherwood*. It was the biography of a lady already admired, for she came from Bridgenorth and may well have been known to the Hanbury relatives there. Mrs Sherwood (whose portrait can be seen, carved in low relief, on her memorial in Worcester Cathedral) had travelled with her husband in India and written dozens of uplifting books for children. Lally's pupils must surely have been brought up on her *History of the Fairchild Family*. Another title mentioned is *The Pilgrim's Progress* ('the outlines'), which was deeply influential despite its nonconformist origin.

At some time not long after Lally moved to Grantchester her mother must have come to join them. She, too, seems to have settled into the ways of the village. It was as well that she seems to have had a calm temperament and was on easy terms with the ladies next door at Mill Farm, Page's mother and aunt, for there was always activity at the Old Vicarage. Children arrived for lessons; visitors came to stay (Mrs Quinsee, indeed, came to stay for a week with her son William, 'he very ill'); and Page's building work was not yet complete. In June 1855 two village men, Watts and Muggleton, started digging foundations for the glasshouse to be attached to the Castle. And a few days later 'Mother had a dreadful fall'.

Three of those summer visitors came over from Worcester – 'Mr Stroud and his two sisters', members of Libby's family. In December there would be a double wedding when those two sisters, Jane and Matilda, were married to two brothers, Alfred and Henry Lapworth. (The eldest of the Stroud sisters, Louisa Williams, had married seven years earlier.) Now, as the 'family' extended (and even in-law connections and second cousins were embraced in that warm circle), there were even more welcoming homes to visit in the metropolis[*], and more of their contemporaries with growing families to be welcomed at Grantchester. Young Williamses and young Lapworths would in due course appear in the Widnall photograph albums, together with Robinsons, Southams, Johnstons and others.

Visitors naturally accompanied their Old Vicarage hosts to church. Lally records, in September 1855:

> A party of 11 went to Church, 10 sat in our own Square pew – Mother[†], Page, Liz, Dick, Lib, Alice, Amy, Mrs & Miss Widnall and Jetty Southam. Lally with the Lilleys

The layout of the church at that time may be clearly seen in the scale model later made by Page. There is only one 'square pew', and it indicates the prominence of the Widnall family in the village.

---

[*]The Johnstons lived at Hampstead; the two Lapworth families at Maida Vale; the Southams at Clapham; and the Robinsons, cousins on the Hanbury side, at Belgrave Place.   [†]Mrs Ann Smith

On a visit by the trio to the family at Worcester at the New Year, 1856, Lally met an artist, Mr Davis, who asked her to sit for him.

> 10 *Jan* Called on Mr Davis and saw his lovely painting 'Punch' and the picture in which I am to appear as a lady taking good things to the poor inmates of a Cottage

One can almost imagine the sentimental Victorian picture: Lally, with her long ringlets, small and gentle, as the benevolent lady. It was surely what the theatrical profession would call 'typecasting'. And one catches hints of the sisters' rather gushing manner of speech now and then – 'Drank tea and spent a pleasant evening with Mrs Deeton a dear heavenly old lady', or exclamations of 'So lovely!'

Back home at Grantchester, life was varied: one day to the Senate House in Cambridge to see young Arthur Robinson (one of those distant cousins from London) take his degree … and a few days later, some village gossip. 'Miss Hawkes called and told us that Mr Searle [*sic*] paid his addresses to Lucy Lilley'. Lucy was thirteen years younger than the Rev. Mr Tearle, who later had charge of the parishes of Gazeley and Kenton; and Miss Hawkes was herself to marry a clergyman and become 'Mrs Dixon of Over'.

The following year, in the midst of calamities – Jetty Southam very ill, Lally rushing to be with her for five days; the dramatic death of one of Page's friends from 'Brain fever' – there comes an entry '18 April Heard the Nightingale'. And then Lally was off with Richard's party to the Continent for 24 days.

> 10 *June* Mr Lapworth Sen. Richd Libby and I arrived at Dieppe in the evening, no carriages about – no gas lights
>
> 14 *June* In Paris, saw the procession to and from Notre Dame on the occasion of the Baptism of the young Prince Imperial
>
> 23 *June* Richd Libby and I first met Mr Buckham in the train between Baden and Heidelburg
>
> 1 *July* Richd, Libby, I and Mr Buckham crossed from Ostend to London on our return from the Continent

In August, Page and Lilly took their own slightly shorter holiday to Wales, accompanied by a Grantchester friend, Mrs Sidney Jackson. A month later it was Page alone who took his mother to see the Crystal Palace at its new location at Sydenham. Three days after that 'Dr

Humphrey removed a tumour from Lizzie's breast'. This was more than a year after the discovery of that lump; but they had called in the most eminent surgeon in Cambridge, and after two and a half weeks Lilly/Lizzie was able to go to church again. Then it was the turn of their friend Miss Fowke, who 'had an operation for tumour like Lizzie's. Lally was with her.' Such surgery would have been done at home at that time; but at least by this date it might have been made more bearable by a whiff of chloroform.

The next year began, once more, with plenty of invitations. Lally's new friend Mr Buckland – Lally was often imprecise in the spelling of names – gave an 'entertainment' in Cambridge, and in the village they spent evenings at each other's houses, with songs at the piano ('Mrs Padley sang "The Lady all Skin & Bone"').

That May, 1857, Richard and Libby brought all four of their children for a long visit to Grantchester. Uncle Page took photographs of Alice and Amy in fancy dress – and a century later the one of Alice as Little Red Riding Hood was still cherished. Shortly after their return there was an emergency, when Lally:

20 *June* Recd Telegram to go to Worcester to nurse dear Libby who is
    dangerously ill
23 *June* Libby who was supposed to be dying bid farewell to all her children
24 *June* I went to Malvern to see Tom & Annie, Laura & baby Tom
31 *June* Returned to Granta after Libby's illness

And the teaching of her pupils must have been resumed. She had a natural rapport with children, being herself so small and serene. The diary mentions a story, *The Little Ash Tree*, which she wrote that year.

In August Page and Lilly were away for four weeks, a more adventurous holiday this time, in the Channel Islands. When, in Guernsey, they 'made the acquaintance of Captn and Mrs Young' it was the beginning of yet another lasting friendship.

In September, at the annual School Treat (an event started by his father), SPW heard of 'Mr Page Howard's trouble'. This was a neighbour only a few years older than himself and known to him all his life, a son of Page Gregory Howard the miller. Now, in October, his wife had died; and 'Mr P. Howard and his daughter left Granta their old servant Kitty Matthews also was buried today to whom they had always sent her Sunday dinner'. Page Howard himself died the following March.

Those new friends, the sea-captain and Mrs Young, came in November and spent a month at the Old Vicarage, perhaps accompanying the trio when they enjoyed tea with young Johnston at Trinity, followed by the evening service in chapel.

They may, too, have shared another experience – going to the University Senate House to hear a notable lecture, and one which was to remain in Page's memory and flourish in his imagination. The speaker was David Livingstone, the great explorer-missionary, launching the Universities' Mission to Central Africa.

*

1858 began in a way that was to become customary – 'theatricals'. This year it was merely 'a party at Mrs Quinsee's' in Cambridge with charades. Bigger and better efforts would follow – although charades could themselves be quite elaborate. An exactly contemporary description of such an evening occurs in the fictional adventures of an Oxford undergraduate, 'Mr Verdant Green'.* There, the hero takes part in New Year charades (four scenes: three syllables plus complete word enacted) and no effort is spared in contriving properties and costumes such as the impersonation of

> ... a footman (Mr Bouncer) attired in a peculiarly ingenious and effective livery, made by pulling up the trousers to the knee, and wearing the dress-coat inside out, so as to display the crimson silk linings of the sleeves: the effect of Mr. Bouncer's appearance is considerably heightened by a judicious outlay of flour sprinkled over his hair ...

Poor Lilly, in May, sprained her knee: an accident which entailed 'setting' with splints for eight days, and crutches for forty-six. Two sea-side holidays, one at Cromer and another at Eastbourne with Mrs Southam, eventually restored her.

*

January 1859 was marked by their own first theatricals, in their own Castle Theatre. Elaborate preparations had been made, in which all three members of the trio played their part. There was scenery to be constructed and painted and endless stitching to be done on costumes. A long poster, printed by Jonathan Palmer with typographical bravura, announced the performance of 'the laughable Farce of <u>Box</u> and <u>Cox</u>', the 'Oriental Extravaganza of <u>Beauty</u> and the <u>Beast</u>' (in eleven scenes); and finally

---

*The Further Adventures of Mr Verdant Green, an Oxford Undergraduate. The author, 'Cuthbert Bede, B.A.', was Edward Bradley (1827–89), a clergyman humourist.

'the universally admired Piece entitled the <u>Railway Station</u>' – which turned out to be a grand buffet supper in which the 'Superintendant of the Goods Department' was their host, Mr Phynditout himself.

The taste for amateur performances of burlesque pieces such as those of J. R. Planché, already becoming popular on the London stage as a contrast to the leaden verse dramas which had been wearying audiences, had been promoted in Cambridge by F. C. Burnand. He, later to write and direct many comic plays, had a few years earlier, while still an undergraduate, founded the Amateur Dramatic Club. The Castle Theatre cast, in true A.D.C. manner, were announced with their identities faintly disguised. The players were:

Mr Phynditout	... Page Widnall
Mrs Phynditout	... Lizzy Widnall
Miss Whaytabytt	... Lally Smith
Mr Aldiborontiphoscophornio- Chrononhotonthologos Crafty	... George Howard
Mr Parallelopiped Sage	... William Howard
Mr Will. D'Espigne	... Mr Wilderspin
Miss Rhozanthyssell	... Miss Buchanan
Miss Convolaria	... Julia Lilley

Similar tricks and puns were to be invented in the following years: Miss La Chasse (Miss Hunt), Mr & Mrs Yelmirg (the Grimleys), and Mr N. O. Nayme (Mr Nimmo) would appear, and George Howard's name be contracted to 'Mr A. &c. Crafty'.

Those two boys with the cumbersome pseudonyms, George, aged fifteen, and his brother William, a year older, lived with their widowed mother and elder brother at Merton House. Their father, Thomas Howard, had married Ellen late in life, and had died before the birth of George. He had left a family sufficiently prosperous for all three of his sons to be sent to St Paul's School in London, and William would gain a Scholarship to Trinity College. But he, thought to be the most brilliant, was never able to take up his award; for exactly three years after his performance at the Old Vicarage, when he was due to matriculate, he would die. Mrs Howard and her boarding-school for 'young ladies' (there were thirteen there in 1851), have already been mentioned; and she and the devoted George would remain among the Widnalls' closest friends.

Later in January 1859, when sister Annie Davis and her friend were staying with them, Page and Lally took William and George Howard to spend 'a delightful afternoon at Ely. The lovely reredos is finished*'. There was evidently still concern about Lilly's health; for after she had spent a month in London with Annie, there is relief in the entry: 'Dear Lilly returned from London looking very well'. And soon she was at work on the 'border of the Church carpet'.

Other diary entries are characteristic of their delights and occupations at the end of the 1850s:

4 *Feb*   Took a photo of the Church with Xmas decorations (P)
11 *March*   Spent a pleasant evening at Miss Fowkes' saw the ancient Doll, read the ancient letters, heard some funny stories and eat [*sic*] hung beef and Banbury cakes (SS)
28 *April*   Our beautiful Peacock was killed by a Cow
10 *June*   Lally started a garden at the back of Swiss Cottage

Emily and Hester Robinson, with the Swiss Cottage

*The cathedral was undergoing a major restoration under the direction of the architect Gilbert Scott.

[58]

The 'Swiss Cottage' was a new addition to the garden, a pretty log cabin which must have been inspired by its namesake at Osborne House on the Isle of Wight, a more extensive playhouse built by Prince Albert for the royal children. Page's Swiss Cottage was approached by a winding path which crossed a stream by a rustic bridge, and at one time it housed rabbits and guinea-pigs. Lally's pupils loved it, and indeed it may have been built with one particular little girl in mind. For in June 1858 brother-in-law Tom Davis had brought his daughter Laura, the niece whose progress from babyhood had particularly delighted Lally. The bright seven-year-old announced on her arrival that she had come 'to stay 6 weeks 6 months or 6 years'. And Laura, who by now had a baby brother Tom, did stay on and off for many years.

1859 30 *Jan* Went to Trumpington Church with Annie & Laura, a little wren sang his pretty song to the accompaniment of the organ and chattered in the litany

12 *March* Laura compared the Tongue to Quaking grass which is never still.

On 25th June that year the old Nursery House – henceforward to be known as Vine Cottage (and later Lyndewode) – was sold to Miss Fowke for £420. Riversdale, offered at the same auction, failed to sell.

Lally and her pupil Julia Lilley were attending the School of Art at Cambridge that year. Page, meantime, was busy making pictures of a different sort.

CHAPTER 8

Photography

——◦•◦——

EXACTLY WHEN DID PAGE WIDNALL first take up photography? The answer is unknown, as his diary record is so fitful. But in July 1854 there is the note about little Alice being photographed lying on the sofa – perhaps ambiguous, for one cannot be certain that SPW was the photographer. It is very likely, though, that he had been experimenting for some months before this.

Among surviving early photographs there are two oddities worth mentioning. One, which may be one of the very earliest experiments, is a curious 'ambrotype': a distant view of Grantchester Church not immediately recognisable – since the effect of that particular technique was to produce on glass a positive image but in reverse. The other is a stereoscopic* view of the village street, with Wright's Row and the thatched school building. There are no figures to offer a clue as to date, and the letters 'FGH' are all that appears on the back. But most likely the picture was taken *c* 1859–63 (at the period when that remarkable amateur photographer, Lady Hawarden, was using this technique) – for certainly the road looks unsurfaced, and no glimpse of the 1867 school building is visible; and at this time Page might well have given such a picture to his young friend Frederick George Howard, or indeed taught him to take it for himself.

Photography was a scientific marvel which had emerged in Page's boyhood. The Frenchman L-J-M Daguerre had perfected a method of fixing a finely-focussed image onto a flat plate of polished metal, which he announced publicly in 1839. The daguerrotype was a great success, but only one copy of each picture could be produced. This prompted an Englishman, Henry Fox Talbot, to announce the results of his own experiments, still at an early stage, which yielded less sharp images but ones which might allow successive prints to be made on paper. In 1844, when Page was eighteen, Fox Talbot produced a small book, *The Pencil of Nature*, which described the stages by which he had developed a technique producing a negative-positive process. This he called the 'calotype'. Perceptively and with clarity, he stated his understanding of the distinctive

*a double image which, seen through a special viewer, would give a three-dimensional impression.

top from left: Tom Davies; Williams children; Miss Hannah Widnall
centre from left: James Nutter; Henry Ellis; Mr Archer
lower from left: Master Grimley; The Fullertons; Sidney Jackson

Typical transport of the 1860s, standing before the Old Vicarage.

nature of photography. There was no magic, simply chemical reactions to light:

> The picture, divested of the ideas which accompany it, and considered only in its ultimate nature, is but a succession or variety of stronger lights thrown upon one part of the paper, and of deeper shadows on another.

It is doubtful whether the Widnalls ever saw this book, but rumours must have reached them through the publications such as *Chambers's*

Journal which they did read. The real breakthrough came in March 1851, when Scott Archer announced a new invention which gave faster and clearer results, the 'wet collodion process'. The Great Exhibition, a month or two later, showed a range of the latest photographic apparatus, and Archer's novel and effective process must have whetted many appetites. From that point, certainly, there was a rush to take up the new activity; for Scott Archer, unlike Fox Talbot, had not thought to patent his technique, and so was to make no profit from its popularity.

Page Widnall appears to have tried several types of equipment. He would have needed a single wide-angled lens for his efforts at Worcester in January 1856 – 'Took some photo's of Worcester cathedral, Chapter-house &c.' A different camera, or perhaps a special adapter, would have been needed for 'a pair of Double Stereoscopic Portrait or Landscape Pictures possessing the requisite angle [to be taken] on one plate'.* That would have enabled him to produce not only the steroscopic view of

Grantchester's High Street, but also those photographs of the little nieces in fancy dress (which, Amy's son was to recall, were both stereoscopic and tinted in colour). But most important to him was the 'Carte de Visite' camera (patented in 1854) which produced four or six pictures on one plate. That was to be given intensive use.

To use the wet collodion process, a photographer had to have a good understanding of the action of the chemicals he was using. It involved a lot of critical work – preparing the exact formula, coating the glass plate with the viscous emulsion, exposing it before it dried, having a sensitizing bath ready for development, and above all handling the large plate so that no smudge or speck of dust could spoil it. It was a daunting procedure,

*Advertisement by Burfield & Rouch, 1862

illustrated by the trials which the friends of Lewis Carroll (the Rev. Charles Dodgson) were to suffer when he came to stay, inflicting not only long sessions in front of the camera but accommodation of all his paraphernalia:

> ... apart from camera, lens and tripod ... a chest full of bottles containing chemicals for coating, developing, fixing and varnishing the glass plates, bottles of various sizes containing stock solutions, a number of dishes, a good stock of glass plates, scales and weights, glass measures and funnels, and, above all, a portable dark tent or cupboard in which all the chemical hocus-pocus took place.*

Dodgson, like Page Widnall, was a methodical worker. The renowned Julia Margaret Cameron, also active in the 1860s, demanded even more tolerance for her inspirational but sloppy activities. She wrote:

> Personal sympathy has helped me on very much. My husband from first to last has watched every picture with delight, and it is my daily habit to run to him with every glass upon which a fresh glory is newly stamped, and to listen to his enthusiastic applause. This habit of running into the dining-room with my wet pictures has stained such an immense quantity of table linen with nitrate of silver, indelible stains, that I should have been banished from any less indulgent household.

SPW's photographs taken in Worcester Cathedral have not, alas, survived. They must have taken several minutes' exposure. Yet it is interesting to find, from the *Photographic News* of March 1859, that early attempts to avoid the cumbersome messiness of the wet process by using Fothergill's new Dry Process entailed an even greater expenditure of time. 'A pretty successful picture of the Choir and Great East Window of York Minster', wrote a correspondent, had to be exposed for four hours.

Despite all its difficulties, the attraction of photography was for Page irresistible: something new which combined technical skill and a certain artistry, something which fitted his talents. He created a studio in the Castle Ruin and began taking portraits. Once listed in the local directory as 'florist' and still as 'farmer', he now assumed a new identity. He had the reverse side of his photographic cards printed with a device: *S.P. Widnall, Photographer.*

*

*Helmut Gersheim, who also quotes the second passage in his *Life & Work of Julia Margaret Cameron*

The remaining evidence of this profession can be found in a few albums. Two are those massive Victorian leather-bound volumes with hard pages into which are set small *carte-de-visite* sized portraits. Some are not by him, and it is at first not easy to distinguish authorship. How can one tell? – for unlike paintings, there is no characteristic brushstroke by which to identify them. But from one album one may, with tweezers, carefully extract some examples. There are enough of them with his sign on the back for one to recognize certain fixtures in his studio: the carved chairs, the checkered carpet, the ornaments. And where there were items of furniture too bulky to be taken up to the studio in the Ruin, they had been painted instead, the false fireplace and the false piano. (The photographic journals of the time were full of advertisements for equipment of all kinds, including 'Backgrounds, balconies, &c., of any design for the ARTIST…' In September 1862 the *Photographic News* would include a scornful comment from a professional portrait-painter: 'The *carte de visite* … is a pedestal with a man near it; it might be catalogued as a portrait of a pedestal, and a column, and a lord.')

In these authentic SPW photographs his skill is evident. With his gentle indoor lighting (and the suggestion of side illumination from a window) his exposures needed to be quite slow; yet he managed to keep his subjects calm and cheerful. There is seldom that fearful rigidity which often gives the impression that our Victorian forbears were people devoid of feeling or humour. (Even today, with the wizardry of fast films and brilliant cameras, a successful portrait reflects a sympathetic rapport between photographer and subject.) In group photographs he achieves a relationship between the figures which is both natural and aesthetically pleasing – the flow of the huge silken skirts in the Fullerton group or the picture of Mrs Buchanan and her daughter, or Professor Grote and his nieces with their chessboard.

Recording the appearance of most of his friends and relations, he included where possible something suggestive of their interests. This iconography provides a book or ecclesiastical-style bookstand for a cleric or an academic; a flower for his botanising ladies; embroidery for Lilly; the piano for the musical Lally; and for his self-portraits either a paper or his microscope.

Besides the portrait albums, two others with fractured bindings and tattered covers contain photographs which are almost all his work. Some have almost faded away, but enough remain to show his range and quality. There are quite early ones taken in Dorset, recording a holiday taken in 1860 ('19 July Went to Tilly Whim and Swanage took Photo's. 21 July Went to Corfe Castle and took Photo's…').

On that occasion the trio were accompanied by Henry Ellis, the son of Alderman Augustus Ellis, a family friend. Henry – young and fit – was with them again in 1862 for a month of travel in the Channel Islands; and once more in 1864 for a holiday in N. Wales. And this young man, recruited as holiday-companion and as the essential porter-cum-lab-assistant for the enterprise, appears himself in the album of portraits. There, he poses at the wicket wearing cricketing togs; and there, too, are his rather solemn parents and his small sister.

It is a marvel that, of the multitude of portraits and photographs of buildings and landscapes, any survive at all. Page had no descendants. His albums stayed in that damp house, or perhaps in the damper Ruin, until some were collected by his niece-by-marriage and her children just before the First World War. The next generation thought them uninteresting, and quantities were destroyed, together with mildewed books and papers, on bonfires. In about 1915 some village boys came across broken photographic plates lying among debris in the crumbling Ruin, and found a brass plate announcing 'S. P. Widnall, Photographer' – all that was left.

(A strange treasure turned up, however, in the 1960s. A new tenant arriving at a house in Grantchester found that a window pane needed mending. 'I think I could mend that myself if I had a piece of glass the right size', he said. 'Ah,' said his wife, 'I noticed a box in the garden shed filled with glass. It looks about right except that it's all dark and dirty. If you cleaned it…' And fortunately John Lester, when he examined these glasses, recognized them as ancient photographic negatives. Being a keen photographer himself, he made contact prints and revealed pictures of Grantchester and Trumpington churches, an interior of King's College Chapel, a portrait of an old lady (Mrs Fowke), and a group taken in the Old Vicarage garden. The box must have been made for the purpose, and have been left amongst old tools and gadgets in the Ruin. The previous tenant of their house had been a gardener at the Old Vicarage who had helped himself to what looked like a useful box.)

And so those albums which remain, though perhaps at first disappointing, do turn out to be interesting. Names written beneath the small portraits point to the identity of many of the sitters – enough to pick out members of the family and many local figures. Old Mrs Widnall and Page's Aunt Hannah are there, his mother looking alert and pleasant, his aunt less so. Mrs Smith and all her children can be seen; also Richard's wife Libby and Anne's husband, the formidably bewhiskered Tom Davis ('Thomas Archibald Lloyd-Davis' as he is styled beneath an appropriately pompous family group taken in a professional studio). And over the years their children and grandchildren were to be photographed in turn.

There are more distant relatives – cousins from London and Worcester – and old family friends. There are, too, figures of interest to the local historian. Grantchester, so close to Cambridge, was in those days exceptionally secluded and yet accessible by light carriage, on horseback or on foot. University dons chose to live in the village (especially when, in the 1880s, they were all at last permitted to marry), and so there was a disproportionate number of academics and 'genteel' people. Although the village, having no squire, had no stately home, no really grand house, there were some exceptionally interesting people among its residents.

The principal families are represented in the big albums: the Lilleys, the Howards; the miller, Mr Nutter; the Vicar, the Rev. William Martin (although his portrait has disappeared); the Vicar of Barton, the Rev. Derisley Harding; and the Vicar of Trumpington, the Rev. John Grote, Professor of Moral Philosophy. The last two both resided in Grantchester for a while.

l to r: the Rev. Prof. Grote and his nieces; the Rev. Derisley Harding; Mrs Ellen Howard

Examining those small portraits while absorbing the contents of the diary, a sense of familiarity develops. It is like overhearing scraps of conversation about people glimpsed at a party: interest quickens, we look again, and begin to form an impression of their characters. And those Victorian ladies and gentlemen who at first appear to later generations to be all clothes, all bonnets and whiskers, reveal interesting personalities – straight from the novels of George Eliot or Trollope.

A late view of the High Street Grantchester. The school of 1867 is visible on the left, and the earlier thatched school on the right. Children are receiving paper windmills from a pedlar.

Page, the mechanically-minded, was also fascinated by forms of transport. Seven photographs show different horse-drawn carriages drawn up for display, mostly in front of the Old Vicarage.* For anyone studying fashion, the costumes and carriages are well worth looking at; similarly, the sailing-ships and paddle-steamer which appear in the Dorset photographs. And characteristic of Page the antiquarian is the eye for ancient ruins: he loved the prehistoric tomb and the romantic castle.

His latest photographs, from the 1880s and '90s, show beautifully-composed scenes – the Red Lion in a misty morning light, sheep and lambs in snow, Byron's Pool, Haslingfield church... but it is impossible to be quite certain whether a picture like the splendid one showing a pedlar distributing paper windmills to children in the High Street is really by him or perhaps by a neighbour, also an amateur photographer, Mr Nigel Pearce.

*The subjects are unknown, but may possibly have come through a connection with Wilderspins the coachbuilders. A Mr G. Wilderspin acted the part of 'Zimri' in the 1859 theatricals, and was photographed by S.P.W.

CHAPTER 9

Early 1860s

————

THE 1860S BEGAN in characteristic style, with 'Our second theatrical performance in which we acted Aggravating Sam, The Victor Vanquished, Twenty Minutes with a Tiger, concluding with a Tableau the "Fairy Glen"': plenty of scope for over-acting and spectacle. Then they all three went up to London for a visit which included an evening at the Adelphi (*The Dead Heart*) and a pleasant evening with friends at Maida Vale. Returning, Lally found that her mother had been gathering exceptionally early blooms – snowdrops, aconites, violets and daisies. (That was before the end of January; but on 23rd April there would be snow two inches deep.)

A new pupil arrived, John Smallman, an eight-year-old from a large house at the Newnham end of the village. The Census record suggests an interesting family: his mother was from 'St George's, Hanover Square', and his father declared himself 'Proprietor of London Dock Stock British Plate Glass Silver Plate House Property &c. C.' They may possibly have been connected with the family mentioned in a diary entry of 1850 – 'Anne and I spent the evening with Mr Smallman at the Castle near B.north!!'.

On 11th May 'Mr & Mrs Jackson and children came to see us for the last time before sailing for S. Africa'. The Jacksons, with young Annie and Clifford, had all been subjected to Page's camera in September 1857, when he had taken a 'nice Photo' of them at the tea-table. Emigration, promising the possibility of dazzling riches to the intrepid, was not to be entered upon lightly. You needed to be prepared. And with this in mind, the editor of *Chambers's Journal*, one of the best of the many periodicals coming out at that time, had promised to provide not only wholesome entertainment for young ladies ('a nice amusing tale ... no trash about Italian coaches and daggers, and ghosts in the blue chamber') but also a variety of well-written and informative articles, including useful instruction about farming and other practical skills for those intending to emigrate. The Jacksons' venture would entail a challenging journey in a sailing ship supplemented by steam. The following year the *Illustrated London News* was to publish engraved illustrations of a terrifying voyage in which that modern marvel, the *Great Eastern*, had nearly overturned in a gale, rocking wildly from side to side.

The Jacksons were not the only ones. A few days later 'Captn & Mrs Young sailed for Australia'; and many other friends were to set sail for distant parts of the British Empire too.

Lally herself displayed great fortitude: on June 29th she wrote, 'I went to London to stay with Louisa and James Williams and the same day to Mr Broadway Dentist and had 6 teeth and a stump taken out'; and the very next day 'Bought some collars &c at Shoollreads <u>Made by the sewing machine</u>!' She visited Jane Lapworth's new home, and James Williams took her to the Opera to see *Lucrezia Borgia* – 'Grisi and Mario were charming'.

Then it was time for a family holiday. Page, Lilly, Mother and Laura came and joined her in London, and on 6th July they were off to Bournemouth. When, on the 11th, Henry Ellis arrived, Page was able to start his own special activity: 'Went from Bournemouth to Christchurch and took some photo views of the Church', and then on the following days along the coast to the Tilly Whim caves and to Swanage, and to Corfe Castle … and of those 1860 Dorset photographs just a few have survived – ruins, churches, sailing ships and rather dismal-looking seashore views with a few sombre figures, men in top hats and women with bonnets, shawls and cumbersome skirts, in the mid-distance. But they show a real photographer at work.

Docks at Weymouth.

Village street (unidentified).

Vessels off the Dorset coast, 1860.

In October they went to see Charles Kean perform in *Louis XI*. The actor, coming towards the end of a career which had not been nearly as successful as his father Edmund Kean's, was evidently admired by Lally.* It was his performance she had seen in *Sardanapalus*; they had all seen him in *Henry VIII*; and now, in Cambridge, he was playing his most effective rôle.

'Our servant Sophy Papworth left has been with us nearly 7 years. Ruth came' (15 Oct.). Sophy, aged thirty, was moving to Wright's Farm (Cedar House), to Mrs & Miss Fowke; and Ruth Rayner, aged eighteen, was taking her place.

On 13th November 'Young Mr James Johnstone died' – one of those cruel early deaths, for it had been only three years before that he had entertained them to tea in his rooms at Trinity.

On 4th December a group met to plan an improvement for the church (an indication, perhaps, that the trend towards tractarianism was touching Grantchester?):

Louis XI, Boucicault's adaptation of a play by Casimir de la Vigne, was said to be 'immeasurably his greatest part'. *D.N.B.*

Mrs Martin, Mrs Hanbury, Mrs Lilley and Mrs Banyard [Lacies Farm] met here to decide upon an Altar cloth Lilly not being able to go out on account of her knee. It is to be maroon Utrecht Velvet with border of fleur-de-lys in gold and a fringe

And on Christmas Day, Page's thirty-fifth birthday, there was 'Very severe frost with a magnificent rime thermometer below zero [Farenheit]'.

*

Page had built himself a rowing boat, and he loved to take it up the river from above the Mill. The narrow stream wandered through a landscape mostly open, with shallow undulations, though in places it became a mysterious tunnel overhung with trees. It was rich with wildlife – with glimpses of water voles, traces of otters, the occasional flash of a kingfisher besides the regular traffic of moorhens and ducks. On his quietly rippling progress through this wonderland he never knew what he might see. On 21st May 1860 it had been 'a Red backed Shrike and some flies he had impaled on a bush'; and a year later it was 'the Prince of Wales at a Pic-nic party'. (The future King Edward VII, who had already spent some time as an undergraduate at Oxford, was now enrolled at Trinity College, Cambridge, though living under discreet supervision at Madingley Hall.)

That summer of 1861, Lally accompanied her mother on a month-long journey, staying in turn in London, Cheltenham ('where we saw dear Annie*'), Worcester and Bridgenorth. The old lady was visiting old friends and old haunts; and when they returned at the end of July they brought Laura with them. A fortnight later Richard arrived at Grantchester with all his family. Once more the square pew was crammed, as

We all went to Church, Mother, Lilly, Page, Laura, Richd, Libby, the four children Mrs & Miss Widnall and I. it was the 12th Sunday after Trin. and Dr George Martin preached from the collect of that day Mother's last Sunday at Church (SS)

It must have become clear that Mrs Ann Smith was by now failing. A friend came to comfort and sleep with her during her illness; and at the end of August she died.

Mrs Smith was buried in the churchyard at Grantchester; and on 1st October 'Mr Naylor brought the tombstone for dear Mother's grave, it

---

*the use of the epithet 'dear' probably implying that Anne Davis was unwell, and perhaps receiving treatment at the Spa

is Gissey's design and we are delighted with it (SS)'. (Lally had adopted
a nickname, 'Gissey', for Page which
now and then would reappear in the
diary. It was pronounced rather like
'Jesse'.) Page's design is distinctive
– a marble cross carved with a broad
ribbon interwoven with ivy wound
about it.* He took a photograph of
Lally kneeling before it on the grass,
to set in the family album beside a
similar one, taken two years earlier, by
her father's grave at Great Yarmouth.

Lally by her mother's grave

*

1862 began with the death, tragically young, of the promising William
Howard. Lally had been to see him on New Year's Day, and three days
later he succumbed to the dreaded consumption (tuberculosis).

A new family had come to Riversdale, with a name which very probably indicates a connection with Lilly and Lally's family. This was Mrs
Hanbury, a widow with a number of sons. Frank Hanbury took his
degree that January; Bernard and Philip were both present at the 1861
census; SPW took photos of Herbert and Folliot; and Charles Hanbury,
aged about 16, appears in the photograph album in full military uniform.

A note of euphoria appears on 1st May that year:

Magnificent Mayday – sunshine – nightingales – cuckoos – swallows
first sprig of lilac. Page has almost finished the sundial. (SS)

It must have been before this time that the earliest surviving photograph of the Old Vicarage was taken. The ladies' heavy dresses suggest
a date not later than 1860. No sundial is visible, but there is a raised
flowerbed surmounted by a 'grecian' sculpture. This last must – rightly
– have been judged to be a mistake. After its removal Page, in 1862,
installed his sundial, carved as an open book whose curling pages throw
shadows which were marked with the hours. Its unusual design was taken
from one seen, perhaps in the Seigneurie Gardens, on the island of Sark.

*still in place, but now largely hidden by a yew hedge

The earliest surviving photograph of the Old Vicarage

As Lally was later to recall, 'I well remember how my Brother used to rush out whenever the sun shone, to mark the spot where the shadow fell'. It was Lilly who painted mottoes on the pages of the open-book sundial; and by the end of May that year she had completed another task: 'Lilly's illumination was framed and looks lovely'. This was an elaborate piece of embroidery designed by Lilly herself to celebrate their happy family life. The text read 'If I take the Wings of the Morning, and dwell in the uttermost parts of the sea; Even there shall thy hand lead me, and thy right hand shall hold me'. Tiny photographs of each family member were incorporated, and the display was still treasured a century later.

Endless attention was given to this home of theirs – not to impose a hard Victorian tidiness on its appearance, but all the time coaxing a little more convenience into the house and a little more romance into its garden.

That July they all – the trio accompanied by Henry Ellis, and so presumably burdened with photographic equipment – set off for an adventurous holiday, sailing to Jersey on the *Alan* from Newhaven, 'a bad passage 21 hours instead of 14'. Fierce currents around the Channel Islands demand skilful navigation; one would like to have fuller details, but their journal of this holiday is lost. They spent nearly a month, crossing to Guernsey and then to Sark, where they 'got lodgings with Mr & Mrs Lepage near the Parsonage'. There they took photographs of the Coupée, the spectacular narrow causeway with a precipitous drop on each side connecting the main island with Little Sark. They visited the Gouliot Caves and perhaps attempted photography there too. A boat had to be chartered to carry them back to Jersey for the final week of their stay.

Safely back at the Southams' house (3 the Grove, Clapham), they 'spent a long day at the exhibition',* where they were joined by Annie and Laura, Libby and the four Smith children. Annie now had a new residence in Bayswater, and Lally went to stay with her there. Only a few days after their return home, they 'heard from Mrs Southam that her sailor son Tom had died at Singapore'.

Laura, now a lively ten-year-old, was spending much of her time at the Old Vicarage. It cannot have felt like an exile from her own home, for there were so many delights around her. In May, Page had taken a 'Photo of Laura and her lamb', perhaps an orphan which had needed hand-rearing. The small farm must itself have provided some of that enlightened education which Lally's pupils enjoyed, and there were other pet animals: rabbits and guinea-pigs housed in the Swiss Cottage, and Lally's cossetted cats. Now, in September, they 'took Laura to the theatre at Camb for the first time in her life, saw the Merchant of Venice'.

Laura aged 10

An agreeable new neighbour had arrived at Merton Cottage†, readily welcomed into village society. This was Colonel Addison, who came round one evening in October 'and read his farce "Dying for Love" it was very amusing'. Next month, when Page went to dine with him, 'His Monkey ran up my back and sat on the top of my head.' Lilly and Laura joined them afterwards for tea, so the little girl must have been able to share the fun.

Increasingly, there were stirrings of activity in church life. The Rev William Martin, an able scholar, was dedicated to his parish, and his parishioners were concerned for his well-being. In March that year,

> Lilly and I began collecting from every house in the village in order
> to present a testimonial to our dear Mr Martin as a mark of affection
> on his recovery from illness (SS)
> A Photographic Album was afterwards presented to him –

*The International Exhibition of 1862 displayed a wide variety of artefacts and included British paintings, but could not be compared with the success of the Crystal Palace Exhibition of 1851.
†now incorporated into Chapel House

Mrs Martin fulfilled her rôle as a Vicar's wife should, attending services and dispensing charity to the almshouses. Needlework, too, was a practical talent which could be directed to the work of the church – either by working an elaborately embroidered altar-cloth, or in providing squares of cambric on which young girls at the village school could learn their hemming; or, occasionally, in more demanding ways.

In the autumn of that year, 1862, the diary records the 'first Dorcas Meeting at the Vicarage for the poor sufferers in Lancashire', meetings which continued for ten weeks. Named after the Dorcas who, in the *Acts of the Apostles*, is said to have made garments to give to the needy, 'Dorcas groups' of church ladies would gather to sew essential clothing for this purpose. At this date news must have just reached Grantchester of the distress of workers in the Lancashire mills who had lost their jobs because of a sudden 'cotton famine'. The dearth of raw material for their looms arose because of the American Civil War. In freeing the slaves who had toiled in the cotton fields of the South, the victorious army had devasted the whole production of cotton and so, distantly, its manufacture.

A reminder of another distant way of life across the seas appears on 2nd December, when, more than a year after his departure, Page 'sent off Gun and other things to Sid. Jackson in S. Africa'. It must have been exciting to receive letters at the Old Vicarage with news of the Jackson family's progress in South Africa, and to hear about conditions there at first hand.

*

Instead of performing in their Castle Theatre in the New Year of 1863, the trio all went up to London to stay with Jane Lapworth. There, besides seeing Lord Dundreary* at the Haymarket, they were able to go to 'some Private Theatricals at the Hanover Square Rooms with Mr Lapworth's tickets'. Then there was a day of fun with a niece and nephew:

> went to the Zoological garden with Annie, Laura and little Tom, were much pleased with the spider monkeys. Went to see a Pantomime in the evening, saw Harlequin cut up and men transformed into chairs…

They left Jane's house, 131 Maida Vale, and spent their last few days with the Southams, going with them to the Lyceum and seeing 'Fechter and Miss Kate Terry in The Duke's Motto a beautiful piece [adapted from a French drama]'. Thanks to those London friends, they saw so many of the leading actors of the day.

*a rather gormless character in Tom Taylor's comedy *Our American Cousin*, whose drooping whiskers were to be adopted as a male fashion for some years

Annie had presented both her sisters and her young daughter with red cloaks. A few days later they were displayed: 'Laura and I wore our Red Cloaks to Church (SS)'.

Page and Lilly were in London again in March, and so were able to see 'the festivities of the Prince of Wales marriage'. (The wedding took place in St George's Chapel, Windsor; but that would not prevent celebrations taking place in the City of London.)

By now, Page's photography had become almost a profession, and he was extending his professional skill. Those large glass plates discovered by chance a century later [see 'Photography' chapter] include one, an interior view of King's College Chapel, which may with some certainty be dated 1860. It is taken from a high viewpoint above the altar – a position only accessible, surely, during that year when there was scaffolding up for renovation work. Another, now cracked across, is a remarkable view taken from inside their drawing-room (either with an assistant opening the shutter or by the use of a long string). This was most probably taken in the summer of 1863 or '64. The sundial is in place – and one can see that the remnants of church masonry used for its base included gothic pinnacles at that time – but not yet the fountain. The family are reclining on the lawn; and Lilly and Lally lean on wooden frames which must have been made for them by Page. (A girl of about sixteen is with them: Miss Grimley,* who was perhaps assisting Lally with her pupils.)

Another of those retrieved plates is a photograph, taken close-up with almost the intensity of a Julia Margaret Cameron portrait, of Mrs Fowke, who lived at Wright's Farm (now Cedar House) and whose age would have been about seventy-five.

*Photographs of Miss Grimley and of members of her family were included in one of the albums, and both Mr & Mrs Grimley took part, as the 'Yelmirgs', in the 1864 theatricals

(SPW had found it necessary to touch up some of the detail of her lace cap, where the collodion emulsion had cracked.)

When, in February 1863, Page took a photo of George Howard, he also 'photo copied an oil painting of Natalia Helena Modesta Gomez y Porta the wife of Fred Howard'. And when, later in the spring, Louisa Williams came with her three children for a fortnight's stay, he not only took her picture 'in Moiré antique dress' but also an outdoor shot, looking upwards, of 'the children standing on the balcony' (a balcony high on the south side of the Ruin, now no longer there). On the final day of the Williams' visit they 'went for a walk in Byron's grove* and Lou nearly fell in the river'…but it was not yet possible to catch moments of sudden drama with a camera.

It must have been at about this time that Page, in his studio, took several photographs of the Fullerton family – Mrs Fullerton and her son and daughter aged about twenty. They had lived in the village for only a year or so: agreeable neighbours who evidently enjoyed posing for the camera. Their group portrait is expertly arranged and lit, and its success must owe something to Widnall's own cheerful personality. He very probably had the Year-Book of Photography for 1862 published by *The Photographic News*, which was full of advertisements for darkroom chemicals, suitable pillars and balconies for subjects to lean against, a 'new and patented magnificent system of COLOURING PHOTOGRAPHS by the ELEPHANTINON PROCESS', and so on. He scarcely needed their detailed advice on portraiture:

> GOOD EXPRESSION is not entirely within the control of the operator, but he may materially aid in causing it… Cheerful, hopeful conversation will materially aid the sitter, and a careful omission of the caution against moving or frowning, which some operators seem to deem necessary. The circumstance that almost all the sitters of some photographers seem to wear pleasant expressions in their portraits, illustrates the fact that the operator may aid in producing a pleasant expression.

In the New Year of 1864 they returned to their theatricals, performing three playlets: *Trying it on*, *A Blighted Being*, and *Our Wife, or The Rose of Amiens*. Before dismantling the set, Page got his actors to pose for photographs, allowing us to see just how carefully they had prepared their

---

*Byron's Pool, a wooded area on the eastern side of the Cam, where Trumpington water-mill once stood. There was a deep pool beneath its weir, a swimming-place enjoyed by Lord Byron when an undergraduate at Trinity.

costumes and scenery. (He may have used Magnesium Light, newly advertised among the many improved appliances.)

It is a year with few diary entries: on 22nd February 'Tweets had a kitten "Puck"', and on 16th June there was one of their boating picnics for a crowd of young girls –

Page, Lilly, Laura, Fanny Southam, K. Howell, Clara Corbett, J. & E. Lilley, Miss Allen, and Geo Howard went up the river to tea

But in the next entry, 24th June, the trio set off for North Wales with young Henry Ellis; and this time the account of their adventures has survived, and provides the following chapter.

AMATEUR THEATRICALS,
GRANTCHESTER,
FEB. 1ST, 1864.

TO COMMENCE AT HALF-PAST SEVEN, WITH THE FARCE BY W. BROUGH, ESQ.,
"TRYING IT ON."

Mr. Walsingham Potts	...	...	Mr. A. &c. Crafty.
Mr. Jobstock	...	...	Mr. Phynditoutt.
Mr. Tittlebat	...	...	Mr. Yelmirg.
Mrs. Jobstock	...	...	Miss Whaytabitt.
Fanny	...	...	Miss Blanche Pier.
Lucy	...	...	Mrs. Phynditoutt.

AFTER WHICH THE FARCE BY TOM TAYLOR, ESQ.,
"A BLIGHTED BEING."

Job Wort	...	...	Mr. Yelmirg.
Ned Spanker	...	...	Mr. Phynditoutt.
Cumming	...	...	Mr. A. &c. Crafty.
The O'Rafferty	...	...	Mr. N. O. Nayme.
Susan Spanker	...	...	Mrs. Yelmirg.

The Arab Chieftain, Mokabula, will now present to the Audience the "Aztec Colombazo Ambassador Extraordinary to the British Realms, from the city of Montezuma."

TO CONCLUDE WITH THE COMIC DRAMA,
"OUR WIFE:
OR,
THE ROSE OF AMIENS;"

IN TWO ACTS.—PERIOD 1634.

Act 1st. Scene : INTERIOR OF POMARET'S SHOP.
Act 2nd. Scene : ANTE-ROOM IN THE TOWN HALL OF AMIENS.

Marquis de Ligny, (Capt. of the King's Guard)	...	Mr. N. O. Nayme.
Count de Brissac (his friend)	...	Mr. A. &c. Crafty.
Pomaret	...	...	Mr. Phynditoutt.
Dumont	...	...	Mr. Yelmirg.
Rosine, (Pomaret's Daughter)	...	Miss Convolaria.
Marriette (her cousin)	...	Miss La Chasse.

Guests, Officers, &c.

CHAPTER 10

Holiday in North Wales

THE TERSE MESSAGE, 'see diary', attached to notes of other holidays, leaves a sense of frustration: one longs for all the colourful details which have been lost. *The Journal of Our Tour in North Wales* was very nearly destroyed, too. Years later, in a great clearance of old papers, 'it hovered over the bonfire' but was rescued by Humphrey Giles, Lilly and Lally's great-nephew.

The leather-bound Journal is in fluent copperplate handwriting – Lally's description of the adventures of herself, Page, Lilly and the indispensable Henry Ellis. (Julia Lilley, 'much to our and her disappointment', had been unable to join them.) It is illustrated with thirty-four of Page's photographs, a little faded but a remarkable accomplishment. Photography, as already explained, was at that time laborious work. And at the very start of this holiday it was made even more difficult. After the ten-hour train-ride from Cambridge, they trailed around Bangor in the rain for an hour, seeing 'a great many Temperance Hotels and not a few intemperate men'. A horse-drawn omnibus took them to Caernarvon late in the evening.

> Now comes a great misfortune – Page's black box, containing all his Photo affairs was dropped off the top of the Omnibus and the greater number of the large glasses broken and many bottles of Chemicals, and the camera too. [But] Page is such a capital contriver that he will get over the inconvenience very tolerably and the chemicals he can fortunately replace in Carnaervon.

Later Lally comments that 'it is a great labour to carry so many things, they will try at a dry process next time'. Still, the great labour enabled Page to record views of the wild countryside; and Henry sometimes served as a figure in the middle-distance to enliven the picture.

One of the joys of the journal is the impression it gives of the four characters – Page, a burly John Bull figure, Lilly tall and grave, Lally a small wren, and young Henry sporting a tam o'shanter. The sisters, hampered by those long Victorian clothes (although dressed less formally than most ladies of that time), found the going hard; the men could be more

The holiday group: Lilly, Lally, Henry Ellis and Page

active. All four had enquiring minds, observing and questioning as they went. No new experience or delight should be missed. Thanks to the railway, North Wales had become accessible to tourists and so hotels were being built. But 1864 was still fairly early in the process, and travellers could feel the thrill of entering a strange land. Rather than select short passages for quotation, it seems best to present almost the entire text.

*

In Carnaervon:
SATURDAY 25th We went to see the Castle, Oh! a magnificent ruin. Page took two Photoes, but no Photo can do justice to this fine old building. One of the pictures is taken from the room where it is supposed the 'Prince of Wales' was born, unfortunately it turned out badly!

[*A photograph of Carnaervon Castle*]

This one shows the Eagle Tower and the centre window of the upper three is the window of the room where the interesting event is said to have occurred. We found *Ruta Muriria, Asplenium Trichomenas, Adiantrum Nigrum* and one little *Scolopendrium*, we got roots of the three former ones. I am so sorry we had to hurry away from this lovely ruin, where really one could spend hours, but we were obliged to do so, as we had arranged with our landlord 'John Lloyd Prince of Wales' (as he signs himself) for a car to take us to Llanberis. It was a lovely ride, the scenery magnificent, – the brawling brooks, the lovely feathery ferns, the mighty hills and the placid lakes, where the water lilies white and yellow literally covered the waters in some places, – I never thought to see such things. We longed to transfer to Grantchester a piece of an old wall, rich in ferns especially dear little *Polypodiums*, growing out of the soft moss among the stones.

(The Latin names are almost all varieties of ferns. Interest in ferns had developed from early in the century, until with the publication of G.F. Francis's An Analysis of the British Ferns *(1837) it grew into a craze – 'Pteridomania'. Known habitats were raided by fern-hunters; and it seems that the young Widnalls had been infected by this mania even on their honeymoon. All three of the trio had, of course, been brought up as botanists through their fathers' occupation.)*

We had a search for lodgings and suited ourselves admirably at a Mr John E. Evans. The Cottage is called *Brynderw* which means 'Oak Bank' from the many Oak trees about it.

I wish we knew a little of the Welsh language, the children we meet are delighted to utter the few English words they know. 'Good bye' is a great favorite, it is so funny to hear the little ones saying to each of us separately 'Good bye, good bye' and then running along by our side, for it is evidently a greeting in their idea.

We dined at the Dolbadarn Hotel. After dinner we went to our lodgings, got a little settled in them and then went to see the 'Ceunant Mawr' Waterfall which is very near us. One wants another set of superlatives, how am I to describe this Waterfall? It is magnificent, grand, beyond description, and the rich deep roar like the 'Falls of Lodore' wants the pen of a Southey to paint.

We met with some ladies above the Waterfall, one of them asked me if we were not at Carnarvon this morning. I said 'yes'. 'And did you lose anything at the Castle?' 'My sister lost a jet brooch' – 'And we picked it up'. Was it not odd we should hear of it again at this spot?

Mr Evans   Mrs Evans

SUNDAY 26th We were informed that the English Service took place at 3 in the afternoon, so went for a stroll along the Pass of Llanberis, found *Polypodium Phegopteris*, and *Lastrea Neoptens*. In the afternoon put on our bonnets for church ....[but found that it] had taken place in the morning and that there was no service in the afternoon, which was a great disappointment. We went for another stroll and saw a dear little bird with a light almost white body, the back and wings a pretty snuff brown, the head and throat appeared a kind of slate colour and it worked its tail up and down continually. We think it was the 'Water Ouzel' or 'Dipper'.

Page and Henry continued their walk to the Slate quarries and Lizzy and I came home. A stoat cross our Path on our way. Page found the *Allosorus Crispus* and brought home a little plant. After tea Page and

Henry went out again and Lizzy and I stayed at home and read. There is a book about the unfortunate Mr Starr of Northampton in our sitting room. He was lost on one of the Snowdon mountains, Page read one of his sermons after supper.

MONDAY 27th Lizzy and I wrote letters while Page and Henry were preparing the Photo affairs for a day's tour. We did not start till nearly 12 in the day. Page took four pictures which promise to be nice. It is a great labour to carry so many things, they will try at a dry process next time. We brought home a splendid plant of *Allosorus* and several other ferns but did not get back to dinner till 7 o'clock, when we fared sumptuously on the last couple of the four fowls we bought at Carnarvon for 4/-. On our way back we saw a Welsh shepherd driving his sheep and a most difficult matter it was especially with one naughty sheep who would jump over the stone fences and dash up every aperture generally followed by its lamb; five times did this same sheep lead its driver a pretty race. On one occasion after great difficulty in catching it, and having to go back a long way for it, he tied its legs together and carried it to the flock quietly grazing in the road, no sooner had he set it free, than over the fence again it dashed. We were quite sorry for the Shepherd and he did look so red and hot.

(The wonders of this area were not just botanical and pastoral. Victorian villas and the long terraces of working-class housing were being roofed with Welsh slate, the product of an enormous industrial site close by.)

TUESDAY 28th June Went to the Dinorwic Slate Quarry which we can see from our sitting-room window. There are 2700 men and boys employed in these slate works, many of them live near Carnaervon and Bangor and come daily to their work in Velocipedes (which are made for work and not for pleasure, as all the Velocipedes we have hitherto seen have been). These Velocipedes are propelled on the Railway and contain some 8 and others 12 men, all of whom help to propel it themselves. We mounted to an immense height on an inclined plane, in one of the trucks in which the slates are conveyed, accompanied by a guide. We were drawn upwards by a descending truck loaded with slates, for it is in this manner that the trucks are raised, as one empty one ascends, another full one descends. It is curious to see the men splitting and chipping or cutting the edges of the slates. We went into the Engine House and saw the Steam Engine which works all the planing and sawing machines. We saw them blasting the rocks, the noise is like thunder and on the explosion of the gunpowder a great mass of rock was flung as by a giant's strength, into a deep chasm below.

It began to rain before we descended, which we did on foot, and a fine state of mess I got into under the impression that, as my dress was short, I need not hold it up. I don't know what's to be done with it, its condition is so bad. It was very rainy all the afternoon but about 8 o'clock in the evening it cleared a little and off went Page and Henry like a couple of boys let loose from school, to fish, and never came back till dark (half-past nine) having caught six trout.

WEDNESDAY 29th Went out to photograph the Waterfall, found it too windy so returned home, and I managed to slip and feared I had sprained my ankle, but I am thankful to say it was not so. We went a pleasant walk along the Dinorwic road as far as the Hospital. On our way we crossed the bridge (formed of one slab of slate 21 feet long) into the Plantation ;belonging to the Victoria Hotel, and there we found in abundance *Hymenophyllum Tunbridgende* and *Wilsonii* growing on the rocks in a damp and dark situation, this was a great delight. We also found what we think is the *Polypodium Alpestre*, and we brought home roots of all these ferns and many pretty pieces of quartz. In the afternoon it commenced raining but in spite of that Page and Henry went out fishing, and having walked as far as some lake famous for its fish, up in a Mountain called 'Cwm-dwythwck', they brought home two fish, which they were too proud to eat; they came home very wet, having walked through some bogs. The lake is about two miles up the mountain.

THURSDAY 30th Set out on an expedition to Twll Du, at half past 10 a.m. We rode down the Pass of Llanberis as far as we could (about 2 miles) and then struck into the fields, and almost immediately began the ascent which was great labour, it is about 3 miles of ascent and then a mile along the top of the mountain, often in very boggy places, the guide told us the mountain was upwards of 2000 feet high. The scenery was very beautiful, as we mounted we often rested and saw the Vale of Llanberis spread out like a map at our feet, the mighty mountains forming a grand and magnificent background.

One must go up one of these lofty mountains to appreciate the difficulty, and the disappointment shall I say, of finding as you get to the top of one eminence which appears to be really the top, that another rises before you. The hills indeed seem to <u>heighten</u> <u>as you</u> <u>mount</u>. Twll Du or the 'Black Cleft' is a mighty chasm between two rocks of enormous height down which runs a stream from the lake called Llyn-y-cwm. After rain this is a tremendous torrent, dashing down this precipice of 150 yards, and thundering as it goes. When we saw it there was only a small stream and here we rested and ate our sandwiches surrounded by the wildest mountain scenery. Page and Henry went to the foot of the chasm, they say it was a wonderful sight to look up and see the rocks almost meet hundreds of feet overhead. They found *Dryopteris, Viride, Trichomenes, Plegopteris lystopteris,* and many delicate little plants which we did not know but hope to find out. Before we reached Twll Du we had found the Parsley Fern in great abundance, it was perfectly beautiful, growing among great masses of rocks, where its dear little fronds had great difficulty, one would think, to get at the light of day.

Lizzy and I found the time rather long as Page and Henry were absent with the guide about 2 hours. Eternal silence seems to reign among these mountains. When we all met again we turned homewards. We found many lovely mosses and lichens in the swampy places we crossed and then came the descent which was no joke, I cannot describe it and had better not try, suffice it to say that we were all thoroughly tired when we got to our lodgings, and no wonder, for we had had a ten miles walk, six of which was either up or down hill. So I feel no compunction in saying that I never was so tired in my life and felt as if I should never have the proper use of my knees again.

FRIDAY JULY 1st Page and Henry went to the Cennant Mawr Waterfall and took three good pictures, Lizzy and I stayed at home and wrote letters and then sauntered to the Post Office with them, and returned and found dinner ready and waited and wished for Page and Henry, and at last were rewarded by their arrival and a delicious dinner of ducks.

After dinner we had a row on Llyn Padarn, we landed on the Dinorwic side and saw many of the quarry men returning from their work on their velocipedes, one of which had 15 men in it, they were going at the rate of nearly 20 miles an hour. Henry took his fishing rod, but caught no fish. Page dropped one of the rowlocks into the lake, we tried to peer into the water for it, but all our peering was vain there was no rowlock to be seen. We measured the depth of the water and found it 66 feet: it is said some parts are 140 yards deep. It began to rain and was very cold before we got home. This lake is 2 miles long and about half a mile broad, the upper lake Llyn Peris is about a mile long.

SATURDAY 2nd Rain, wind, and storm until about half past 4 o'clock when we went to see the Waterfall. We had not seen it in perfection till to-day, the rain has so greatly increased its beauty, it is a magnificent sight, the foaming waters dashing down the precipice and over the side, white with foam and feathery as delicate wool and such a depth (I mean the depth of the sheet of water) the particles of water seemed to strike out separately like a mighty and beautiful moss. We went on and saw some falls higher up which are exceeding beautiful, there are five platforms on which the water dashes and the last is rounded so that the water seems to bubble up like the top of a fountain.

Waterfalls in full spate are simply indescribable! But after this a wonderfully interesting photograph is inserted, which illustrates the following passage.

Page has had some talk with our Landlady, she says she has a dairy of two cows, the butter is churned by a waterwheel worked by a little mountain stream at the back of the house. They do not skim the milk, but pour in milk and cream together, this makes a great deal of butter-milk which is the general drink of the inhabitants.

Church attendance, and the reading of sermons, were of great importance.

SUNDAY 3rd Went to Church, the service is at present performed in a part of a building erected for a club-house. In the afternoon there was a collection towards building a Church for the Visitors which I am sure is needed, fancy, two, three, four, five large hotels and <u>no</u> church.

In the evening Page & Henry went a little way up Snowdon, they met with the shepherd who had such trouble with the sheep in the Pass, he was accompanied by another shepherd, who sent his dog up after the sheep to bring them down the mountain oh! so cleverly. These men presently produced their hymn books, printed in Welsh on the new System something after the manner of the Hullah* & then began to sing, one had a good bass voice and the other sang treble, shortly afterwards they were joined by two companions who took the tenor, and they sang hymn after hymn with great enthusiasm; their voices too were very good, it really was a treat among the glorious mountains, the setting sun shedding its beams on all around and tinting the clouds with its colours of fire…

MONDAY 4th …Page took likenesses of our kind good-natured landlady, her husband and their two children, one of them such a black-eyed black-haired little girl. Also our little waiting maid Sydney, a niece of Mrs Evans's and a pretty little girl 15 years of age. She has managed to frown in her picture tho' and it therefore does not do her justice.

We saw the top of Snowdon for the first time today. This mountain is like an Eastern Lady rarely raises her veil, does not like being gazed upon by vulgar eyes. We met some pleasant people who had come for the day and were delighted with the Waterfall. There was a Welsh Funeral coming down the mountains from some cottage, accompanied by such a great number of people….

On the Tuesday they trudged all the way up 'and though the view was fine we do not think it altogether worth the labour'. *Still, its attractions are described, and Henry took a much longer and steeper way home over Capel Curig while Page rambled about searching for ferns. Arrangements were made for their departure next day* '& sorry indeed am I to leave this lovely spot and our comfy lodgings'.

Before leaving, Page had a final photograph to take.

WEDNESDAY 6th The old Welsh woman who promised to come to be photographed arrived before we had done breakfast. She was tall and must have been very good-looking when young, she was very poor but very tidy and dressed in the old Welsh Costume. A tall black hat, white

---

*A sort of tonic-sol-fa devised by J. P. Hullah, a Worcester musician and so familiar to the Smith family. His reputation was such that he had been entertained in the Master's Lodge at Trinity twenty years earlier.

cap, a coloured handkerchief over her head under her hat, a blue cotton jacket very much patched and the striped black & red petticoat. To complete it her name was 'Jenny Jones'. Mrs Evans says she is a very religious old woman, we were much pleased with her, and she is going to knit us some socks for next winter. Poor old woman! When she was asked to come she said 'I hope there is nothing wicked in it'. She could not speak a word of English though, so I ought to say that is the interpretation of what she said.

Regretfully, they left, and had a lovely drive through the Pass of Llanberis to their next lodgings –

We obtained lodgings at Colwyn Cottage 34/- a week, 4/- more than we paid at Llanberis and far from being as convenient or as comfortable. I may as well say here that for this sum we have three bedrooms and a sitting-room. The river Colwyn flows in front of our room and makes a pleasant rippling sound. After tea we took a walk to Pont Aberglaslyn, a bridge situated in the most romantic and beautiful scenery, altogether the walk was a lovely one and we greatly enjoyed it. Of course the ferns were abundant and never did we see so many and so fine *Blechnums*. As Henry had brought his fishing rod he stayed to fish and Page stayed with him, Lizzy and I walking back towards our lodgings. As we walked on we met a nice pleasant looking boy (perhaps I ought to say man). Presently we found that the owner of this pleasant face had turned back again, and he came up to me and said 'I think you are Miss Smith', in great surprise I said 'yes'. 'And you', turning to Lizzy 'are Mrs Widnall'. Our astonishment was at its height, but he gave us no time for expressing it, adding 'I am Adolphe'. It was Adolphe Flower who formerly lived at Grantchester, and whom we knew a bright happy boy 8 years ago. He is really quite handsome, he walked home with us talking of old times, we find he lodges close by.

Six days were spent at Beddgelert. There, Lally was deeply impressed by the legend of Prince Llewelyn, 'who slew his dog in anger and ever after so bitterly repented the act'. She copied into the Journal page after page of the poem

written to commemorate this tale, and a photograph was taken of Gelert's
Grave. Their interests continued, as before, to extend beyond mountain scenery –

... Page was interested in a Water wheel about 30 feet in diameter, which worked a pump in a mine three or four hundred yards distant, by means of a rod the same length and which then descended to the bottom of the mine, which is 140 yards deep, where the pump is situated; so that the pump is actually more than a quarter of a mile distant from the wheel that works it.

SATURDAY 9th Photography will go wrong; messing after the provoking plates most of the morning. In the afternoon Henry went to the Lake Dinas to fish, his usual luck attended him, the fish object to being caught and indeed are rarely visible. Page, Lizzy and I went out fern-hunting and brought home a splendid lot of *Trichomenes, Phegopteris* and *Oreopteris* &c...

On Sunday the English Service at the local church was of course important, but as it took place in the afternoon they were able to enjoy a delightful walk, on which they gathered 30 different sorts of flowers in one field; 'among them was a pretty white Orchis the root of which we brought home'. Henry caught one or two tiger beetles 'for microscopic objects'.

When we returned home it was dinner time and after dinner we went to Church, the Clergyman was a Mr Priestley and he told us that a man's character was <u>himself</u>, and made many remarks on this subject which much pleased us. His manner of reading was rapid and monotonous, and reminded me of little Alfred's way of saying grace 'Thank-God-for-my-good-dinner-please-Ma-may-I-get-down'. The Hymns and Psalms were given out and the first verse read in one tone and without any apparent pause. They have a very singular custom in Wales of hanging up on the walls of the Church the coffin plates inscribed with the names and ages of the deceased; it has a very ugly look....

And so they continued, wandering, observing, reading pious books; Henry ranging more widely, collecting 'lovely pieces of quartz with bright bits of copper in them', Page taking photographs. But then the last days of their stay in Wales became a terrible muddle. After a 'long hot ride' from Bedgellert to Bettws y Coed ... they discovered on arrival that no lodging place could take them in. They were forced to retreat and eventually found themselves back in Llanberis, arriving past midnight to find beds in the big hotel there. Two or three days were then thankfully spent with the Evanses again, recovering from the fruitless journey and the annoyance of having paid 7/-for the carriage of their luggage to Bettws y Coed only to pay the same extravagant sum for its transport back.

*On Saturday 16th they set off at 6 a.m., at first revelling in their ride
through the vale – 'the mountains were visible through a thin mist, really it
was very beautiful to observe the sometimes soft and graceful and then jagged
and abrupt outlines of the hills as they rose one above another...' – and then
realized with horror that their barrel of ferns had been left behind with Mrs
Evans. They eventually reached Tenbury by train, to stay with their friends
Mr and Miss Home. On the way they parted with Henry, who took with him
his carpet bag but not the tightly-packed barrel of ferns which should have
accompanied him from Stafford to Cambridge. And when they reached
Tenbury, they found that Lizzie's box and the hamper had mistakenly been
taken off the train at Craven Arms. They, like the barrel, did in the end
reach their destination; but on the Sunday 'we could not go to Church, for our
bonnets happen to be in the missing box'. (Evidently the straw hats worn for
mountain walks would not do; but consolation was found in yet another volume
of sermons.)*

*The Homes, middle-aged brother and sister, were old friends. With their
hostess, on the Monday, they went for a drive in a carriage and pair up to the
Clee Hills and picnicked there. Next morning was spent indoors, learning
'how to tack Pamphlets together' – probably to do with church activities; and
while Page prepared for more photography, Lally 'read Mrs Gatty's tale
"The Poor Incumbent". It is very touching'. An impression of the harmony
among these companions follows:*

... I was telling Miss Home at dinner to day the state of mind I was
in, on finding that our Ferns were left behind and added 'There was
Page as placid as possible, of course he was vexed, but even that you had
almost to guess, I don't believe there is anybody like him.' 'I think we
have just such another in the house' said Miss Home. 'On one occasion,
when I was carving a goose, I had on a new black silk dress, and I had the
misfortune to upset the gravy all down the front of my dress. Of course I
was exceedingly vexed and coming to my brother I said "Oh Benjamin I
have had such a misfortune, I have upset all the gravy on my new silk
dress". "Dear, dear" said my brother, looking very serious, "What a
pity! And I'm afraid there is no more *gravy*."' We all had such a laugh.
Was it not a climax?....

WEDNESDAY 20th Mr Home took us to the Wells to taste the mineral
waters (which are not over nice). There is an exceedingly pretty Pump
Room, the walls are of brick and wood work in various devices, and look
so very cool and foreign like, something Moorish, I think. [*A good photograph shows this attractive building.*]

... After tea went with Miss Home to see St Michael's Church. It is about two miles off, over the bridge and across the fields, but never were there so many styles I should think in so short a distance. This church (to which there is a College attached) was built by the Rev Sir Frederick G. Ouseley and is a perfect gem. Every thing is exquisite from the locks on the doors to the lovely pillars of grey stone, with their delicately carved capitals in white stone. The Roof, the beautiful Font of white stone inlaid with green Marble, and its elaborate cover in the baptistery, where there is a well for the baptismal water, the lovely windows all of which are ultimately to be filled with stained glass, the exquisite Communion Table or Altar with a kind of Canopy, and the Organ which has four rows of keys and no end of stops, the tone of which too is wonderfully grand, and with its choir of young voices, the choicest that can be culled in England, how overpowering must be the service in this Church.

... Sir Frederick is an accomplished musician, his character too must be harmonious for he is greatly beloved. The Cloisters, the Dormitories, the Dining Hall, Sir Frederick's own Drawing-room, Dining-room and Library, Oh! All is exceedingly lovely and perfect.

... Sir Frederick's father was ambassador to the Court of Persia which accounted for the precious inlaid Persian furniture in the Drawing-room &c. There was a portrait of the Duke of Wellington, who was Godfather to Sir Frederick, the Duke of York was his other Godfather. there was too a portrait of Sir F. but it was too dark to see it well. A cousin of ours John Capel Hanbury was here not long since (*actually appointed organist to the foundation*) ... we have not seen him for many years though. There is accommodation in this College for 40 pupils I believe.

St Michael's College, Tenbury, was indeed a remarkable foundation, which owed everything to Sir Frederick Ouseley. His father had hoped for a diplomatic career for him, but he, a musical prodigy from childhood, had instead gone into the church, and resolved to do what he could to rescue English church music from the apathy which had settled upon it for a century or more. S.S. Wesley, when organist at Gloucester Cathedral, had tried to stir up reform in 1849 with a pamphlet in which he claimed that the choir of St Paul's, in London, in ancient times numbering forty, had currently 'but six voices'. That long-established enthusiasm for choral music in the west of England, the Three Choirs Festival enjoyed by Lally and her sisters, the lusty performance of oratorios composed for mixed voices, was something quite different from the devotional music of services in cathedrals and parish churches day by day. It was this tradition of singing, once so abundant and now decayed, which the baronet clergyman was using his private wealth to restore.

The church building so much admired by Lally was regarded more coolly by a later critic, C.A. Nicholson, who commented that 'details are on the whole good and carefully thought out but give the impression that the architect [Henry Woodyer] aimed at producing a collection of reproductions of 13th and 14th-century ornament; a genuine mediaeval building would have been much simpler'. After more than a century and a quarter, this whole establishment, to which Ouseley had committed his inherited fortune but with insufficient endowment, was closed in 1985.

*

Examining the intricacies of the old railway system, one can only marvel at the intrepidity of those travellers. Compared with the package-tour holidaymakers of today, their undertaking was heroic. Page must have been one of those men who revel in complicated timetables and connections with lines run by tiny railway companies. The move from Llanberis to Tenbury involved changes at Carnaervon, Stafford, Ironbridge, Craven Arms, and Woofferton, with at least three different companies. But, provided you had planned carefully, it worked; and because such journeys were now possible, tourists in increasing numbers were reaching previously remote valleys.

There were minor adventures on their journeys: a realisation that they had boarded the wrong train when jaunting from Tenbury to Ludlow, set right at the first stop; and a glimpse, at the station at Stafford, of a horrifying drama —

… we saw a poor mad woman who was being conveyed to some asylum we suppose. It was a very painful sight, the poor thing was confined in a *sack* and her legs were tied together, so the men seem to lift her about like a bag of grain.

*

It was with gentle regrets and great contentment that Page, Lilly and Lally returned to Cambridge, arriving earlier than expected

... so of course the Chaise was not at the station to meet us, we therefore walked home and greatly to the surprise and pleasure of Mrs and Miss Widnall walked in just as Brown was preparing the horse to start to meet us. Mrs and Miss Widnall were both pretty well and our dear home looked exceeding charming, though the garden thirsts for rain. We had too the pleasure of finding 'Tweets' and the kitten safe and sound...

The Village

*A wonderful old chap ... Nothing in the village ever
happened without him.*   HUMPHREY GILES

PAGE WAS ABOVE ALL a village man, and spent his whole life in the same
corner down near the river and the Mill. Although he loved to explore
other territories, although he took a close interest in the progress of the
in-law families and pride in their successes, and although, increasingly, he
would become adopted into the fringes of Cambridge university life, his
devotion to Grantchester and its affairs was always total and unwavering.

*

Then as now, Grantchester attracted visitors wanting a stroll or short
ride out from Cambridge. It was not far, and the village appeared satis-
fyingly picturesque: its huddled cottages were mostly thatched, many
showing the dilapidation which looked so pleasing in the paintings and
popular engravings of the period. There was a kindly spirit among the
occupants of the larger houses, but a wide social division between them
and the 'labouring poor'. Those thatched cottages had from the start
been poorly built and overcrowded; and the few examples which remain
owe their survival to the Cottage Improvement Society (formed in the
1920s). At that time, life for many of the cottagers was hard.

Most of the men worked on the land, and ten or so were employed in
the mill. Women found employment in 'service', working as cooks or
housemaids in middle-class homes, or as 'bedders' in the colleges three
miles away. The village was largely self-supporting, having its own
butcher, baker, tailor, shoemaker, blacksmith, four public houses, a
brewer and even a brickmaker, in addition to the miller and several farmers and market-gardeners. There were the carriers, ready to transport
goods to and from Cambridge – a regular service being the carriage of
laundry, which a number of housewives washed, ironed and packed into
wicker baskets. Everything entailed hard physical labour: many of the
women living in the cottages and, later, in 'the terrace' (a long row of yellow brick houses with slate roofs, built in 1878) would regularly do
laundry work. For this, water had first to be drawn from a communal

pump and then carried to a big copper vat which needed to be heated by a fire; and when all the pummelling and rinsing was done, wet sheets and clothing were carried across the road and over a stile to the meadows, where they were pegged onto clothes-lines to dry. Ironing was itself a heavy chore, since irons had to be heated in turn on the stove, a stove kept burning with the coals which needed to be shovelled and carted about.

All these activities were the essential daily grind of village life. The children who presented themselves at the village school came from these homes, and the school year reflected the seasons of both church and farm. For a rural parish, 'Plough Sunday' at the beginning of the year was a moment of real significance, and was celebrated by men and boys. May Day meant gathering spring flowers for the girls. The long summer holiday was the Harvest Holiday; and if there had been a difficult harvest the autumn term might have to be delayed. When the church held its first Harvest Festival, in 1860, the congregation knew the meaning of harvest: the culmination of all those months of preparing the land, sowing and protecting the seed in its germination; weeding and hoeing, and finally gathering and storing crops which had come successfully through capricious weather. The cottagers gleaned the last of the fallen grain, and kept their own pigs and hens. 'All is safely gathered in', they could at last sing with relief and thanksgiving.

Two successive diary entries of 1865 may, however, be evidence of rising discontent among farm labourers. In January there was a fire in Page Widnall's stackyard; and the following month 'Part of Mr Lilley's farm burnt down'.

Few surviving photographs give any impression of general village life at that time. In a view of the Green Man and nearby houses, there are a child, a dog, a couple of farm carts and what seems to be a pedlar's van laden with wares. A man in the wide-brimmed top hat and frock coat which suggest a date *c.*1858–62 may be the pedlar himself. In another picture (*c.*1862–66) the extreme contrast in social class is illustrated: it is one of Page's series of horse-and-carriage photographs, in which two young men loll in a fine new gig, one wearing a tall silk hat and the other the fashionable shallow bowler, while the lad who holds the pony's head is in loose rags and a flat cap. Men actually at work in the fields were likely to be in smocks and simple hats of felt or straw.

Parishioners of every degree came together in church, although much of the seating there was reserved for the better-off families. In the Widnall household the church was of central importance. In the village history he

was later to write, Page would record some of the alterations in the church fabric which had occurred during his lifetime so far. As a boy of about seven he must have been fascinated to watch the carpenters enlarging the gallery at the back of the nave, and the installation of a barrel organ (at a cost of £60). Then in 1835 a vestry had been created under the church tower, which meant that the old west-facing doorway was changed to a window, and a small outside entrance had to be provided for the spiral staircase up to the bell-chamber. Some of these significant events were noted in Page's diary, such as 'Grantchester organ altered from Barrel to Finger' (Feb 1849); the repewing of the eastern part of the nave in 1856; or Lilly's work on the border of the church carpet in 1859. Her embroidery on the fine new altar-cloth was part of the next major improvement:

> 3 *March* '61 Chancel of our Church re-opened after being re-seated.
> The Master of Corpus Coll. Preached. The Russian serfs
> were freed today.*

Corpus Christi College, patron of the living, is responsible for the fabric of the church's fine 14th-century chancel; but with sublime Victorian self-assurance its 1861 restoration included some 'improvements' which may confuse present-day visitors to the church – the addition of authentic-looking sedilia and of poppyhead finials to carved niches.

Much more will be told about S.P.W.'s involvement in the church in due course. Something closely connected, which engaged his attention in the 1860s, was the need for a new building to house the village school.

---

*This non-sequitur is included to indicate the manner in which events were noted

Page could recall the erection of the original building in 1830 – a simple thatched room which still stands and is now used for minor meetings, as an annexe to the Village Hall. Although there had been some provision earlier – a Sunday School run by the nonconformists who had their small conventicle on the Coton Road – that day school was one of the first in the area, supported by the National Society and built at a cost of £80. As he himself was later to write:

> ... the parishioners erected what they no doubt thought was a very neat and pretty little room for the education of the children of the poorer classes.

Though 'neat and pretty', with its patterned window-panes and its small bell-tower (now gone), the accommodation was inadequate. Children came not only from Grantchester – whose own boundary extended in those days to Newnham Croft, now part of Cambridge – but from surrounding villages, walking the field paths in all weathers. As years went by the small building became impossibly crowded.

The Widnalls had certainly taken an interest in the little school from its very beginning, and the annual tea-party started by Page's father seems to have been kept up. But now in the 1860s the population of the village was rising: in 1841 the Census had counted 284 people, living in 56 houses, and by 1864 there were nearly 700 in the parish (but many of them at the Cambridge end). And by that date the school was in the charge of a determined young woman, Miss Charlotte Snelling.

Miss Snelling seems to have taken over from a married couple* in 1854, and moved into the School House adjoining the small thatched building. Sometime, probably in about 1860, Page took her photograph. It is there in the big album among other village worthies. She confronts the camera wearing her best silk dress, her hair done in the tight hanging ringlets no longer fashionable, standing erect with a book in one hand. Although still in her late thirties, her looks are already careworn.

* John and Mary Butler

Miss Snelling was 'certificated', better-qualified than many teachers of that time, and – dare one say? – 'better class'. Yet what was most essential for that job must have been sheer strength of character. With up to a hundred children of all ages crammed into that room, there must have been days when the noise and smell were almost beyond endurance. She subdued the clamour and imposed order; and we still have the Log Book kept in her elegant handwriting from 1872 onwards, recording the daily struggles and achievements of the school.

But for now, it was clear that larger premises were needed. The National Society had of course to play a major part; Corpus Christi College, Cambridge, as patron of the parish church, was appealed to; and King's College, as Lord of the Manor, was asked to provide a site for the new building.

This was to be an altogether more costly enterprise than the original one. £730 had to be raised, not only by subscriptions and the annual School Sermons in church, but by fund-raising events. Special concerts took place, with ladies and gentlemen from far afield singing and playing. And the greatest of these events was planned and hosted by Mr S.P. Widnall – a grand two-day Bazaar held in the Old Vicarage garden. 'The Bazaar being a thorough success', as the newspaper reported, 'the committee immediately set about the beginning of the work they had undertaken'.

That was in May 1866. King's College conveyed a piece of farmland to the school's Trustees, stipulating that the purpose of the building should be 'for the education of children … of the labouring manufacturing and other poorer classes in the Parish of Grantchester'. When the new building, with its steeply-pitched roof and tall bell-spire, its decorative ridge-tiles and barge-boards, and the carved buttress-stones which, showing lily and rose, acknowledged the contributions of Corpus Christi and King's Colleges – when all was complete, the *Cambridgeshire Chronicle* reported thus:

> A very tasty and an, in every way, adapted building has been erected,
> in the gothic style, from the designs of Wm. Fawcett, Esq., and we
> congratulate the parishioners on having been so successful in their labours.

The opening ceremony, in February 1867, was a great event for the village. Dignitaries, including the Archdeacon of Ely, and well-to-do subscribers congregated in the church, where they heard the Senior Fellow of Corpus give a fitting sermon; after which the church choir, with banners, led a procession to the new building. There, the Master of Corpus knocked on the door, which was opened by the Vicar, the Rev. W. Martin. Then they all entered and sat down to luncheon. 'After the repast', says the newspaper, 'the several toasts were proposed and responded to in some very terse and well-chosen remarks, and were drunk with much enthusiasm'.

Enthusiasm was, indeed, running so high that the committee, having raised the necessary £730, were now hoping to collect enough extra for a harmonium. That evening some of the more ordinary villagers may themselves have been able to afford tickets at 6d or 3d for the lengthy concert given in the new schoolroom. The newspaper rather patronisingly suggests that this was so –

> At the concert on the opening-day it was remarked that the humbler ranks among the audience accurately distinguished and more loudly applauded the *best music*. This fact must have been very gratifying to the numerous ladies and gentlemen of Grantchester, Cambridge, Ashley, Hampstead, &c., to whom the parishioners are so much indebted for that delightful entertainment: it is certainly very encouraging to all who are endeavouring to promote the welfare and innocent enjoyment of the working classes.

No tickets were needed for the next day's event, a great tea party for 60 women, mothers of school pupils and needy widows, given by the Vicar and his wife.

But that was not all. To add to the funds the resourceful Mr Widnall gave, on the following two days, an entertainment called 'Natural Magic'. He 'exhibited various illustrations with great skill and ingenuity, and much interested large companies'. With satisfaction he noted 'Proceeds £3.16.9'.

The splendid new village schoolroom provided a hall in which public entertainments could take place (the old thatched building having become a 'Reading Room' for smaller gatherings). Here the Church Missionary Society might hold a meeting (subject: 'The Search for Dr Livingstone', June 1867), or the Pitt Press Reading & Musical Union give a concert (proceeds towards the cost of a harmonium for the school, Jan 1868). It was here that Page gave lectures on divers subjects. It was the place where the ladies from the Old Vicarage, after joining their friends and practising a few times at Merton House, could present their Grand Concert too. Over the years other performances would follow – a 'minstrel' entertainment, readings, *tableaux vivants*, a spectacular conjuring show given by a Cambridge don, an illustrated talk given by the Curate...

*

In April 1867 Page made another contribution to the parish. One of Lally's diary entries says 'All the candlesticks put up in the church and look so pretty'. Those candelabra are in the church still, though they were once – as seen in Page's photograph of the church interior a few years later – more numerous and provided the only illumination after dark. He had made them very simply, mounted on slim square-cut poles. The branches are thin curved straps of metal, painted in matt blue and red. Ivy leaves cut from sheet tinplate hang down; and the candle-holders are little cake-tins which cannot have cost more than a ha'penny each. Their naivety and economy do not appeal to everyone, but those who know a little about Page Widnall regard them with affection.*

Tragic events in the village appear in the diary now and then. In a place whose cottages were mostly thatched, fire was a constant hazard. Early in 1865 there were two bad fires, one in Page's own stackyard, where hay, peas and straw were burnt; and another a month later, when part of Mr Lilley's farm burnt down. (The local newspaper suspected 'an incendiary' as the cause.) But in 1867 there was a more tragic disaster:

> 24 *Aug* The 'Rose & Crown' and some cottages burned down at Grantchester a girl named Smith who is supposed to have caused the fire was so frightened she ran and threw herself into the river and was drowned.

That must all have been the sort of terrible accident which could so easily happen in dry summer weather when a fire kindled by the careless use of candles, oil lamps or greasy cooking over an open stove got out of control.

But it was always possible that damage might be caused by deranged minds. Just before Christmas 1869

> Mrs Howard and George came to tea a man came and broke 8 panes of glass in our drawing room window he had previously broken some at Mrs Nimmo's [the Mill House, just around the corner].

And next spring, 'Mrs Jas. Stearn set fire to her house and had to be taken to the Fulbourn Asylum' [a huge edifice with tower and castellations, the County Lunatic Asylum, which had been built in 1851].

*unlike the Best Kept Village judges of 1972 who expressed scorn for 'sconces made from old cake tins'. See Appendix IV

CHAPTER 12

Daily Life in the late 1860s
Extending the Circle

———•◦•———

VILLAGE AND FAMILY – that network of connections stemming from Page's in-laws – were the main themes throughout his life. It is time now to resume the story, with attention to his own corner of Grantchester and developments in the family circle.

Their home gave the trio such delight that they never ceased to make improvements and additions. Early in 1865 Page got some men to bore a deep well, so deep that from it arose a perpetual fountain. Indoors, that spring, he made alterations to the drawing-room and turned its staircase. And he and Lilly came back from an auction sale at Impington with some small treasures, a decanter, a clock and other things.

It was a year when they were preoccupied with the health of Page's mother. Instead of taking off for some more exciting destination, they took old Mrs Widnall to the east coast. In June they stayed for a fortnight at Aldeburgh, during which Page and Lilly escaped for a day to go 'egging' at Orford-ness. For the rest of that month and July, Page occupied part of his time with successive broods of chickens hatched in his (probably home-made) incubator, eagerly recording the results. Just one visitor, Miss Hunt, is mentioned.

The senior Mrs Widnall was in decline. In August, Lally accompanied Page to Hunstanton in a search for suitable lodgings for her, and three days later he and Lilly took the old lady (now aged seventy-eight) there, hoping that sea air would bring improvement. For more than a month after that the trio, and Annie and Laura besides, went 'backwards and forwards several times' to be with her; but she was brought home on 18th September, and died a fortnight later.

It was not long – 12th January the following year – before the other old lady for whom they had been caring, Aunt Hannah Widnall, died too. From now on, attention shifted to the younger generation, and they would acquire some very interesting new friends from the University.

*

There was that long-standing friendship with the Howard family, now into the third generation. Young George Howard had become an undergraduate at Trinity College; Alfred Robinson, at St John's, was a year ahead. On 20th October 1865 'Mr Palmer and Mr Hope called', both studying at St John's. A few days later there were new arrivals at the Mill House close by, Mr & Mrs Nimmo and their large family. The ladies quickly got to know each other, and in January 1866

> Lilly, Lally, Mary Nimmo and Miss Hudson went in the early morning to Mr Hudson's rooms in St John's [actually Trinity] and he took us to the Senate House to hear the degree list read. G. Howard 26th Wrangler we then went to Mr Niven's rooms and breakfasted and met Mr Clifford who is expected to be Senior Wrangler next year

The Mr Hudson in whose rooms they met was a Tutor at Trinity at that time.* George Howard had earned a very respectable degree, and the following day they attended the degree ceremony, lunched with the new graduate in his rooms and met his friends, including Mr Coneybeare. They were a remarkable group. Mr Hudson's own interests ranged beyond classics and theology to musical scholarship. Niven would become Professor of Natural Philosophy at Aberdeen, Coneybeare a clergyman and local historian. And Mr Clifford was indeed an outstanding undergraduate, who at the end of the year would be chosen to deliver a 'declamation' in the hall at Trinity College. Although in the event he became only Second Wrangler, his declamation displayed a keenly original mind. Taking Sir Walter Raleigh as his theme, he considered exploration, pointing to the momentous implications for society in the discoveries which might be revealed not only to an explorer over sea and land, but to a scientist. His own mental explorations would conjure-up mathematical structures on which far-reaching developments were to be based long after his death.

*

Early that spring the Old Vicarage trio went over to Worcester. While Page (who was anxious to see how the first hundred eggs of the year in his new incubator house were hatching) returned fairly soon, Lilly and Lally spent several weeks with the families there. This was the year when

---

*A Yorkshireman, Hudson would some years later become Rural Dean of Helmsley. But in 1900 he was to assume the name and arms of Pemberton when his wife, as heir, succeeded to the ownership of Trumpington Hall.

the Widnalls hosted their great two-day Bazaar in the garden to raise money for the new village school building. When preparations were almost complete Annie came over from Malvern, bringing Laura for the occasion. It was May; the weather was fine, the garden at its best … and one at least of their undergraduate friends must have been there among the stalls and refreshment tables, that unusual young man whose intro-duction to the Widnalls may have come about through a relationship to their old friend Jonathan Palmer. For only a fortnight later, on the 22nd, 'Mr Palmer proposed to Laura'.

It was a day or two before her fifteenth birthday. Laura was still far too young for marriage, but she accepted Edward's proposal. Many years later Aunt Lally, writing a description of the garden for a friend, conveyed her own delight at the event:

> … Then comes the Nut Walk, bordering a sort of wilderness of fruit trees, &c. This walk leads down to the Bathing House, for the river Granta flows along the bottom of the garden, and the path is overshadowed by a row of fine Chestnut trees. In this Chestnut path, many loving words have been spoken. I have two pretty poems, one written by my niece Laura, and the other by her husband (the well-known Professor Palmer) some years after the little words that linked them together were spoken beneath the 'Shady Chestnut trees', and both describing the all-important event…

Two of Edward's poems are quoted in the biography of him written by Sir Walter Besant.* One, in Italian, is an acrostic spelling LAURA DAVIS. The other is the one mentioned by Lally –

> I felt the flood-gates open fly,
> And poured my secret in her ear,
> And paused awhile for her reply
> With hope, though somewhat mixed with fear.
> It came – a little word that sent
> Through all my frame a joyous thrill;
> And gently on my arm there leaned
> Those tiny fingers, trembling still.
> The merry stream flowed on apace
> Beneath the shady chestnut trees;
> And lo! another smiling face
> Was turned to catch the balmy breeze.

*Sir Walter Besant: *Life & Achievements of Edward Henry Palmer*

Laura's whirlwind romance must have astounded the family, a family in which dynastic arrangements had always been made with such care. Libby brought her own girls – Alice now seventeen, Amy sixteen – for a visit shortly afterwards. They had reached that moment when they, too, were ready for some shy introductions to be made with Lilly and Lally's help to some young university men.

A few days after their return to Worcester, Richard brought the boys, Bertie (fifteen) and Car (fourteen). Page arranged a great river treat. Boating picnics do not always go quite according to plan, though:

> Page, Lilly, Lally, Mrs Young, Bertie & Car went for a long day up the river, went as far as Malton farm [beyond Barrington], got the boat on a stump on our return and made a hole in the boat reached home about 2 a.m.

The boys stayed for the rest of the summer – six weeks, a time when they were sure to be having many happier experiences with their uncle. Much of that time, one guesses, was spent fishing, absorbing bits of country lore, tales of antiquity and ingenious experiments in Uncle Page's work-shop. Messing about on the river must have included swimming, for on 11th July Lilly and Lally themselves 'began river bathing for the season'.

After their visitors had left, it was time for their own holiday, once more an adventurous one. 'Page, Lilly, Lally and Julia Lilley went to the Channel Islands see diary' is the abrupt entry; and, annoyingly, all the details are lost.

Towards the end of that year, another family arrived as close neigh-bours at Riversdale – the Greenes, new friends to join in the Shakespeare readings (*Julius Caesar*) just starting at Mrs Howard's. They had come from Henley-on-Thames: William Greene and his wife Charlotte, with at that time three daughters and three sons, the youngest newly-born. The girls, Florence, Alice and Polly, came at once to Lally for their schooling. The family were to spend six years as Riversdale tenants and to remain lifelong friends.

*

For Page Widnall, New Year's Day 1867 was an exciting moment. 'Placed a model of my patent folding Form* at the Educational depart-ment of the S. Kensington Museum', he recorded. Now he was not mere-ly a 'capital contriver' but an inventor-craftsman of (he hoped) some significance; for there was always, with him, that urge to seek fame and

*See Appendix V

fortune through activities other than farming. (Fame, in the end, would scarcely extend beyond the village; and fortune always eluded him.)

The South Kensington Museum was at that time

> ... a strictly functional hall, with aisles and a gallery, built with corrugated iron sheets and lit by skylights. For displays its simplicity must have had, by modern standards, many advantages, but its brutalism, relieved only by a light, cast-iron porch, not unlike the platform covering of a small railway station, shocked contemporary taste.

> [T. S. R. Boase, *English Art* 1800–1870]

This building was, of course, replaced by the extravagant Victoria & Albert Museum we know. But even in 1883 Ruskin was to speak scornfully of its contents – 'the miscellaneous collection at Kensington, where Gothic saints and sinners are confounded alike among steam thrashing-machines and dynamite-proof ships of war...'

While the Old Vicarage was full of his ingenious gadgets, this seems to have been the only one patented. Page had caught a good moment – in 1863 an exhibition in Vienna had displayed *Mannstein's Patent Folding Furniture*, which packed beds, easy-chairs and tables into compact units which might be swallowed by a wardrobe. He may, indeed, have seen pictures of these wonders in the *Illustrated London News*, and felt challenged to invent something on the same lines. How many of his own folding forms he sold at 20/- (one pound) apiece is not known.

1867 was to be altogether a varied and busy year. In February there were the ceremonies for the formal opening of the new village school building, followed by two evening performances of Page's 'conjuring entertainment'. Next month he took himself, through deep snow, to Shepreth to give a lecture. In April he installed his candelabra in the church. Further carpentry followed: now he was 'very busy at the new bathing house'. This stood near the riverbank where a shallow gravelly bottom provided a possible entry to the chilly waters – a place formerly known as Hog Hunch, where gravel had been excavated. Bathers could change in the 'picturesque' [Polly Greene] bathing house, and swing from ropes attached to the overhanging chestnut branches.

They had visitors, Jane Lapworth with three small children and their nurse. And the summer social season began with croquet at the Nimmos'. But the weather changed, and four days later, when the Lapworths left, there was a great flood.

Far more serious was the shock to them all, on 15th May, of 'Lilly's dreadful operation for cancer by Dr Humphrey'. Once again Page had called in the very best surgeon in Cambridge – possibly in the whole country at that time. When the worst of the ordeal was over, Richard and Libby came. The day after, the 29th, Lilly was able to come downstairs for tea; and after another fortnight her brother and his wife left.

In the meantime, summer entertainments carried on. In June, Alice and Amy came to stay with Mrs Ellen Howard at Merton House, to be 'finished'. With their younger cousin Laura now informally engaged to Edward Palmer, they too needed to contemplate their inevitable destiny – and few places were richer in suitable young men (clever, charming, athletic and possibly well off) than Cambridge. The game of croquet was an ideal pastime; the Old Vicarage garden a romantic setting. One particular croquet party on the Old Vicarage lawn called for some patience, as the guests were posed for a series of photographs.

It was 14th June 1867; and three surviving pictures preserve for us that paradisal Old Vicarage way of life which was always to be treasured in the memories of those who experienced it. In the first the trio are all there, dispensing tea to a group of young people, Lilly smiling cheerfully. The girls gathered about them are at that stage of emergence from childhood, the younger ones with Alice-in-Wonderland hair, their ankles visible beneath flounced dresses, while those a year or two older have put their hair up and wear longer skirts. Laura Davis is recognisable, her hair already a 'crowning glory', while the two beside her at tea seem to be her cousins Alice and Amy. In another photograph they are supposedly playing croquet (on rather rough grass) beside the new fountain. And in

the third, taken on another occasion in front of the Castle Ruin, Lilly is again the smiling hostess; Lally is wearing a curious hat and has allowed her ringlets to hang loose; and between them sits the young William Clifford, a sombre figure (perhaps in the throes of the shift in belief which took him, during those years, from High Anglicanism to agnosticism*). Three young girls and a boy sit on the grass, and two older girls and their parents complete the party.

Towards the end of June, Alice and Amy left, and the trio set off for their summer holiday, this time to Devonshire. They arrived at Brookhill House, Kingsweir, where they were to stay with Tom and

*See *Such Silver Currents, the story of William and Lucy Clifford* by M. Chisholm

Annie Davis, and found that not only Laura was there but Edward Palmer as well. The engagement had evidently been approved: in spite of his stuffy appearance in the family portrait, Tom Davis must have been persuaded of Edward's respectability (after all, his late father had been a schoolmaster) and prospects of success.

The Teign provided all that they most enjoyed – wildlife, churches, castles, and a mild climate for Lilly's convalescence. It seems to have been a characteristically energetic holiday:

1 *July* Went from Kingsweir to Totness [*sic*] in a boat had tea and a wet row back. Saw a great many pretty jelly fish

24 *July* Page, Lilly, Lally, Annie and others went for a pleasant row and caught 4 mackerel at Kingsweir

and after a month in Devon they returned as far as London to stay with the Lapworths, with whom they had broken their outward journey. This allowed them, on 2nd August, to see 'the grand fireworks at the Crystal Palace'.

Then they were home again, back to their Grantchester friends. There is a rather odd diary entry for 29th August: 'Page went to Merton House to play Croquet with Mr Jones (alias Cavendish)'. At first one wonders whether this could possibly be the future Duke of Devonshire or one of his family ... but it turns out that there actually was a famous Henry Jones* known as 'Cavendish'.

In the autumn they went for a 'lovely drive to Hildersham with G. Howard to see the church &c'. Over the Gog Magog hills they went, a brisk and airy drive with their new pony, Dapple, clip-clopping between the shafts. Despite the eighteen-year difference in age, George Howard was a natural companion for Page. As amateur antiquarians they would have examined the ancient carved oak effigies and medieval brasses in the church at Hildersham, but perhaps paid particular homage to one image, the gruesome skeleton of a Richard Howard who had died in 1499.

Turning from antiquities to science, Page gave a lecture on Geology at Coton, and in November another on 'Fire & Water' in the schoolroom at Grantchester. And this winter the Shakespeare-reading group were gathering at the Old Vicarage for *Richard III*.

*Dr Henry Jones (1831–1899, whose writings about the game of whist were thought sufficiently important for his inclusion in the *Dictionary of National Biography*

1868 opened with Page being invited by Edward Palmer to dine in Hall with the Fellows of St John's College. He must have been delighted and impressed, finding himself in such surroundings; and it provided proof that young Palmer might actually be going to be able to support Laura – might, indeed, have a brilliant future.

Edward Palmer was altogether an extraordinary man. Both his parents had died when he was a boy, and so he was brought up by a sympathetic aunt and sent to the Perse School at Cambridge. He achieved little at school, and left at sixteen to work as a junior clerk in an office in the London docks. While at school, though, he had used his pocket-money to pay gipsies to give him sixpenny lessons in Romany. And again while in Dockland, he befriended Italian immigrants – political exiles, organ grinders, waiters, sailors – and became fluent in their language and dialects; likewise French. The three years as a clerk were also filled with theatre-going (from which he formed a lifelong friendship with Henry Irving), attempts at photography, wood-carving and mesmerism.

Then he was found to have tuberculosis at an advanced stage. A herbalist prescribed strong doses of lobelia, and the response was dramatic. He became more violently ill and very nearly died; then recovered and was free of the disease. During convalescence he wrote amusing pieces for the theatre and himself began to act, appearing three times on the stage of the Cambridge Theatre.

But the stage was set aside. He had got to know an orientalist called Seyd Abdullah, and from him learnt Arabic. He acquired a scholarship at St John's, Cambridge, and in due course was to add Greek, Hebrew, Syriac,Urdu and Persian to his vocabulary. At the time of his proposal to Laura he was still an undergraduate running late, and with a very uncertain future. Now, in spite of a poor performance in the Classical Tripos, a special examination in oriental languages had revealed his exceptional ability, and he had been elected to a Fellowship of his college. His biographer, Sir Walter Besant, was to describe him thus:

> In appearance Palmer was of short stature, a little man, with narrow, sloping shoulders and contracted chest. His figure had, in later years, a slight stoop, caused by continued bending over his desk; his arms were long, and he had remarkable fingers, delicate, long, thin; fingers which seemed endowed with a separate individuality...

Unpromising as his appearance was, he had courage, energy and charm.

At the Old Vicarage, the trio were free to resume activities in their Castle Theatre this year. On 23rd January, Libby and all four of her children arrived to see the dress rehearsal of the three short plays performed next day:

> Our theatricals 'Delicate Ground' 'Cousin Tom' & 'Blue Beard' very successful had a dance afterwards, 41 guests broke up at 3 a.m.

It was their most ambitious entertainment ever; and one of their guests, Mrs Greene, gave birth to a baby boy next day. A few days later, Page took photographs of some of the players: Lally wears 18th-century costume as 'Pauline' and Mr Capel as 'Sangfroid' in *Delicate Ground*.

They were all in creative mood. 1868 was the year of the great singing class, started in February, when

> Mr Capel proposed a singing class a delightful evening. Mrs Clark* sang 'Home sweet Home' 'Last rose of summer' 'Wreath of Roses' &c. Libby sang 'Should he upbraid' 'Lady of the Lea' & 'Auld Robin Gray'. Mr Capel sang 'John Brown' 'Once I loved a maiden fair' 'Barbara Allen' &c. Alice & Amy sang a duett

They had all dined at Mrs Howard's and afterwards supped at Mr Capel's. And then, in May, they gave their 'grand Concert in the Schoolroom', when they not only sang, but performed Haydn's 'Toy Symphony' on two successive nights. Page himself was no musician (although he might have been persuaded to play the cuckoo or tap a drum on that occasion); but he was again in demand as a lecturer at Coton and in

Grantchester, where he gave a talk on 'Old England', during which a replica of the Corpus Horn was passed around – the original being an ancient drinking cup belonging to Corpus Christi College.

Since the two attractive girls, Alice and Amy, needed chaperoning, Page and Lally were able to share the entertainment provided by that Trinity undergraduate, Mr Clifford. They all went to hear a debate in the Union, and spent a 'Delightful

*wife of Prof. E. C. Clark, who lived at Grove Lodge

evening at Mr Clifford's rooms read "School for Scandal" he gave a noble supper'. Then 'Mr Clifford & Mr Crotch came to take Alice & Amy to Trin. Chapel. Lally went with them had tea in Mr Clifford's rooms'. At the end of May, all three – Lilly, Lally, Page – were taken with Laura by Mr Palmer to the A.D.C. to see *The Contested Election* and *Popping the Question*.

Soon her aunts and uncle took Laura off with them for a holiday. This time they left the Old Vicarage in the care of Jane Lapworth while they travelled down to the Isle of Wight, at first lodging with a Mrs Carter at Freshwater. The island was already becoming popular, having been 'discovered' by the Royal Family and the Poet Laureate. The group walked from Freshwater 'to Alum Bay by the downs in a tremendous wind'. (No mention is made of the reclusive Tennyson, or of the photographer Julia Margaret Cameron, by then installed in the vicinity.) Then they moved to Chale, and drove over to Carisbrook to see the Castle one day, to Ventnor and Bonchurch another. Finally, on 6 July:

> Left Chale, went in a carrier's cart to Newport, by sail to Cowes, by steamer to Lymington, by rail again to Christchurch and in a carriage to Bournemouth

and on 10th July arrived home to find Jane and little Alfred still in residence.

*

A diary entry for 3rd August 1868 is of special interest. Page boasts '"The first apple pie from our orchard" I planted in the spring of this year'. He had filled the acre of ground between Yew Garth and the Old Vicarage with a variety of trees, apples, cherries, plums, pears and medlars, all chosen to provide fruit for as many months of the year as possible. Of the 116 named varieties listed in his meticulous record, one at least seems to have been of his own grafting* – the *Hannah Widnall* apple, named in tribute to the aunt who had died two years before. Other apples – the *Golden Spire*, the *Winter Peach* – had probably come from Richard Smith's nursery; and in the Vale of Evesham he may have found, too, many more of those 32 varieties of apples, 13 of pears, 10 of plums and 7 of cherries. Page Widnall's orchard became, some years after his death, the Orchard Tea Gardens, a favourite resort for Cambridge undergraduates and intelligentsia. Visitors take their refreshments, reclining on

---

*A skill perhaps learnt from old Arthur Biggs of the Botanic Garden many years before

deck chairs, beneath those same trees still; and where replacements are needed, they are made as far as possible with the original varieties.

Daily life had such a regular pattern – farming, housekeeping, teaching – that the staccato diary entries note only a few exceptions now and then. On 11th August, for instance, 'Laura went with Mr Palmer to have her likeness taken in her silk dress'. The resulting studio photographs, preserved in the family album, show the betrothed couple at this stage of their lives, he aged twenty-eight, still needing 'reputation and an income of some kind', and she only seventeen, '… a singularly beautiful girl, fair and with a lovely complexion, taller than her *fiancé*'.*

It must have been a warm summer. On 5th September Lally noted: 'Lilly, Laura and I bathed and succeeded in swimming without our belts' – beside which Page scribbled 'Oh!?' And as an addition to their already splendid garden: '31 October Received our Peafowls "Jacko" & "Pieco"'.

Page was busy in his rôle as scientist – for always, tantalisingly, there was that dream of the fortune he might make through discoveries or inventions. Now, at the beginning of November, he made a journey into

Wales 'to inquire about a lake … said to have a valuable deposit of clay'. No more is heard of that; but a few days later he announces having made 'some thermo instruments for G. Howard'. Another entry, 'Bought the Brass work for our Banner screens 18/-' sounds like preparation for an enterprise in embroidery by Lilly.

*Sir Walter Besant: *The Life & Achievements of E.H. Palmer*

[113]

Several diary entries refer to young Mr Clifford and his friends. In December the Old Vicarage group 'went to see Mr Clifford, Crotch, two Pollocks and others at the Gymnasium'. As at Oxford, gymnastics had become a fashionable form of exercise, and William Kingdom Clifford was worth watching, for he was not only spectacularly good on the bars but is said to have once 'hung by his toes from a weathercock'. His life was to be cut short by tuberculosis; but his work as a mathematician was so outstanding that the applications of Clifford Algebra have in recent times made possible advances in many scientific fields – computers, space technology, medicine and astronomy. His philosophical argument was formidable, yet he could present his ideas simply, as in a booklet of elementary science, *Seeing and Thinking*.

> The vivacity and quaint humour of his addresses, and the remarkable felicity of illustration, interested popular hearers, and persuaded them (not always correctly) that they could follow his reasoning. [*D.N.B.*]

They were altogether a remarkable group, members of the 'Apostles'*and as agile mentally as physically. While Clifford was to become Professor of Applied Mathematics at University College, London, Frederick Pollock would go to Corpus Christi College, Oxford as a law professor[†].

*

Friendship with the latest Riversdale family was also flourishing. Mrs Greene, the birth of whose seventh child had perhaps been accelerated by the laughter and dancing at the rumbustious New Year theatricals across the road, shared her neighbours' tastes. In December she took Lally to 'a delightful Concert at the Town Hall to hear Mad. Titiens'[‡]. Once again, Lally was witnessing one of the great personalities of the age: a prima donna who, that same year, had brought a performance of Weber's *Oberon* to a standstill with prolonged applause and demands from the audience for their favourite songs.

For the Greenes, as for the Widnalls, this was to become a very special friendship; and when, seventy or more years later, Polly Greene wrote down some memories of the six years of her childhood spent in Grantchester, she would acknowledge that it had been 'the people who lived in the Old Vicarage', who had influenced her sense of 'beauty and cheerfulness' most deeply. [See Chapter 13]

*The Apostles, a discussion society composed of the most original minds, mostly drawn from Trinity and King's Colleges.
[†]and in due course join Leslie Stephen in editing the *Lectures and Essays of W.K. Clifford*
[‡]Teresa Tietjens

*

The final year of the decade is one suitable as an illustration of 'the diary', showing how Page and Lally set down events – and the consequent puzzle for the reader in interpreting them. Before giving this example, a little explanation is needed.

Laura Davis, still too young for marriage, stayed with her aunts at Grantchester much of the time. Edward Palmer had been recruited to take part in an expedition to survey the Sinai desert. A photograph of the explorers shows Palmer alone having adopted bedouin dress and hookah, for it was he whose task was to approach the leaders of the various tribes and learn their names for geographical features. Actual contact with these people in their own land suited him well: his health improved in the dry climate and he added new dialects to his knowledge of Arabic. When, on 22nd May, 'Mr Palmer returned from the East...' it was after this journey. And – not recorded in *Uncle Page's Book* – at the end of the year he was off again, this time with only one companion, the surveyor Tyrwhitt Drake. The two of them,

> without escort or dragoman, walked the six hundred miles from
> Sinai to Jerusalem, identifying sites and searching vainly for
> inscriptions. They explored for the first time the Desert of the
> Wanderings (Tik), and many unknown parts of Edom and Moab,
> and accomplished a quantity of useful geographical work. [*D.N.B.*]

They went on 'with many adventures and close shaves', to Damascus where he met and became friends with Capt. Richard Burton. It was a huge experience, in which he developed his intimacy with the desert people and became accepted among the Arab sheikhs as 'Abdullah Effendi'.

Another development, in the summer of 1869, was the result of the nieces' encounters with the young men from the university. When Alice and Amy were in Grantchester once more, they all went to a concert at Christ's, where Mr Crotch (spelt 'Crouch' in the diary) again met them. Soon Mr Crotch reappeared, taking Libby and the girls to the ADC, Cambridge's very active Amateur Dramatic Club. His attentions turn out to have been a discreet courtship; for in September Lally 'heard of Alice's engagement to Mr Crouch'. Alice was not quite twenty-one at the time, and seems to have felt uncertain, later, of her feelings. A year later this engagement would end.

*

29 *Jan*	Had a party of 21 Charades 'Black-leg', 'Wax-work', 'Phantom' all went well thanks to Mrs Young
19 *Feb*	I gathered some Hawthorn in leaf even the flower buds were visible (SS)
[1] 8 *March*	Went to the Gymnasium
[2] 11 *March*	Laura and I slept in my newly papered room (SS)
15 *March*	Page gave a lecture 'On an Unseen World'
18 *March*	Mrs Young came intending to stay with us
5 *April*	Chas. Williams came to Grantchester
24 *April*	Mrs Young left us
28 *April*	Hawthorn in bloom
1 *May*	Bought our Alderney Cow Buttercup £17.17.0 [17 guineas]
4 *May*	Alice & Amy came. Our concert in the School room 'Son and Stranger' &c.
[3] 22 *May*	Mr Palmer returned from the East he came to Cambridge today Page and Laura went to meet him
28 *May*	Grand Performance at the Gymnasium Mr Frost did wonders–
31 *May*	Libby came and joined Alice and Amy We went to the Concert at Christ's Col. Mr Crouch met us there (SS)
[4] 5 *June*	Mr Palmer came for Laura Mr Crouch for Libby, Alice & Amy to go to a Promenade Concert, the 3 latter to the A.D.C.
[5] 10 *June*	Mr & Mrs Higginbotham returned to Scotland taking with them Mary and Polly Greene
[6] 20 *June*	Mary Ann Fordham and Ellis Lewis asked in Church
[7] 20 *July*	Had tea at the Hardings and went to see the Marionetts
[8] 30 *July*	Church Clock put up
2 *Aug*	Page Lilly & Lally went to see Mr Swan (artist) and saw his drawings
[9] 14 *Aug*	Went to Wicken Fen, crossed the Ferry at the inn '5 miles from Anywhere & no hurry'
[10] 16 *Aug*	Page & Lilly went to Dunmow Flitch of Bacon Day – saw Mrs Clark Miss Kelsey & Mrs Tofts &c
19 *Aug*	Polly Greene returned from Scotland
[11] 4 *Sep*	Had a pleasant drive to Orwell took Annie Creeke saw the Maypole
7 *Sep*	Heard of Alice's engagement to Mr Crouch
[12] 13 *Sep*	Louisa Bensley and Eddy came to school
14 *Oct*	Laura went to school to Mrs Sharp at Dallington
25 *Oct*	Lally took part in Moliere's play of 'Le Bourgeois Gentilhomme' at Merton House
[13] 29 *Oct*	Lilly not very well has gone to London for a change
[14] 2 *Nov*	Went to Mr Palmer's lecture on Sinai Capt Palmer also spoke very interesting altogether
13 *Nov*	Page went to London to join Lilly
22 *Nov*	Page & Lilly returned from London Lilly very ill with Rheumatic Gout scarcely able to crawl
25 *Nov*	Reading at our School Room Page read 'Lord Dundreary or Poor Richds Proverbs', G Howard read 'Boots at the Holly Tree Inn' Our Ram knocked little Polly Greene down and hurt her knee
6 *Dec*	Dr Humphrey came and prescribed for dear Lilly
16 *Dec*	James Williams died
18 *Dec*	I dismissed my children as Lilly continued very ill (SS)
22 *Dec*	Mrs Howard & George came to tea a man came and broke 8 panes of glass in our drawing room windows he had previously broken some at Mrs Nimmo's

Here are a few explanations of the above

1 The Gymnasium was in Cambridge, and at that time popular with their young undergraduate friends.

2 Lally's room had been papered in response to a suggestion the previous April: 'Mrs Howard & George brought some wall-papers for us to see (they are going to paper their drawing-room) We fell in love with one a large Chintz pattern'.

3 Mr Palmer's return from the East was the homecoming of Laura's fiancé Edward Palmer after his exploratory journey across the Sinai Desert

4 'Mr Crouch' was a Trinity undergraduate, earlier recorded as 'Mr Crotch'

5 Mr & Mrs Higginbotham & Mary do not appear elsewhere. Polly Greene at this time was aged 8 or 9.

6 Mary Ann Fordham was one of the family servants: now having the banns of marriage called.

7 Hardings: the Rev Derisley Harding was Vicar of Barton, and had for some years lived in 'Widnall's cottage' in Grantchester, but was now at Caldecote Vicarage

8 This was Grantchester's church clock, later to excite the interest of tourists because of the final couplet of Rupert Brooke's poem about the Old Vicarage:
> 'Stands the Church clock at ten to three?
> And is there honey still for tea?'

9 The old inn known as the 'Five Miles From Anywhere – No Hurry' was at Upware, 'the tiniest and most sequestered of hamlets, where the wide Fens spread all around, bare, treeless, houseless, open to the sweep of every breeze, and giving the same delicious sense of space as a sea view.' [Coneybeare]

10 An ancient tradition awards a 'flitch' of bacon (the local product) each year to the most happily-married couple to present themselves at Dunmow, in Essex. Page's cousins Mrs Clark and Mrs Tofts were both widows. Could they have been there as witnesses to vouch for the success of the Widnall marriage?

11 The Orwell Maypole was an ancient post marking the boundary between Harlton and Orwell, one of the last in the country used in the originally heathen dancing ceremony, on top of White Hill. 'It stood almost exactly upon the meridian of Greenwich, so that it was a valuable and far-seen landmark.' [Coneybeare] Annie Creeke was a former pupil of Lally's.

12 Louisa and Eddy, children of new residents in the village. Their father was a Fellow of Caius.

13 Lilly's illness was to persist for 14 weeks.

14 Captain Palmer had been a member of the Sinai Exploration team. He was not related to Edward Palmer

[CHAPTER 13]

The Greenes

———◦•◦———

THE GREENE FAMILY have already been mentioned a number of times, Riversdale tenants who became such close friends that they were almost honorary members of the Old Vicarage household. Mr Greene, who was to describe himself for the 1871 Census as a 'Law Student' (aged 46) scarcely appears in the diary: he had private means and, being in weak health, lived quietly at home or went off to Matlock Spa to take the waters. He did, however, have the strength to beget nine children; and although from childhood considered delicate, there had been an experience during his adolescence which must have coloured his view of life ever after.

William Greene was himself the youngest of a family of eleven children, and his father, Benjamin, had been a wealthy city merchant. Years later a member of the family* would write a description for her children:

The wealth of the family was derived from large sugar plantations at St Kitts in the West Indies, managed by an agent and run entirely on slave labour. Benjamin Greene sent out one of his younger sons (Charles) to act, nominally, as 'Manager' and William joined him there, making the long journey in a sailing ship quite alone when he was barely 14 years old. His brother was only two years his senior and the two boys must have had a wonderful time together. The actual work and supervision of the Estate was done entirely by the agent, and free of all duties and responsibilities they spent their days in riding, bathing, and roaming over the island. To the end of his life William looked back with longing to those fabulous two years, when slaves waited upon their every want and the days were filled with sunshine and joy.

The St Kitts idyll came to an end with the death of Charles from yellow fever. Young William returned and read for the Bar but never practised; and because he had no need to earn a living was able to follow his literary interests:

*Mrs Eva Greene, widow of Edward Greene

Being fond of walking he spent whole days wandering about the countryside with a volume of Plutarch or Bacon's Essays in his pocket, resting and reading from time to time in the shade of trees or hedges.

He had in 1854 married Charlotte Smith, a strong character, daughter of a master mariner in coastal shipping. When they arrived in Grantchester in 1866 they had six children, and a further three were born during their residence at Riversdale.

Polly (Charlotte Mary Greene) was the fourth child, after Florence, Graham* and Alice. When they came to Grantchester she was five years old, and all three girls were sent across the road to be taught by Lally – and little Polly, greatly impressed by the Old Vicarage 'magician', supposed his name to be 'Mr Windmill'. Graham, slight but strong-willed, managed to dominate a reluctant donkey which bore him daily to school in Cambridge. In old age Polly was to set down her remiscences, providing sympathetic descriptions of the people she grew to love so well.

Mr Widnall [whose name she, as a five-year-old, had at first taken to be 'Mr Windmill'] *was rather short and stout. He had a bald head with a fringe of hair at the back, a fine Roman nose and a benign boyish expression. He had broad blunt fingers but with these fingers he fashioned the tiny details of the wonderful models that he made...*

Mrs Widnall was tall. She had grey hair, walked with dignity and her expression was sweet and grave. She wore simple dresses with skirts that hung straight down.

So simple were her dresses that, in those days of amplitude and furbelows, they were remarkable. She made wonderful jams and preserves, often from uncommon fruits such as Pyrus Japonica, hips, mountain ash berries, mulberries, the nice sour fruit of the barbary and from huckleberries. She gardened a good deal and carried round with her as she walked in the garden a long wand to keep off the peacocks who were either too tame or too fierce.

Aunt Lalley, her sister, was very small. She wore lace caps with pretty ribands in them. Three white curls of hair came from under the cap on each side and framed her face. She wore beautiful flowered silk shawls and often her hands were mittened. She was fond of her white fantailed doves which she fed. They sometimes followed her into the house. All the pets in their house were white. They had three white

---

*Later Sir Graham Greene, Parliamentary Secretary to the Admiralty, and uncle of the novelist cats, many white doves, and the ducks, which walked back from the river to their shed every afternoon at the same time, were snow white.

Mr Widnall called himself a farmer. I know that he planted the Orchard which is now a favourite resort of those people of Cambridge who like to take their tea under the shadow of appletrees. I know that he had calves for one day when I was playing in his paddock with a little friend I saw them but was undisturbed by any fear of them and we began to dance round an old pollard elm. My friend had on a white dress tied round the waist with a broad emerald green sash. One of the calves watched the sash fluttering from her as she danced and made for it. She ran away but the calf caught her up and got hold of the end of what it thought was a luscious morsel and little by little it disappeared down its throat. If it were not for my knowledge of the apple tree planting and my memory of Mr. Widnall's anxiety over the health of the calf I should not have known that he owned and farmed land for he always had time for the village and for us children. I am able to say that the calf recovered with the aid of a Vet.

Mr. Widnall had a printing press, – a wonder and a joy to us. He printed and published books of his own writing, amongst them an interesting gossiping guide to Cambridge for he knew much of its history. He printed notices of every entertainment held in the village as well as programmes for the plays that were acted there all of which he got up. He painted the scenery for them, made the properties, and he coached and held together the amateur actors. Most of the plays were acted in the big room of his "Castle Ruins".

The garden of the Old Vicarage is large and goes down to the river. Along the river is a line of huge chestnut trees, in his day at their best. They sent their branches far over the river which was there a swift stream flowing from the nearby mill. Under the trees was a picturesque bathing shed.

> "And there the chestnuts summer through
> Along the river make for you
> A tunnel of green gloom."

When lessons were over we would run down the lawn, through the woodland and soon we were in the river drowning the sound of the mill wheels with our shouts and splashings. Then we would run back avoiding the peacocks but with a keen eye for any dropped feathers. There was much to look at that tempted delay but hunger usually prevented us from getting home too late for our dinner. However I would sometimes pause to see, on sunny days, the rainbow in the fountain spray. The lovely fountain was designed and made by Mr. Widnall and the water then spouted up high. The sundial, like an open book, was also his work. Mr. Widnall built a Swiss Cottage of wood and plaster work in a glade reached by a bridge over a tiny stream. In it lived rabbits and hares and guineapigs. We children found them delightful creatures to call on. Above all he architected and built with his own hand his great work, the "Castle Ruins".

His Castle was in a corner of the garden backed by a grove. Winding stairs led to a long, well proportioned room hung with old tapestry. The mantel piece was of ancient carved oak. Chippendale chairs stood round the walls. Mr. Widnall had bought the tapestry, chairs and mantelpiece for a pound or two. They were regarded as old fashioned rubbish. When, years afterwards, the furniture of the Old Vicarage was sold, these brought in as much as all the rest put together.

At the end of the long room was a smaller one almost forming part of it. It was easy to turn it into a stage and acting often took place in the "Castle Ruins". My first really clear memory is of being taken to a performance (or perhaps it was a dress rehearsal) of a play in these castle rooms. In one scene the stage seemed covered with sand and Mr. Palmer of St. John's College, afterwards Professor Palmer of Arabian fame, was acting as an Arab. He was then courting the beautiful Laura, the Widnall's niece whom he married later. No doubt she was acting too but I have no remembrance of her. Mr. Palmer striding about the stage, wearing a dress that would be sure to strike a child, I can still see.

Mr. Widnall once lent his garden for a bazaar for the church. To be sold at a stall was a little pamphlet which he printed. He got his friends to write amusing little articles for it. Professor Clifford of Trinity, a mathematician, a great lover of Grantchester, was one of his friends who wrote for it. Mr. Widnall made me learn by heart a specimen of his pieces of nonsense. I remember it still.

"Among the things not generally known is this – the report of a pistol, seen at the distance of five ounces, smells like the taste of half an hour, only it is not white."

Professor Clifford was fond of children and always ready to joke with them. One day Aunt Lalley, my two elder sisters and I had walked into Cambridge. He saw me in King's Parade when I was separated from the others and had my nose glued to a picture shop window gazing at the one picture displayed in it. It had a card placed

near it and on the card was the word "Turner". The word "Turner"
meant nothing to me. Professor Clifford came behind me and said:—
"I will tell you how that picture was painted. The artist squeezed a lot
of his paints on to a canvas and sat on it". I remember turning round and
looking silently at him with the scornful tolerance of the very young for
those much older. I again became absorbed in the picture. It mattered
nothing to me how it was done. It <u>was</u> done. I gazed at it until Aunt
Lalley fetched me away.

Polly would later herself become a landscape artist; and Clifford,
whose whimsical humour reminds one a little of his contemporary mathematician at Oxford, Charles Dodgson, would always be known for his
rapport with children. This was in spite of his appearance, which might
have been thought piratical; for he wore a great black beard, and in 1870
actually experienced shipwreck when with the Royal Astronomical Society's expedition to Sicily to observe an eclipse of the sun, met with near-
disaster on the coast of Catania. Some, like Polly, may have found his
nonsense vexing yet memorable and mind–stretching. Marriage, in 1875,
to the novelist Lucy would give him two daughters of his own; but their
happiness together was to be cut short by his death only four years later.

And now we have a closer view of Lally's little school:

Aunt Lalley – how can I describe the charm of the little fairy God-
mother of Grantchester? We were lucky children to be taught by her.
She made learning of geography a travel-joy, history an exciting story,
the Bible a living and beautiful book. Even grammar was not dull with
her. She guided us through "Little Mary's Grammar". She taught me
all I have ever been able to learn of arithmetic and that I fear is not
much. One afternoon in every week was spent in reading poetry. I was
considerably younger than my clever sister Alice who was next above
me in age yet, with Aunt Lalley's help, Shakespeare, Milton, even
Spenser, down to the modern poets were all studied by my small brain
with great joy but I daresay with little understanding.

The Old Vicarage was of course haunted. A bedroom on the upper
storey had two windows, one looking East and the other West. One of
the old vicars of Grantchester must have been very wicked for one night
when he was sleeping there as usual, the Devil came in at the East
window and carried him out by the West. I have slept in the room but I
was not disturbed by either of the couple. The back stairs, near the dark
cupboard where Mr. Widnall kept his press for printing sheets, was

supposed to be favoured by the spirit of a little old woman in a red cloak but I never saw her.

… Mr. Widnall, Aunt Lalley and two of us children would sometimes go on botanising expeditions. We were driven in a chaise drawn by an old white horse once dappled grey and still called "Dapple". We would perhaps go to the Roman Road to pick the clustered Campanula or to the Fleam Dyke to pick Dane's Blood or to the deserted railway cutting for what we called "the blue fleabane" which is a Canadian plant naturalised in very few places in England. This plant grew nowhere except near the railway cutting and we were always interested in guessing why and how it suddenly should have sprung up on the banks after the high ground had been cut through for a railway that was never completed. Did some workman in digging drop from his pocket some seeds which he had unknowingly brought from his home in Canada? Or was it perhaps once a native plant and seeds had lain dormant in the ground for hundreds of years? Every summer we went in Mr. Widnall's big boat to the field called Florida full of uncommon wild flowers. It lies between the two rivers, the Ribb and the Rhee, which join at the end of the field and form the Granta.

One day Mr Widnall asked me to come with him. He said that he was going to tell me a profound secret. We went to a huge field near the Bourn Brook and there, by a series of clues, I was taught to find the tiny Adders Tongue fern. It was like looking for a needle in a bottle of hay but there it was. It was declared, in the then edition of Babington's Flora of Cambridgeshire, to be extinct in Grantchester and Mr. Widnall and I knew that it wasn't! It was a grand moment to be told something that the great Dr. Babington did not know. When I was out with Mr. Widnall he would teach me to know the names of all the trees, by their bark, growth and twigs in winter, and by their leaves in summer. He knew a great deal about geology and I began to understand it a little. He was a splendid companion.…

CHAPTER 14

Into the 1870s

———•◦•———

IT HAD BEEN A HARD WINTER. The river had frozen, and beer was found frozen in the barrel. The local paper reported that 'The cold has, of course, been severely felt by the poor'; but at Christmas-time people were skating and playing games on the river, and several had to be rescued from drowning down by Baitsbite Lock.

The diary for 1870 begins with local concerns: Mr Lilley having a bad accident, Lally hurting herself with a fall at the church gate. More seriously, Lilly was still prostrated by her 'Rheumatic gout'. It was a severe and protracted illness, causing Lally to 'dismiss' her pupils in order to attend to her; and five painful months passed before she was able to venture out to tea with Mrs Howard, and a further month before she could go to church again. The church, meanwhile, catching up with the livelier congregational singing of nonconformist rivals, adopted the 'New Hymn book' (*Hymns Ancient & Modern*, published in 1861), and regular practices were organised to learn the new tunes.

'18 March Page went to tea at Mr Fyson's'. It is the only mention of that name, yet entries in the diary generally have more than casual significance. Fyson lived in what was known as the Widnall Cottage and would be described in the 1871 census as 'Retired Farmer, aged 30'; and in the parish there was another man described as 'Farmer out of business, aged 45'. Certainly there are signs that Page himself was growing uneasy about the profitability of his farming at this time. East Anglia was the region chiefly reliant upon arable farming, and the price of corn had dropped since its strong level at the time of the Crimean War. There were to be poorer and poorer returns as the century advanced. Competition from the North American prairies, difficult weather conditions and demands for increases in labourers' wages all made farming an anxious business.

For little Polly Greene – 'Mr Widnall called himself a farmer' – the occupation which provided the main family income seemed barely perceptible. But very likely Page attended to his farming activities before breakfast, in much the same way as a minor character in Trollope's

Framley Parsonage:

> (Frank Gresham, no doubt, went round his farm before he came in for
> prayers, and his wife was probably looking to the butter in the dairy)

and a reliable bailiff would see that his directions were carried out. In the
year of the publication of that Trollope novel, 1861, Page was employing
seven men and three boys: a modest enterprise compared with Henry
Banyard of Lacies Farm with his 570 acres, twenty-three men and nine
boys, or Frederick Lilley at the Manor Farm who worked 316 acres with
twelve men and five boys. Now, at the 1871 count, Page farmed 78 acres
and had reduced his workforce to five men and three boys.

Needing a steady income from his land, Page was having to think, as
his father had done, of other ways. 'Diversification', in modern parlance,
might offer a solution. Rather than offer the land for desperate and
unprofitable sale, a farmer in this area might lease some for coprolite-
digging. This had already become a thriving industry around Cambridge and in the village, and accounted for some of the sudden increase
in population during the 1860s and '70s. The parish register records the
death of a young man in 1863, adding, 'He was the first of the strangers
who came here to dig coprolites that died amongst us'; and the following
year of another twenty-year-old: 'He was killed by a fall of earth in a
coprolite pit'.

So what were coprolites? They were 'phosphatic nodules' deposited
in prehistoric times by the creatures who once roamed the area. Popularly known as 'dinosaur dung', this treasure could be crushed and used as
agricultural fertilizer. The shallow deposit was found in Cambridge
Greensand, lying beneath the chalk layer and above the gault. Once
extracted, the topsoil could be restored and the land returned to farming. (The industry closed down when it became uneconomic by the end
of the 1880s; though there would be a short revival at the beginning of
the First World War, when phosphates were needed to make explosives.)

Part of the land which had been farmed by the Widnalls had been put
up for auction in 1865 when Mrs Widnall's tenancy ended. It was a ten-
acre field sloping down to the millstream and the Bourn Brook, and was
advertised as 'containing valuable beds of coprolites'. Page may or may
not have bought the freehold himself. But certainly one effect of the
coprolite boom was to stir up his interest in geology and palæontology;
for, among the nodules, fossils were emerging of prehistoric sea-crea-
tures and even fish-eating flying reptiles (pterosaurs) – exciting stuff for

a man with a keen imagination. These revelations were no doubt discussed with Clifford, now a Fellow of Trinity, who might be hearing of the latest discoveries at first hand from Adam Sedgwick.

*

The coprolite boom, which lasted for a couple of decades, affected the village in various ways. Labourers, attracted by good wages, were drawn in from far away and had to be somehow accommodated. The local farm workers grew restive, and Page Widnall is said to have grumbled that they were now demanding an extra shilling a week. In April 1871 he travelled down to Wiltshire 'to inquire about Coprolites', a sign that he was hoping to find some way of profiting from the industry himself.

If the farmers felt hard-pressed, they cannot have been entirely unsympathetic to the aspirations of their labourers. Village society is revealed in some detail in the Census returns which, decade by decade, recorded those present in each household. In 1871 the contrast between life in those primitive cottages and the houses of the 'leisured classes' is very clear. The comfortable houses were frequently occupied by people – 'fundholders', clergy without livings, widows with private means – with no need to work. For the lower orders, work was essential the moment a child could be released from school. Looking at Wright's Row, for instance, that pretty row of thatched cottages still preserved with discreet reinforcement and additions in the rear, we now see five houses. In 1871 the row (cruelly nicknamed 'Bugs Row') was divided into seven – possibly nine – dwellings, six of them with young families. William Pawley (43) and his wife (41) had sons aged 20, 19, 14 and 12, all 'labourers', as well as children of 11, 7, 6, 4 and 5 months. Next door, Charles Dilley and his wife had seven children. The conditions indoors in winter must have been stifling, with barely room to turn. On summer evenings there was some respite: older people would rest on a hard chair outside and watch the children play and their parents do the last chores, pumping water, feeding poultry, unharnessing horses, returning from the evening milking with a brimming jug. And for thirsty menfolk one of the village brewers could supply beer at 1d a pint.

But now in Grantchester the world of the 'agricultural poor' had been invaded by the coprolite workers – an injection of new blood which was to enliven a previously closed and inbred society. In 1871 the Cambridgeshire & Isle of Ely Chamber of Agriculture was formed (with Mr Banyard of Lacies Farm a council member). Its first meeting was held in

1872, and viewed 'with apprehension the compulsory attendance of children in Elementary Schools' since it allowed secular rather than purely church-controlled education, and would increase the burden of taxation. Only 'a certain moderate amount of elementary knowledge' was needed for employment on the land. But at their second meeting, less grudgingly, they considered 'The Expedience of Endeavouring to improve the dwellings of the Agricultural Labourer'. That was an urgent need. For besides being overcrowded, cottages in this area were very poorly built. In the mid-20th century a description was written by George Rogers, himself a village man and a builder, of many of the practical details concerning the daily lives of villagers in his boyhood: the construction of cottages,* the wells and pumps upon which they depended for water, the state of the roads and the work of the 'carrier' trundling daily along them into Cambridge. The quiet and almost self-sufficient village of 'Old Grantchester' had its own tradesmen – butcher, baker, blacksmith, cobbler and so on. By the 1870s, though, a whole area at the northern end of the parish was filling up with streets of new houses, destined to become, forty years later, separated off as part of Newnham. There, the occupations were more varied, providing services for the expanding University of Cambridge.

*

On 20th July 1870 the Old Vicarage trio set off for one of those great month-long holidays, this time picking up the nieces, Alice and Amy, in London on their way to Southampton, where they embarked for Guernsey. After a few days they moved on to Jersey, where the womenfolk 'bathed from the ladies rocks' and went on an excursion to Grève de Lecq. Then they sailed to Sark, 'where Mr Cachermaile [*sic*] has taken a little house for us', and spent a week there, showing their favourite places to the two girls. Lilly, apparently, was able to clamber and swim in spite of her recent illness.

Of the three islands visited, Sark had always been the least accessible; and it was Sark which seems to have appealed most strongly to them. To start with, the approach was exciting: their boat, probably with a single high smokestack, foresail and mizzen, was piloted around the island and between savage rocks and cross-currents into the one tiny harbour. They would climb a steep track to reach the nearly-level landscape of small

*See Appendix VI

fields divided by stone walls. The island's residents at that time all belonged to the place and spoke its peculiar French *patois* – all, that is, except for the Seigneur, the doctor and the clergyman. The island was divided into sections and farmed by the Forty Tenants, each tending his portion of land, and every family was likely to be involved in fishing, and making and mending tools or clothing – the essentials of subsistence living. Just as their language was distinctive, so was their costume, the shape of their implements and, indeed, their superstitions.

Day-trippers from Guernsey had by the 1860s started to come in large numbers to Sark, mainly to admire the gardens at the Seigneurie (where, perhaps, Page had, on his first visit, seen the model for the sundial he was to make for his own garden). Certainly our trio found a great deal more to interest them, and to test their young companions' nerves as they ventured across the narrow path of the Coupée with precipices falling to surf-washed rocks below. As botanists they would study the many varieties of wild flowers peculiar to the place; Page would consider the geology of that craggy coast; and there were hosts of birds and sea creatures new to them. They were thrifty and so their lodgings were simple. Inevitably Page – Page the churchman, antiquarian, naturalist – struck up a friendship with the Vicar. St Peter's Church had been built earlier in the century, and the Rev J.L.V.Cachemaille, its first Vicar, was deeply interested in his parish. During the 1870s the knowledge accumulated during his 40 years' ministry was published in monthly instalments of the *Guernsey Magazine*.* His stories and observations must have fascinated the Widnall group. The idea of gathering material for local history may already have been forming in Page's own mind.

One of the natural wonders of Sark had been discovered by the previous Seigneur – a whole system of caverns called the Gouliot Caves. These, filled with sea anemones and other creatures, could be entered at low tide, and Cachemaille deplored the way these rarities were being taken away as souvenirs. But he obviously admired two visitors (could it possibly have been Widnall and Ellis, on a previous visit?)

...who chanced to be excellent swimmers, [and] were impelled by an irresistable desire to inspect these caves when half-filled by the sea. This they more than once succeeded in accomplishing during calm weather, and, of course, described the effect as most singular and enchanting ... a vast natural aquarium ... [They were able to see

*Originally in French, it appeared as a book in English translation in 1928

previously] almost unobserved denizens of the mysterious deep, playfully disporting themselves in brilliant clothing outside their dusky shells; myriads of anemones in blossom; madrepores and tubularias, bursting as it were into flower! Now seemed the arched roofs and rocky walls to live – so covered were they with gorgeous colour and moving forms …

Cachemaille well knew how desperately dangerous this exploit was. He had himself watched, horrified, the drowning of Seigneur Le Pelley when his small boat was engulfed in a high sea, and was ever after nervous of leaving the safety of the island.

(But Mr Cachemaille did make a sea journey in 1872, when he and his wife paid a short visit to Grantchester and were photographed by Page.)

*

Alice and Amy had evidently gone home to Worcester after their Channel Island adventure; but later, towards the end of September, Libby brought them again to Grantchester. The elder sister had been feeling troubled, and 'the next day Alice wrote to Mr Crouch to break off the engagement'. George Crotch, a close friend of William Clifford and an energetic walker and entomologist, was no doubt an attractive man.

But like their aunt's entanglement with Mr Stickland, it had all been an embarrassing mistake, perhaps encouraged by Laura's happy engagement to Edward Palmer. It cannot have been easy to be certain of one's choice in those days of limited social contacts and extreme decorum. A year after Alice freed herself from 'Mr Crouch', Amy too was to change her mind about a young man. Marriage was such a huge undertaking, and not all families were as sympathetic and supportive as these girls'.

The later events recorded in that year are unrelated but of some interest. In October, Lally and Florence (the eldest of the Greene family, a former pupil of hers) began to attend the French lectures given by a M. Boquel – a tutor to Newnham students who, with his wife, would later join their circle of friends.

'Laura came.' 'Mrs Clark and Miss Kelsey came.' The entries do not tell much, except that from the date (24th December) it appears that the two ladies had arrived to spend Christmas at the Old Vicarage. Those two names would occur together in later diary entries. Mrs Clark had already been mentioned, with her sister Mrs Toft, on that visit to Dunmow a year or two earlier. They were cousins of Page, daughters of his mother's brother Robert Freeman; and although both widows, Elizabeth Clark and Sarah Toft must have been comfortably off. Sarah seems to have run the village school at Little Abington before her marriage to Charles Toft, who was a major farmer. A useful inheritance had probably come to the sisters from their father, a share in the legacy he had received at the death of Great Aunt Sarah Page. If so, some of that money might well have provided capital for Mrs Clark's small school, Bishop's Stortford's Ladies' College, where Miss Kelsey was her assistant. The two visitors were probably present at the village's winter entertainment, a lecture given by George Howard in the schoolroom on 'Pocket Handkerchiefs'. George, now Curate of Grantchester, had prepared his talk with care, giving a 'very interesting and instructive lecture' about the manufacture of cotton and linen, illustrated by samples, diagrams and a handloom. The evening ended more light-heartedly with readings, songs and other music.

CHAPTER 15

The First Book

AN ENTRY IN LALLY'S DIARY, 1ˢᵗ March 1870, reveals her brother-in-law's latest activity: 'Page has finished his story "The Miller's Daughter"'. The story came out in book form the following year, with a Preface:

> I must ask my readers not to be too severe in their criticism on this little book, as it is my first attempt as an author, my first attempt at printing, (in a press too of my own construction,) and the illustrations are my first attempt at lithography.

And Page introduced the tale with a Prologue, a little fantasy set in roughly his own time. A man in a boat rows up the river Granta. He passes the old Trumpington Mill, at work with its 'click-clack' sound;

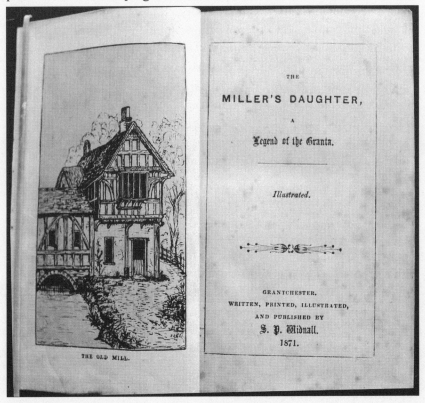

then, 'leaving the deep pool said to have been a favourite bathing place of Lord Byron on the left; ... here comes in sight an old ruined boathouse wreathed with ivy, and above, a dead tree extends its withered arms...' He lands on an islet formed by three ditches and the river, which contains four old fishponds. (By now his young readers, perhaps Lally's pupils, would have been hugging themselves: they knew exactly the place, and indeed it is still recognisable on Baker's 1830 map.) There the boatman notices little paths passing under branches too low for ordinary folk ... and encounters a moorhen which turns into a fairy. 'Have you come for the book?' he is asked. And the book, a diary begun in the year 1470, is preserved in an iron box, buried centuries ago and locked with a 'key' which – being an ash-key – has grown into the old tree. A great gale blows that night, brought about by fairy magic, and the tree comes down; the casket is revealed, opened, and the diary – the real narrative – begins.

Page Widnall had always been excited by old buildings, and had built for himself the gothic ruin of his fantasies. But that fascination led him beyond fantasy: the enquiring mind was endlessly seeking and absorbing information, finding nuggets, perhaps, among the ancient books and manuscripts in Corpus Christi College library. From popular historybooks and from his own surroundings, augmented by imagination, he could recapture something of the 15th-century setting for his tale.

At that time most ordinary readers would have been familiar with Tennyson's poem *The Miller's Daughter* [*c*.1852], supposed to have been inspired by the mill of Chaucer's *Reeve's Tale*. For Tennyson, as a Cambridge undergraduate walking or boating upriver, the site of that mill must have been merely the spot (perhaps with some decaying remnants) called 'Old Mills'. Nearby, though, was Grantchester Mill to provide a model.

> I loved the brimming wave that swam
>   Thro' quiet meadows round the mill,
> The sleepy pool above the dam,
>   The pool beneath it never still,
> The meal-sacks on the whiten'd floor,
>   The dark round of the dripping wheel,
> The very air about the door
>   Made misty with the floating meal

These lines evoke the Old Mill at work, the setting for his slight story of the love of 'the long and listless boy/Late-left an orphan of the squire' for the humble daughter of the miller.

'And slowly was my mother brought
To yield consent to my desire:
She wish'd me happy, but she thought
I might have look'd a little higher'

[*not the poet's best lines*]

And now Page Widnall, having been born and brought up so close to the place, set himself to weave a much fuller story from the same theme. He knew not only the area but some interesting episodes in its history.

The Miller's Daughter, a Legend of the Granta is a love story, with twists and trials before reaching its happy conclusion. Yet it is more than a costume piece, for great care has been taken to convey authenticity. The villain is an officer under the Earl of Warwick on the Lancastrian side in the Wars of the Roses, and dies at the Battle of Barnet. A virtuous supporting character is Father Eustace, from 'the Monastery of St Tartar on the Hill' (close by, one may suppose, Tartar's Well, a curious Grantchester antiquity on Widnall's own farmland). Stourbridge Fair, the introduction of

BURGHERST TOWER.

PLANNING THE HOUSE.

the printing press, the Priory of St Rhadegunde, Denny Abbey, the Lady Chapel on White Hill at Haslingfield, the hermit on the bridge to Shelford ... all these and many other references to the locality and the period are worked into the story. To add to the entertainment, Page had set the whole thing as a fairytale; and he had even given his heroine, in her troubled dreams, a vision of the future in which a terrifying monster – recognized by his readers as a railway train – roars and clatters over a bridge spanning the Granta.

After composing his text, the versatile author had drawn lithograph illustrations for his story; constructed a small printing press; set up his type; and printed the whole book – 174 pages. His drawings are those of an amateur but not at all bad: a little weak on figures, yet remarkably good when one considers how ambitious the whole project was. For by doing the drawings himself, he was able to show a reconstruction of the Old Mill; the romantic old building – 'Burgherst Tower' – where his hero, Walter de Merton, lives; and the betrothed couple planning their future home (the Manor House), with the tower of Grantchester Church in the background. A blurry photograph – probably not one of his – actually survives of a mill building which could be related to his drawing. 'Burgherst Tower' is similar to his own Castle Ruin (which at that time did have a tower); and both the ground plan of the Manor House and the church tower are quite convincing. (The picture of the betrothed couple planning their future home together echoes, indeed, the romance he and Lilly had experienced in creating their own home.) The names Burgherst and de Merton were taken from actual medieval records concerning the Manor of Grantchester.[*]

Altogether that first little book, now a rarity, is well worth reading. It is the romantic outpouring of a mind dwelling, as so many Victorian minds were, on the enchantments of the Middle Ages (or their own stylized version of those times). Into his exactly-chosen period his plot includes abduction, near death by drowning, imprisonment and narrow escapes, and the Battle of Barnet; and into it he works ideas about protestantism and social rank. He had several friends (young George Howard especially) with whom to discuss the early history of the parish; and he also had a brother-in-law, Richard, who himself had joined an antiquarian society and was nourishing a dream of recovering the ancient glories of his family. It is very likely, though unverifiable, that Page had grown

[*]Merton College, Oxford, owned Grantchester Mill and a good deal of farmland in the parish. This association lasted into the 20th century, and now survives only in the possession of one cottage.

up with two large volumes, published *c.*1840, entitled *Old England: A Museum of Popular Antiquities.* This book, if his family indeed possessed it, is the likeliest source of his lifelong interest in history and of his lecture with that same title. Its copious illustrations are of just those ancient ruins that he loved to photograph, and its medieval kings and peasants are just as they appear in his own drawings.

How many copies of *The Miller's Daughter* were produced is not recorded, nor the price asked. But printing had become a new enthusiasm. Page's press must have been quite small, for it used to be carried into the drawing-room in the evenings so that he could be with his family while working at it. (The old powder-closet halfway up the back stairs was used for the storage of paper.) His type-setting improved with practice: in that first effort the n's and u's were sometimes inverted, and small errors are still to be found in later books, though not too often.

Page now found himself becoming a jobbing-printer, producing notices and programmes of village entertainments and printing other people's literary efforts. There were certainly many small pamphlets such as a surviving playlet about King Alfred. Somewhere there must be copies of the little volume, *Thoughts in Verse,* of Laura Palmer's poems, printed in 1876. This is described by Besant in his biography of her husband as 'only intended for private circulation', and so almost certainly the printing was undertaken by her uncle. Each book was marked with his device, and he used ornaments bought as 'printers' flowers' or small wood-engravings resembling Bewick's work.

In a critical account of Page's six main publications (a seventh is included, but scarcely qualifies), Bruce Dickins* says:

> Though Widnall was middle-aged before he started printing, he had always shown marked mechanical aptitude and manual dexterity. He built his own press, and it worked. He does not seem to have been able to print more than four – sometimes only two – pages at a time, and, as he never used signatures, it is not always easy to determine the exact make-up of his books without pulling them to pieces, a proceeding not encouraged by librarians...
>
> [*Transactions of the Cambridge Bibliographical Society* 1958]

*Bruce Dickins, 1889–1978, Fellow of Corpus Christi College and Professor of Anglo-Saxon

CHAPTER 16

Daily Happenings

IT MAY BE THAT LILLY WIDNALL, that winter, had little energy. There were no family theatricals for the 1871 New Year. Instead, Lally went to stay with her friend Miranda Newman at Maida Vale and saw some enjoyable London performances, and 'Gissey' joined her for the final three days. They were thoroughly congenial companions, those two. So, after seeing *A Midsummer Night's Dream* at the Queen's Theatre with Miranda (when they found that 'Phelps as "Bottom" was capital'), Lally went with Page to see *Ages Ago* at German Reeds, and Buxton in *The Palace of Truth* at the Haymarket.

But in March the family were all three together for a Shakespeare reading in 'Mr Walter Leaf's[*] rooms in Trin. Col. "Romeo & Juliet"'; and two days later they heard Dr Humphrey's lecture on 'Sleep', an evening which concluded with the singing of 'God save the Queen and cheers for Princess Louise who was married today'.

In April they took the short train ride down to Bishop's Stortford, and had a few days with Mrs Clark, wandering one afternoon with friends of hers about Warberry Dells. In May there were Tableaux Vivants – 'The Lord of Burleigh' – in the schoolroom; and one guesses that some of the Greenes were among the Tudor figures in the cast. Shortly after, they all spent 'a delightful day at Bartlow with Mrs Greene and family'.

*

Lally, though by now very much a Grantchester person, was still naturally drawn to Worcester and her family there. In July Page accompanied her on a visit to Richard and Libby at their new and grander home, Barbourne House. There was a good deal to admire, and much to discuss. Richard had prospered and become a respected figure in Worcester, where his nursery gardens at St John's, just south of the city and well placed for communication by rail and river, surpassed even the late Samuel Widnall's.

---

[*]Dr Walter Leaf (1852–1927) later became a Fellow of Trinity and was joint translator, with Andrew Lang, of Homer's *Iliad*.

His four children were now young adults. There was some anxiety just then about Bertie, who was still recovering from 'concussion of the brain' sustained in a bad accident six weeks earlier. But Bertie (Herbert Hanbury), aged twenty, came through this with no lasting harm. He was a determined young man, and was doing outstandingly well in an engineering firm, Hardy & Padmore.

The younger son, Car (Richard Carington), was a more easygoing fellow, in no hurry to contemplate a career. During that visit Page and Lally called to see him 'in camp at Malvern', where he was probably taking part in Territorial exercises. It was to be four years before his matriculation at St John's College, Cambridge.

The two sisters, Alice and Amy, were living at home, no doubt meeting 'suitable' young men but feeling nervous in the family's expectation of betrothal. One imagines Libby confiding her anxieties to Lally.

Between Richard and Page there must have been discussion about the progress of the boys, about farming and horticulture and much else. A topic dear to them both was the family history of the Smiths. Richard had joined the Society of Antiquaries and hoped to trace the links with his noble ancestors. Having grown up with rumours of the family's lost fortune and dignity, for him success as a businessman could only reach true fulfilment when he had established his pedigree. Page Widnall was, of course, the very man to assist him. The quest would call upon all his skills – rummaging in old documents; hunting for gravestones and photographing or making plaster casts of their inscriptions; setting the information in order and finally printing it. It is most likely that the whole project was set in motion at this time, and that the two men had already visited or read about the village of Ashby Folville in Leicestershire where tombs of some of those ancestors might be found.

*

Late that summer there was a shock for the village, the sudden death of Ellen Howard. For the Widnalls the loss was keenly felt: she had been so close to them all – someone Page had known since she first came to the village as Thomas Howard's bride when he was a boy, and a warm friend to all the womenfolk of the family. Now her youngest son George was undertaking a major part of the pastoral work in the parish while the Vicar was away recuperating from illness.

The diary tells how George, as Curate, had preached on the text 'Thy will be done' shortly before taking his mother for a holiday in Switzerland. Six days later, on 3rd September, she had died at Interlaken. Lally, writing to tell the Vicar's wife the news said, 'Truly Grantchester will not be like Grantchester without dear Mrs Howard, and what will poor, dear George do? Oh dear, it is grievous…' After her burial in the village churchyard, George spent the evening at the Old Vicarage. When he preached for the first time after this event: 1 Cor. XVI.13 ('Watch ye, stand fast in the faith, quit you like men, be strong') there was 'scarce a dry eye in the Church'.

*

Whether as a result of consultation with Richard or not, Page had by the end of that summer made a momentous decision. On 21st September 1871 much of his farming stock was auctioned, realizing £75.9.5; and on 19th October the rest made £175.17.2.

Probably the September sale was mostly of livestock, sheep and cattle. The advertisement for the second sale indicates the range of his mixed farming, now ending with the tenure of the land.

> 2 useful Cart Horses, 1 Cow, 3 Sows, some Store Pigs, and a Boar, carts, ploughs, harrows, drill, dressing-machine, incubator, sacks, hurdles, and other Farming Implements. Also 100 Bushels of POTATOES.

That same issue of the *Cambridge Chronicle* in which this notice appeared gives ominous news for farmers in the region. There had been great harvests of grain in the prairies of North America, soon to be imported and to drive down prices at home; and for livestock farmers poor prospects, since foot-and-mouth disease was spreading.

Now, at forty-five, no longer a commercial farmer (although there would naturally continue to be a dairy cow such as the Alderney 'Buttercup', bought for 17 guineas two years before, some poultry and the essential horse), Page had to turn to his more studious and creative talents. It was perhaps a relief. After all, the S.P.W. depicted in his photographic self-portraits had been a literary man, and a man with serious scientific interests, rather than the John Bull character suggested by his build and occupation at the time. A new start had been made with *The Miller's Daughter*.

He might, too, be able to compensate for his farm income by shrewd investment. There had been that enquiry about coprolites in Wiltshire, and a visit to London 'to attend a meeting to start a Cooperative Store' (although that is a venture which sounds more altruistic than concerned with moneymaking, and was not mentioned again).

Of the various possibilities, some sort of involvement in the coprolite boom must have seemed attractive.* Artificial fertilizers were selling well at a time when arable farmers needed to increase production to compensate for the falling price of their produce. Peruvian Guano, brought as ballast on return voyages from South America, had been found to improve yields. But now there was competition from a closer source with the manufacture of fertilizer from the local product. At Duxford, a few miles from Grantchester, the Cambridge Manure Company ground-up coprolites and made mixtures suitable for particular crops. Two of Page's photographs hint at an involvement with this enterprise, one a portrait of a Mr Bond (the name of the chief entrepreneur in this business), and the other of an unpicturesque subject, a large factory building with *Cambridge Manure Company* painted across its front. One cannot tell for sure. What is certain is that he had not the Smith family's flair for business; and as great-nephew Humphrey was to say years later that, apart from his patent folding form, 'Page never made any money out of anything!'

*

On 11th November Laura and Edward Palmer were at last married. At eighteen she had been sent to school with a Mrs Sharp, near Northampton, to be 'finished'. Now, at twenty, she was surely ready.

But there were hindrances: Edward had no secure income, nor was he permitted, as a don, to marry without a Professorship; and in that he was at first disappointed.

In 1871 the Professorship of Arabic fell vacant. Palmer stood for it, but was not elected, and though a man of merit was preferred, circumstances in the election made the result peculiarly mortifying. The electors were the Heads of Houses; men, at that time, on

Edward Palmer (*right*) and friends

whom knowledge of the unusual dawned slowly, and who were afraid of the unconventional. That Palmer certainly was, even in his amusements – conjuror, an adept at all tricks of sleight of hand, mesmerist, about his only outdoor pleasure was a day's fishing in the fens. Report says that

*In 1883 *Kelly's Directory* lists Mr Lilley, of Manor Farm, as 'farmer and coprolite raiser'

coming to College one evening from the river, very wet and dirty, he met Dr Bateson, then Master, who enquired: "Is that Eastern costume, Palmer?" "No, Master," was the prompt reply, "Eastern counties".

And so that principal chair, well-endowed, was denied him. A few months later a lesser chair, the Lord Almoner's Professorship of Arabic, fell vacant and was awarded to Edward Palmer. 'It was a poor thing, worth about £40 a year, but it had the advantage that he could marry without losing his fellowship.'*

But even then there was delay because of 'an unlucky and ludicrous accident' [Besant]. Marriage was dependent upon the appointment, and that required various formalities, the crucial one being the reception of a seal in a japanned box. The craftsman was tardy in delivering the japanned box, and so more time was wasted. At last on 11th November Lally could write in her diary, 'Dear Laura was married today at St Pancras Ch. to Professor E. H. Palmer'.

While those two were away honeymooning, a letter arrived from Libby announcing Amy's engagement to J. Stallard (a young man from a good and well-to-do family). It must have seemed very satisfactory.

*

Edward and Laura set up their home at Brookside, on the southern edge of Cambridge, and Lilly gave them a piece of her own painstaking embroidery, a banner screen† worked with the arms of St John's College. A less successful gift was that of a kitten, Little Dot, who did not settle well. A fortnight later she was brought back, and Lally was 'Amused at her recognition of her mother Tweets'.

1872 was to be a year in which friendship with the Greene family flourished. Clever Alice Greene (aged fourteen or fifteen) had written a story, *The Three Princesses*, which Page printed for her and took to Grays for binding. Then in March the Old Vicarage trio went over to Riversdale to watch the children perform Alice's play of *Cinderella*. Later in the year, in September, 'Page and the Greenes went for a long walk to Shepreth' (described by Coneybeare as 'a little gem of a village, with a clear and copious brook running across its maze of thick-shaded lanes'). It was indeed a long walk, a trudge of twelve miles or more, there and back. Three days later the family left; and Polly would later recall: 'When we

*Quotations from the biographical sketch by Dr T. G. Bonney, quoted in *Cambridge Revisited*, by Arthur B. Gray
†A brass stand supporting a screen as protection from the scorching heat of a fire

left Grantchester for Bedford I left my heart behind'. The move was judged necessary for the children's education, and they would stay in Bedford for eleven years. But it was not so very far away. The families were never to be apart for long.

*

A year, almost to the day, after Laura and Edward's wedding the first baby, Ethel, was born, and Lally became her godmother. Their home at Brookside was not far from Grantchester, and so contact remained close.

And then in the New Year, 1873, Lally went for her first visit to the Greenes at their own new home in Bedford. It was a huge, rambling house close to the river, and it had an enormous drawing-room, added by a former Mayor of Bedford for his public receptions. Although icy cold in winter, this vast room would accommodate many parties and private theatricals, and under their mother's guidance the family would thrive there. As the wife of one of those children (Edward) would later write:

> The Father remained always somewhat apart. He was a nervous, highly-strung man, with no real occupation. He shut himself up in his study with its many beautiful, leather-bound books and it was his wife who had to solve the problem of bringing up a large family of nine children on a slowly, but steadily, declining income..... It was around the mother that the whole household centred. With a calm and serene temperament and great commonsense, she adjusted herself, without fuss, quietly and firmly, to changing conditions and did the best she could for every one of her children....

*

The Diary notes few events for that year. But one is of a stunning entertainment given by Edward Palmer in the village schoolroom. Adopting the name 'Professor Hermann Frikell' – surely in imitation of Herr Adalbert Freikl, 'celebrated conjuror and humourist', who was travelling with his show at that period – he, with a lady assistant, performed similar feats. His advertisement, printed with great panache by S.P.W., rivalled the professional's: 'Wizard of the East, Professor Hermann Frikell, Illusionist and Prestidigitateurinordinary to His Imperial Majesty the Shah of Persia...' (In the *Cambridge Chronicle* of October 1871 Freikl had announced 'Sparkling comicalities! Rapid changes! Startling effects! Great surprises! Transformations! Explanations!') And Edward Palmer's entertainment was enriched with musical interludes provided by friends.

[141]

GRANTCHESTER SCHOOL ROOM.

MAY the 5th. 1873

PROFESSOR HERMANN FRIKELL,

WIZARD OF THE EAST!!

ILLUSIONIST AND PRESTIDIGITATEUR

IN ORDINARY

TO HIS IMPERIAL MAJESTY

THE SHAH OF PERSIA

will give his celebrated entertainment of

MAGIC AND MYSTERY!!!!

In the course of which he will perform his

WONDROUS EXPERIMENTS OF

THE LUMINOUS HAT,

or the Feast of Lanthorns.

COCKALORUM or the **HUMAN HEN!**

EXCALIBUR or the **ENCHANTED SWORD!**

Also the unprecedented and astonishing feat, of
extracting a live person from an ordinary box,

LOCKED and CORDED by the AUDIENCE.

Together with other illusions never hitherto attempted
by any living professor of the art.

Tickets may be had of MR. CHS. DILLEY.

NUMBERED SEATS ... 1s   RESERVED SEATS ... 6d

BACK `SEATS ... 3d

Doors open at 7 30. performance to begin at 7 45

Next month, when Annie and Tom had come, Laura and Edward gave a dinner party at their Brookside home; and a few days later they and their friends were entertained to tea at the Old Vicarage. A second child was expected, both a joy and an anxiety; for Edward needed to earn more, by translating work and journalism, to support his growing family.

Presently Lally was off to visit the rest of her family, Richard, Libby and their children who were holidaying at Weston-super-Mare; and after that she enjoyed a long stay with her old London friends, the Williamses and the Johnstones. Home via Bishop's Stortford, she arrived at last at the beginning of August carrying a gift from the Johnstones, a canary in a cage.

She was back in time for a great 'pic-nic to Toft, Dr Clark and others 31 altogether'. Dr E. C. Clark* and his wife, who lived at Grove Lodge, had sent their children, Eddie and May, to Lally as pupils. Again, it was a warm friendship which linked the Old Vicarage trio with university society.

And that special friendship with the Howards was marked when George 'gave us a likeness of our dear Mother framed as a companion

*later Regius Professor of Civil Law

picture to that of Mrs Howard'. Another of the old village connections was maintained, too, when in September they made 'our first visit to the Vicarage at Over'. This was the home of the former Miss Hawkes, now married to the Rev W. Dixon. The Hawkes family were cornmerchants; and after the sudden death of Ellen Howard 'Mr H. Hawkes and his two sisters Emma and Jane [had come] to stay at Merton House' to support the bereaved George. Page would make the journey to Over, some eight or ten miles north of Cambridge, a number of times to give his various lectures.

Lally had found a new resident in the village who shared her academic tastes, Miss Loxley*. Together they went (Lally, perhaps, to serve as chaperone) 'to the first of Mr Skeat's lectures on the English language and literature'. It must have been a notable occasion: the idea of English Literature as a serious subject for study at the university had a long way to go before acceptance in the next century, and philology at that time was the sort of thing one went to Germany for. Skeat, the compiler of the great Etymological Dictionary, had begun his career as lecturer in Mathematics before becoming Professor of Anglo-Saxon. (In its obituary after his death in 1912 a new publication, the *Cambridge Magazine*, would comment:

> Professor Skeat was a familiar figure in the streets of Cambridge. His long beard and his curious gait could not but make him an object of interest to passers-by. In his earlier years he was a remarkable skater, and it is interesting to recollect that he was the first Cambridge Professor who ventured to trust himself to a cycle.)

Through Lally's enthusiasm for intellectual pursuits, another valuable friendship was initiated at this time, when she and Lilly invited the French tutor M. Boquel and his wife to the Old Vicarage.

---

*living with her mother at 'Merton Cottage' (later Chapel House). The name was probably Locksley.

CHAPTER 17

Village Matters: Church & School

———•·•———

A GREAT DEAL WAS GOING ON in the village during the 1870s in which the Widnall household was concerned, although the diary often fails to mention these events.

It was a time when many parish church congregations were stirring themselves to missionary efforts and church alterations. The old plain buildings must be restored to something of their supposed former gothic glory; and there must be pews available for ever larger gatherings. After all, the dissenting chapels were gaining ground and must not be allowed to find the Church of England lacking in zeal.

The northern area of the parish adjoining Newnham, now becoming known as 'new Grantchester', was developing fast and the occupants of its terraced houses were forming a community separate from the old village. If they did not feel part of the parish of St Andrew and St Mary, they lacked a place for their Sunday worship. So thought the worthies of 'old Grantchester'; and on 5th June 1871 at a meeting held at 11 Park Terrace, Cambridge, it was proposed by Mr Banyard and seconded by Mr Widnall that funds be collected for 'the erection of a temporary church in the Gardens belonging to the Master & Fellows of Corpus Christi' beside the Barton Road. Unlike the parent church, 'the seats of the proposed church [were] to be free and unappropriated without pew rents'.

The project took off without delay. The money was raised in six weeks, and a small wooden church was built in 157 days. (As tends to happen with 'temporary' buildings, it would be thirty years before a permanent one appeared, and even then the wooden structure remained in use as a meeting room for several more decades.) Old Grantchester contributed handsomely to the new little church. The *Cambridge Chronicle* reported its opening ceremony, on St Martin's Day, 1871:

St Mark's Temporary Church, Barton Road
...The altar cloth was the last work of the late Mrs Howard, whose recent decease all deplore; the alms basin is of turned and carved oak, purchased with small sums collected by the Vicar's servants; the

offertory bags were presented by a lady in Lincolnshire; Mrs Widnall
and friends have executed other needlework and have decorated the
telbeams [*sic*] and other salient parts of the interior with illuminated
texts of Scripture…. The cost of the church, including fittings and
furniture, will be about £400.

*

In May the following year the burial ground surrounding the old
church of St Andrew and St Mary was extended by the enclosure of an
extra plot on the west side. It was an event in the church's long history
which fascinated Page. Because of Grantchester's location and associations, he later wrote*, over the centuries 'many persons who were not
parishioners have desired to be buried [in its churchyard] … and the
ground is consequently much crowded'. Attempting then the impossible
task of reckoning up – taking into account the number of years this
piece of ground had been used for the purpose – the total number of
burials, he was to conclude:

> …more than 5000 persons have been buried there! What a multitude is
> this to rise from "God's acre" at the last great day …. In consequence of
> the churchyard being so full a quarter of an acre of ground has lately been
> added, it was consecrated by the Bishop of Ely on the 10th of May 1872.
>
> The first funeral in the new ground, which took place on the 23rd of
> July in the same year, was interesting. It was of two persons, the widow
> Carter, aged 89, and her great, great grandchild, one, probably the
> oldest inhabitant of the village and the other certainly the youngest,
> being only a few days old; they were both laid in the same grave!

(This particular grave, almost in the centre of the second churchyard, is
marked with a quite striking headstone: a celtic cross 'erected by relatives and neighbours' in memory of the old widow whose home, shared
with her great-granddaughter, had been one of the almshouses.)

*

And now all the dignitaries involved with Grantchester Church
approached a further project, the extension of the church building itself.

One might think that this church, which had undergone a series of
improvements earlier in the century, was scarcely in need of major alteration now. Even in 1843, when Joseph Romilly paid a visit to the church,
he had observed:

*in his *History of Grantchester*

... it is very nicely fitted up with an organ & stalls, the East End
very well done up: it used to be damp & green & miserble.

Yet the great restlessness of those years, when other churches round about
were changing the pitch of their roofs and making additions[*] to the fabric, had spread to this parish. At a Vestry Meeting of 7th June 1872, it
was proposed by Mr Banyard (the farmer recently retired from Lacies
Farm to Cedar Lodge), seconded by Mr Widnall, 'that it is desirable to
endeavour to enlarge the Parish Church'. The Committee members were
the Provost and Bursar of King's, the Master and Bursar of Corpus, the
Deans of the two colleges, the Vicar, the Churchwardens (Banyard and
Lilley, both farmers), the Rev J. Martin[†], the Rev F.G. Howard
(curate) and Mr Widnall. The argument in favour of the proposal
involved the inadequate provision of 'sittings'. The recent Census had
revealed the total population of the parish to be 845, of which 220 were
in the St Mark's district. For the remaining 625 persons there were
insufficient sittings, since a large number were 'appropriated' by the principal families or reserved for children.

The resolution to enlarge the church was supported by the signatures
of many of the Householders of the Parish, followed by the names of 90
Labourers who declared that '... we have no doubt that many are kept
away from Divine Worship by the want of room'. (Among those 90,
many surnames are familiar still to those who have lived in the village for
some years). What of course is not mentioned is the presence in the village of a strong nonconformist body. James Nutter, the miller, had provided a small meeting-house on the Coton Road, and – perhaps roused
by the activities of the churchmen – that congregation were to build a
proper little Baptist Chapel down the Broadway and open it the year
before the re-opening of the Church.

...For from proposal to completion, the church enlargement took
three and a half years, much longer than expected. An architect, Mr
Blomfield, was consulted, but his first scheme – to make both north and
south aisles – was rejected. By 1874 his revised design had satisfied the
Committee; but now Corpus Christi College 'refused to sanction the
proposed plan of placing the Organ Chamber against the Chancel'. That
matter was decided: the organ was to remain on its gallery at the west

---

[*]Trumpington, Barton, and Harston are known to have reverted to the medieval high-pitched
nave roofs at about this time; and at Dry Drayton the nave was extended.
[†]The Rev. John Martin, Vicar of St Andrew's Church in Cambridge but whose family home was
Croft Lodge, a large house beside the Barton Road, in the parish of Grantchester.

end, and the 14th-century chancel was to be left intact. But in 1875 a more
tiresome obstacle arose.

Mr Crisp objected to the application for a Faculty for the church
alterations. Quite what sort of a man Mr Crisp was is now mercifully
forgotten; but he is the one person for whom the even-tempered Page
seems to have felt a strong dislike. Horace/Horatio Crisp, by now aged
74, described himself for the census as an 'apparitor'; his wife, one of the
Lilley daughters, was half his age; and their son was articled to a solicitor's firm. (One suspects that they had an appetite for litigation.) They
lived at Byron's Lodge. His Objection begins with a description of the
Church. It is

> ... a beautiful building of clunch and Rubble with stone quoins and
> Buttresses ... it has a Nave, Chancel, Tower and Porch the Nave being
> in the perpendicular and the Chancel in the Decorated style.

The difficulty was the destruction entailed in the proposed enlargement: the S. wall would have to be pulled down, all seating removed
except for the organ gallery, and the floor taken up. He claimed that an
additional S. aisle was quite unnecessary since

> ... one third of the church as it presently stands being unoccupied at
> Divine Service [there was] always vacant space for from 50 to 100
> persons.

He offered other arguments, pointing out that the Church had undergone renovations and reseating about twenty years before. But his chief
obstacle was the presence, on the S. side, of an old family vault known as
the Manor Vault, where some of his ancestors lay and where there was
space still left 'for a great number of coffins'.*

His objections sounded, to an impartial Court of Arches, quite rea-
sonable; and so on 3rd February 1876 an Inhibition was issued, with the
costs evenly divided between Crisp and the Committee. The Committee
were horrified by the expenses, and asked for an 'abatement' and
appealed for further funds.

In the original subscription list, the better-off had given generously:
George Howard had shown his enthusiasm with a gift of £100, and
Page Widnall's contribution was £10. Miss Snelling the schoolmistress
gave from her meagre salary 5/-, and collected 15/- from her school-

---

*The vault cannot have been so very ancient, for it seems to have contained the remains of his
wife's family only, tenants of the Manor Farm since early in the century.

children. Donations from friends of the village included 10/- from the Rev Ch. Wordsworth, nephew of the Poet Laureate. Further sums were raised in practical ways: Miss Arabella Cowlard, sister of the Vicar's wife, made £6.6.0 by a Sale of Work; Miss Nimmo £5.5.0 by a Sale of Pictures; the Vicar's wife herself, Mrs Martin, £5.0.0 by Flower Painting; and the Christmas Carol Singers added £1.10.0. In the end the largest contribution of all these came indirectly from the Old Vicarage household, who once again ran a Garden Party which raised £100; and to that must be added the profits (unrecorded) from the sale of Page's *History of Grantchester*. The 1879 accounts give the grand total – 'By Subscriptions & Garden Party £2217.18.0' with the quaint note '[by Farthings, to make even money – 1d]'.

And so, after an expensive referral back to the Court, permission was at last granted. (The crucial legal document is more than usually impressive, headed as it is by the name of the Chancellor of the Diocese of Ely, ISUMBARD BRUNEL, who must have been son of the famous engineer.)

On 12th April 1877 there was a contested election for Churchwarden, and Page recorded with satisfaction that Mr Banyard had been given 128 votes, while Crisp had only 36. A few days later the work of enlargement began. Considering what a major task it was, they did well to have it completed by the beginning of December. An account from the Organ Builder A.T. Miller shows that his firm took down and removed the organ to their warehouse on April 23rd and returned it, duly restored and tuned, on December 4th. Next day the Bishop performed the re-opening ceremony. As the *Cambridge Express* commented, there had been an 'unusual obstacle' to the work.

> However, all now is happily ended, and the Vicar, assisted as he was by an influential committee, has seen the reward of his arduous and protracted labours for the good of the parish and the glory of his Divine Master.

We do not need to consult the newspaper report or builders' accounts to have a fairly exact impression of the alterations made in 1877. F.G.(George) Howard, the curate, wrote a description for the local antiquarian society of the ancient pieces of stonework uncovered in the course of the demolition work. These curiosities were, accordingly, set into the new flint-faced south wall*. And the appearance of the old church interior is recorded in a fine photograph taken by Page Widnall.

*Other pieces of church masonry discarded by the Victorian 'improvers' may still be found in the gardens of Merton House and the Old Vicarage.

*

At the National School, Miss Snelling was obliged, from 1872 onwards, to record her efforts to educate the children of the 'labouring poor' in a Log Book. Her entries, written in a graceful sloping hand, tell of an uphill struggle. By now the invigorating smells of new pine and fresh paint must have faded, and the schoolroom carried the atmosphere generated by nearly a hundred closely-packed young bodies.

Small children clustered, some forty of them, in Class IV; but Class I was seldom so fully attended, since the pressing demands of their home life often kept the elder children away. In June 1873 the Log Book reports: 'Several children gone to field work, some under 7 years of age ... Girls kept at home for their mothers to go out haymaking'. Next month there was 'Feast week, numbers very low' as children went off to the fun of the fair, set out on the meadows near the Red Lion (an annual village feast which was to continue until the 1920s). And on Plough Monday that year twenty boys had been absent, having joined their dads with blackened faces for the traditional song and dance from house to house.

Since field work was assumed to be the destiny of most boys, and housework that of girls, it was not surprising that parents grudged the payment of a penny a week for schooling. In January 1875 three reluctant pupils turned up – 'boys from the fields. Ages 10 and 8, and obliged to be worked ... with infants of 5 years of age'. Even older boys completely lacking the rudiments of reading and writing were to appear; and in October 1877 there was 'a great influx of children who have been at home, or at work a long time' all needing instruction and raising the school roll to 114. (Great indignation was aroused when, in 1878, the weekly school fee was raised to twopence – though still a penny for second or later children.) Pupils were meant to continue their studies until they had attained a certain Standard; but a number would slip away for employment, leaving the Headmistress with a reduced claim for a school grant.

Conditions in overcrowded cottages and in the tightly-packed school itself encouraged the spread of infection. Those children who had survived their early infancy seem to have had a good resistance to (or managed to ignore) the more everyday ailments. But if a serious new infection arrived, an epidemic might develop.

Most stressful of all was Miss Snelling's constant preoccupation with her assistants, young girls who, barely out of childhood themselves, were her only help in controlling and teaching so many children. Her

Pupil Teacher and Monitors had themselves to receive instruction out of school hours: this was part of her duty. And then, to her annoyance, they were sometimes lazy, or disruptive to other classes when they tried to command attention by loudness. But they seem to have tried their best, and there are few entries such as this, December 1873: 'Teachers – Emily, Lucy and Annie, neglected their lessons and spent time in play'. When one became lethargic and rebellious ('I know <u>not</u> why') she was eventually found to be unwell, needing many months at home. Even worse was the case of poor Rose Benton, in 1879:

Jan 27 Monitor Rose Benton ill, and unable to attend...
Jan 31 ...Monitor Rose Benton still absent (sick)
Feb 4 She died this day. A new Monitor wanted.
Feb 12 Assistant not at school (Flood prevented her) Timetable
          cannot be kept, as two teachers are away (one is dead).

The school regime allowed for little variety. The Rev George Howard, as curate, came on Friday afternoons; the Vicar occasionally gave religious instruction, and even provided an annual prize for proficiency in scripture; and his wife would bring in pieces of cambric for the older girls to practice their sewing. In November 1873 'Needlework sent from the vicarage – consisting of 12 Glasscloths, 12 Teas Do. And One Dozen dusters (for Schoolroom)', and later 'Three dozen pieces of needlework (for Poor Women's box) sent from Vicarage to School'. Perhaps the work sent by Mrs Locksley, from Merton Cottage, 'Parts of 4 night shirts', was also destined for charity. If the light became too poor, singing might have to be substituted for sewing.* They did have a repertoire of six Infant Songs and twelve General School Songs, probably accompanied by the harmonium provided by money raised from successive village concerts.

At the end of the Harvest Holiday, in October 1876, the children came back to find a much-needed second classroom ready for use. The Inspector would now urge the authorities to provide some low desks for the Infants; three years earlier he had recommended that 'a set of good desks for the third class would be a great help to the Mistress'. Year after year he praised the efforts she was making with so little support from assistants or equipment.

Altogether, what went on in the village school was very different from the cosy lessons given in Aunt Lally's little school.

*Oil lamps were not replaced by electric lighting until 1937.

CHAPTER 18

Church Enlargement
SPW's Model & *History*

DURING THOSE YEARS OF PREPARATION, frustration and finally the great structural upheaval of the church's enlargement, Page Widnall, as an initiater of the whole project, contributed to the fund-raising mightily. But, characteristically, he did it in his own way.

The whole process of enlargement entailed close examination of the church building; and while the architect was taking his exact measurements, S.P.W. was making his own observations, photographing and sketching to make sure he had recorded every detail of the building – a building soon to be so drastically altered.

The result of this survey was to appear in three-dimensional form. In his Castle Ruin workshop Page constructed a scale model of the church, about half a metre in length, standing in its churchyard. External details

of windows, porch, steeple and weathercock were reproduced, as were gravestones and memorials (and the slab under which he himself in due course would lie). More wondrous was the intricacy revealed when the roof was lifted. Inside, every part of the furnishing and decoration was displayed: the organ on its gallery, the pews (including the big square Widnall family pew), the altar-table, the pulpit, memorials and inscriptions, and those many candelabra which he himself had made – all were there in miniature; a tiny mechanism allowed the viewer to open and close its doors. Just when this first model was completed is not known; but the diary records his making a second, for George Howard, in 1878, and later another for the Lapworths.*

At the Old Vicarage at this time they seem to have been hosts to a paying guest, or possibly someone assisting with Lally's pupils. In April 1874 there was a Miss Pennell, who came with her maid and stayed for four months. She overlapped with Mrs W. Tennant, who 'came to live with us' and stayed for four years, during which period a Mrs Thompson spent some time with them and Mrs J. Tennant also made some visits. Certainly there were some interesting young pupils around: Connop and Arthur Perowne, sons of the Rev. Dr John Perowne, a future Dean of Peterborough and Bishop of Worcester; Eddie and May Clark, children of Prof. E. C. Clark, and Ernest and Clement Borissow, children of the Precentor of Trinity College, are all named in the diary.

The Garden Party Bazaar to raise money for the church enlargement has already been mentioned. It called for earnest preparation by the household. First, an advertisement was placed in the *Cambridge Chronicle*. The event, in the grounds of Mr Widnall, was to be held on 12th May 1875 from 1 p.m. to 7 p.m., and for Cambridge residents 'conveyances [would] leave the Bull Hotel at 1.30, 2.30 and 5 p.m. … Horses and Carriages [would] be provided for'. The band of the Cambridge Town Rifle Corps would play, and there would be two Amateur Concerts during the afternoon. Everything was planned, and the garden was in early leaf, with an abundance of blossom and spring flowers. But the weather…?

All turned out well. As the newspaper reported later,

> …The weather was splendid, with a light refreshing breeze; and the
> rain of last week, followed by sunshine, had brought out the great
> beauty of Mr Widnall's garden. Stalls, filled with useful and beautiful
> articles, which had been supplied by a large circle of friends, and several

---

*One example of the model, probably the first, is still, more than a century and a quarter old, on display in the church as a record of its former appearance.

of these of the labouring class, were held by Mrs W. Martin, ... by
Miss A. Cowlard ... and by Mrs Widnall ...; while in the centre was a
table covered with choice specimens of Honiton lace, under the care of
Mrs Tennant and Miss Rolfe. In a detached part of the grounds stands
a very tasteful summerhouse, beautifully shaded by trees; here Mrs
E.C. Clark, assisted by the Misses Heaton and Miss Mary Nimmo,
presided over a separate department for tea, coffee, ices and other
light refreshments. Further on, and on the other side of the garden,
Mr L. Manns kept a stall for the sale of lemonade, &c.

*

But this great effort was not all. During the previous year Page had had
another project on the go, and its culmination is announced in the diary
entry for 26th April 1875: 'Paid Gray for Binding His. Of Granta. 202
copies £6.14.8'.

The *History of Grantchester* was a remarkable achievement: a book
still treasured, the rare surviving copies priced accordingly. Out came
the little printing press again; and this time his text was illustrated with
three fine photographs – the church outside and in, and the Manor
House; also a reproduction of an 18th century etching; a facsimile of part
of an inscription on a brass; and seven woodcuts – 'my first and only
attempts in that line'. All that store (comparable to the 'general store' of a
village shop in its rich variety of the useful and the random) of accumulated knowledge is there.

To start with, he tells of the prehistory (the geology so recently
brought to farmers' attention in the coprolite diggings) and adds his
homely comment on the evolution of the countryside:

> People are apt to boast of the long line of their ancestors, but probably
> the sparrow that sits on the house-top could, if he knew all, boast of his
> family living in the same neighbourhood for a much longer time.

The first chapter, called *Fabulous and Ancient History*, recounts many
of the stories about this area, some of which, as he says, may contain 'a
smattering of truth'. What is impressive is the extent of his reading: he
had consulted Dyer, Cole (who quotes Leland and Caius), Bede,
Blomefield and so on. He had pored over maps and related what he saw
there to the fields and pathways he knew so intimately, and to these often
bizarre ancient chronicles and to traditional lore. A sort of wisdom and
insight emerges from it all.

Then comes *The Church*, again a sort of narrative based on quotations from history books, a confection filled with plums and spices as he digresses into explanations of old words. *Bedroll*, for instance, suggests 'bede' or 'bead' and 'bidding prayer', and leads to a verse from Spenser and references to Pepys' diary. The word *Derige* or 'dirge' comes from the 5th Psalm. '*IIII pellys of the Bellys*' – four peals of the bells – brings quotations from an Old English Homily for Trinity Sunday and from Durandus. An explanation of *pike* and *curols* is illustrated with snippets of Chaucer and Gower, and references to George Herbert and Archbishop Parker.

He tells how at Grantchester the old registers from 1539 were transcribed and continued; how an infamous Vicar called Whatton was ejected in 1644, leaving the church without an incumbent until 1662, but how – as suggested in Lingard's History of England – during the Commonwealth period pulpits were 'occupied by Presbyterians, Independants, and even by sectaries of a less orderly description'.

After many more colourful items which bring the story up to his own time, Page ends this chapter:

> … I am principally indebted to Master's History of Corpus Christi College, and have in many cases given it in his own words, though not always within marks of quotation, as I have in some cases condensed, and in others expanded them, where I thought explanation necessary…

All this is followed by *The Church, pt. II*, a more direct account from his own observations. First, one studies that photograph of the interior – the long nave well-lit by windows with clear glass. The centre aisle is interrupted by a tall cast-iron stove, obviously the only heating provided for the entire church. The great east window has an inscription, 'I am the Bread of Life', and a painted ribbon-decoration with another text echoes the gothic arch; and all the other windows have similar texts above. The Ten Commandments are

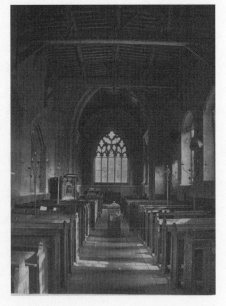

inscribed on boards fitted into the carved recesses each side of the altar. The altar itself is of a modest size and has the velvet covering which Lilly and her friends had embroidered. The nave roof is nearly flat: its very shallow pitch is supported on beams and trusses, those at the east end of the nave lightly decorated with carving.

Grantchester Church as it was in the early 1870s had an austere simplicity – its austerity lightened by Page's own candelabra, dancing silently up the nave and into the chancel. (Their slender branches lit the organ loft too.)

Page's other wonderful photo-graph of the church, used as fron-tispiece to the book, shows the east end of the church as seen when approaching uphill, with the Manor Farm Lodge on the left. With what skill he had persuaded the two elderly men to pause and chat in a happy and relaxed way to com-plete his composition! Another of his surviving photographs of the exterior shows the strange low roof of the nave at that time, and anoth-er the neighbouring Trumpington Church with a similar nearly-flat roof. Both churches changed to their present steeply-pitched roofs in the late 1870s; and the same thing happened at nearby Barton a decade later.

And now Widnall, in this chapter, tells about the more recent history of the church. Descriptions and anecdotes are supplied from his own memory, from rummaging in the parish chest, and from tales told by the old people of the village.

There had, for instance, been a great three-decker pulpit – the present pulpit plus reading and clerk's desks – until 1856, when the east part of the nave was repewed (visible in his photograph as wider pews); and the carved oak separate reading-desk had been installed in 1860, a gift of the Vicar. There were memories of the former screen between nave and chancel, surmounted (in the late 18th century) by the King's Arms and the ten commandments; and also of the closed door in the wall by the N. side of the chancel arch, once an entrance to the small staircase leading up to the top of the old rood screen.

He discusses Grantchester's ancient tombs and memorials in relation to the neighbouring churches – Coton, Impington and other places. And he quotes Cole's report of figures of saints high up in the windows, and of a wall painting at the west end. After examining the structure of the building he draws his conclusions about probable dates (mostly confirmed by later 'experts'). His conjecture about the lowering of the roof gives a date *c.*1635.

Everything is described, including the font, which at that time was placed under the staircase up to the organ loft. The specification of the organ is set out, and its history. It had been converted from a barrel organ (with two, then three barrels, each playing ten tunes) which was installed *c.*1833. Before that, the gallery had been much smaller

> … and was occupied by the village choir who performed on Violins, Flutes &c. But even this was an improvement on the former state of things, for it is related that at the end of the prayers the old clerk would get up and say "If there's anybody that can pitch a tune I'll give out a hume [*sic*], but if there aint t'aint no use".

Moving up the church tower, he describes the clock (1870, cost nearly £100, from Munseys); the three bells, 17th-century but probably recast from earlier ones, and once four; and climbing out onto the tower, he explains the presence of what Coneybeare, later, was to call 'a weird piece of ironwork' standing there at that time. Widnall supplies a picture of this, inaccurately spelt 'Collameter Mark'. But his account is otherwise correct: when the University Observatory was built in 1823, it was essential to have a *collimator* mark by which to set the main telescope, and so the exact positioning of the western end of the Observatory had to be 'the spot which has the tower of Grantchester Church [about three miles off] in the meridian to the south'. (This structure was still in place at the beginning of the 20th century, by which time trees and houses intervened, and the observatory had long since been equipped with collimating telescopes for greater accuracy.)

Page's rambling descriptions and speculations end this chapter with his complicated reckoning of the number buried in the churchyard and account of the newly-opened extension.

St Mark's Church A short section tells of the provision, in 1871, of a separate place of worship for the growing population at the Newnham end of the village. With all the promptitude and efficiency that the Victorians (when not delayed by a Mr Crisp) could muster, the decision had been made on the 10th June; sufficient money was collected in six weeks;

and on the 10th November the Bishop had opened the wooden building – a temporary but sufficient church to which a belfry was added two years later.

Ancient Houses The Manor House: again Widnall quotes from Cole and from oral tradition. He knew the house well from the Lilleys' tenancy and had examined the building carefully. Although his speculations about its former glory may have gone beyond the reality (could it really have once extended to a whole range of buildings like a college court?) he was certainly right in perceiving that there was a hidden fireplace, and that a lofty hall with gallery had been lost in later alterations. There were in his time still distant memories of the 'Doctor's Garden' (a medieval herb garden) and of a separate high building known as 'The Library', though used in its last years as a storeroom. And in his historical summary he says that before the Manor was bought by King Henry VI for King's College it was known as the Manor of Burgherst and owned by Henry Somer.

The Old Vicarage: this is his other Ancient House, and once more he takes the opportunity to draw on a variety of sources. The building in which he lived had been 'new built' in the 17th century; but he talks about the much earlier Rectory and the Guildhall, both utterly disappeared. At the Old Vicarage, 'the part of the garden by the river was formerly used as a parish gravel-pit and called Hog Hunch'; and he points out that the old building opposite Wrights Row now known as King's Cottage is 'the only other house in the village with chimneys of the same style'.

Page's intimate knowledge of field-names and the land itself leads to speculation. Could there once have been a castle ('Castle Furlong')? Might the quantities of red bricks turned up by the plough in one place have come from the ruins?

> It is worthy of note that all the old houses in this neighbourhood were built of red brick, and one cannot help wondering from whence they were procured, as they have now to be brought from long distances which must have been a great difficulty in olden times.

The Parish In a wonderfully rambling chapter, Page's close knowledge of every inch of his village is again shown. (His gossipy style is rather more engaging than that of the Rev Dr F. A. Walker, who in the following year published his History of Dry Drayton and entitled a similar section *Diversa Parochialia*.) For instance, he says that a kink in the boundary-line between Grantchester and Trumpington, otherwise defined by the river, is explained by an ancient dispute. At that spot the body of a drowned man had been found, but the parish of Grantchester refused burial; whereupon Trumpington, having undertaken the duty, claimed that patch of land. 'This story seems to rest on oral tradition so must be taken for what it is worth.' (Scholarly habits distinguish firm fact from legend.)

Speaking of the duties of the Overseer in providing comforts for the poor, he tells of 'old Mr Page who was a farmer here' at the end of the 18th century, a 'very tender-hearted' man who could be moved by embarrassment to give to old women who showed their need for new stockings by lifting their petticoats immodestly. This was the same Thomas Page who had married his own Great-aunt Sarah.

Going through the records of parish expenses, Page is moved to exclaim about changing costs ('in 1761 an item appears of "63 Load of Gravel for the Road £1.1s" – 4d a load! whereas the sum now paid is nearer 4s…') and estimates the yield of parish rates:

At the present day a rate of 1s in the pound raises about £160,
and the whole annual sum required is upwards of £700.

It is at this point that he describes the eccentric Samuel Peck who lived in the village in the 1780s, probably in the house called Yew Garth. *Gunning's Reminiscences* had devoted some pages to Peck, the Trinity don who was made Vicar of Trumpington but was best known for his expertise, dispensed to poor farmers, in land law and his habit of accepting generous gifts of game and produce as a reward. Page was able to illustrate this passage with a copy of a caricature of the fat old cleric returning home to Grantchester after giving advice in his rooms at Trinity College, laden with offerings of food and drink. He was also able to quote a rhyme on the reverse of this etching,* and a clause from Samuel Peck's will. For the biographer of Widnall, his possession of this additional material is interesting; for it was by Peck's will that Great-Aunt Sarah Freeman, who later married Thomas Page, had acquired some valuable land and property.

These tales are not ordered chronologically: there are scraps about late eighteenth-century farmers' protests against the damage to crops caused by 'gentlemen, barbers, or gyps of Colleges' shooting and coursing; there is a suggestion (ill-founded) that Gray might have written his

*See Appendix VII

famous *Elegy* in the churchyard at Grantchester; and there is reference to Queen Elizabeth I and her retinue's progress through the village in 1564, perhaps commemorated in the name (already forgotten) of a piece of land, 'Procession Piece'. Then he goes back further, to recall that Archbishop Matthew Parker had in 1533 preached his first sermon in Grantchester Church. Random as these stories appear to be, Widnall has scholarly habits and so always refers to his sources.

But now he proceeds to some parish history within his own time, and tells about the establishment of the village school in 1830. He comments:

> It is interesting to look back to those times before the days of School Boards, when instruction was so difficult for the poor to procure, and when the children came miles to obtain it, instead of being compelled to attend by Act of Parliament.

By the time he was writing, children were no longer trekking to Grantchester School from Comberton (7), Barton (15) and Trumpington (25). The new building was in use; and the Headmistress was writing that Log Book which reveals the persistence of problems with regular attendance.

What do you hope to find in a village history? Page realized that old customs were worth recording, and local dialect as well. So under a heading *Local Customs* he described the happenings season by season. On Plough Monday men and boys, decked out with ribbons, one dressed as a woman, went begging for ha'pence, with a fiddler to lead their dance in the evening. The girls had their turn on St Valentine's Day, going around with a chanted rhyme to beg for buns and sweets. Then May-Day was celebrated by the children gathering flowers and decking themselves with wreaths and garlands, and stopping at each house to dance and sing. The 25th July was the Village Feast – a country fair which lasted for two or three days. Then, of course, in Advent the carol singers trooped around, one party after another,

> ... all singing the same thing,
>   "God bless you merry gentlemen
>   Let nothing you dismay, etc."
> which may not be bad advice to a stranger hearing the discordant
> performance for the first time...

On Christmas Eve itself it had been the custom for boys to go 'mumping' with blackened faces and sticks to thump on the ground at peoples' doors, crying 'Mump, Mump, if you don't give me a ha'penny I'll give you a thump'. But that ritual, not producing many ha'pence, had nearly died out.

There is a description of the Harvest Supper, or 'Horkey', a feast given by the farmer to his men. But times were hard, and labourers would now rather have extra money and forego the merrymaking.

Page has a short chapter on *Charities*, the various bequests which had provided the row of almshouses, the Clerk's Cottage, maintenance of the church and churchyard, and coals and bread for the poor. They yielded small sums but sufficed when goods were cheap and the population small. As he shows, the population had crept up from 294 in 1801 to 845 in 1871.

Finally, Widnall lists *Grantchester Words* – four pages of strange words and phrases, very few of which would be recognized nowadays even by the last of the old village families.

…Except that his book was not, after all, quite finished. After printing the text so far, Page found more details about the history of the Manor and the Mill. An Appendix makes his corrections and gives additional material. But still he could not stop:

> In looking over old books and papers I have been struck with the
> great number of ways in which Grantchester is spelled. I subjoin
> a list of twenty-four of them…

And then, with an Index, his great work was concluded.

CHAPTER 19

Domestic Life

⬩━•◦•━⬩

POLLY GREENE'S RECOLLECTIONS of the Old Vicarage trio are valuable, but leave one still a little curious.

They give a tantalising impression of that elusive individual, Lilly: Lilly, familiar to us as the smiling figure in her husband's photographs yet so little assertive that she might be supposed to be quite colourless. The truth seems to be that in that *ménage à trois* they were all independent spirits. They lived in a harmonious companionship which allowed any two to go off together as their interests drew them. Page was the robust Mr Phynditout, forever pursuing new lines of enquiry and trying new techniques; Lally, with outpourings of delight, revelled in music, art, literature, botany – unselfconsciously 'cultured'. For Lilly too the current of creativity flowed, a private attention to all the domestic arts, deeply responsive to every detail of the natural world. That old house and its leafy, flowery, watery surroundings, a place of refuge and enchantment for so many, owed much of its spirit to the quiet Lilly.

There must have been so many of her imaginative touches about the house. We know about her *magnum opus*, the embroidered text, and her inscriptions on the sundial; but it is impossible now to say what, in their great partnership, were her own contributions to the costumes and scenery for theatricals. Yet, in spite of decay, change of ownership and much alteration, the Castle Ruin has some tiny examples of – surely? – her work. In its little gothic windows, part stained-glass, there are those panes on which have been painted, in loving detail, garden birds.

One time (Jan '76) when Lally returned from one of her New Year stays with the Lapworths – seeing Irving as Hamlet, visiting Windsor Castle – she 'found my little bedroom so prettily done up for me by dear Lilly'. And successive little touches of new décor were to be noted over the next few years which indicate a taste in sympathy with the Aesthetic Movement.

It must have been before all these developments that Page made one of his most delightful models, a small* representation of the Old Vicarage

---

*Its stand measures $c.\,10\frac{1}{2}$ x $7\frac{1}{2}$ inches (27 cm x 19 cm).

itself. It is quite light in weight, but again full of detail. Taking off its roof, one may peer into the main bedrooms, seeing the four-poster beds; and when that storey is raised, the ground floor is exposed to view, with drawing-room (Buhl clock on mantelpiece, walnut table, the chairs bought in Tottenham Court Road for £3.15.0, the upright piano), the dining-room with its narrow doorway through to the big kitchen, scullery and larder – plate-rack, saucepans on shelves and all. The details of their domestic life mattered to them all and were celebrated: the cats, the pony, Buttercup the Alderney cow (bought for seventeen guineas in 1869), the peafowls, the fantail pigeons and even the new poultry house all deserved mention in the diary. Their servants, too, whose loyalty to the family is suggested by long years of service.

*

All the young people they had watched through childhood and adolescence were by now moving into the next stage. There were engagements and marriages: Edith Williams, Susie Stallard, Ida Lapworth. Laura Palmer's second little girl, Maud, had been born in December 1873, although her cousins Alice and Amy Smith, older than Laura, were still unmarried. They, with their father, in April 1874 went to Southsea to see a brave sight: 'the Duke of Cambridge [reviewing] the 42nd Highlanders on their return from Ashanti War'. (But it had not been a very glorious victory. The Highlanders had arrived in Ashanti, on the west coast of Africa, when the enemy's feeble resistance had already been overcome, and withdrew after leaving the capital in flames. The Ashanti chief had conceded a humiliating tribute of gold; but subsequent inaction by the British was to allow his brother to seize power and tyrannize that region for many years. It was just one of the many episodes in the progressive European exploitation of Africa which, a century later, would be regarded as shameful.)

Richard Smith himself was prospering. The following month he 'went with the Directors to the opening of the new Railway at Bromyard',* and his son Herbert, although only twenty-three, had already done outstandingly well in the engineering firm for which he had been working: '12 May 1874 Bertie left Messrs Hardy & Padmore and was presented with 100 guineas and a testimonial in August'. In September he was to start working with Whitworths of Manchester.

In June Richard was made a J.P. And in that same year he won a First Class Certificate from the Royal Horticultural Society for the *Worcester Pearmain* apple, developed by him from a chance example grown in the area. His St John's Nursery now issued ten catalogues. They were impressive lists, with descriptions of plants and hints about their care. A typically Victorian tree, the *Wellingtonia gigantea*, for instance, could be bought at 12in for 9d; at 2ft for 2s 6d; or at 7ft from 12/6 to 21/-. And the horticultural historian, Miles Hadfield, notes that

> At this period Smith had 50 acres of fruit trees, 50 acres of conifers and evergreens, 12 acres of rose trees, as well as space given over to other plants; there were 32 miles of walks and 2-and-a-half acres of glass.

All these glories 'poor dear Libby' was able to share with him before, in March 1875, she died.

*

The following year, at Grantchester, 'Easter Sunday F.G.H. preached morning and evening his last Sunday as our curate'. George was to become Chaplain of Trinity College, and Chaplain of Non-Collegiate Students. During his remaining time at Merton House he would walk daily into Cambridge, arriving at Trinity in time to conduct the early morning service. And although his attention was now upon his new duties, the old intimacy with his Grantchester friends would never be lost.

---

*– the first suggestion of interest, and perhaps involvement, in one of the great moneymaking ventures of the Victorian age. The younger generation were to participate in the engineering boom.

In that year, 1875, Page had plenty to occupy him at home. First there was the great Garden Party Bazaar and the publication of his *History of Grantchester*. Among other projects was a rather mundane one concerning poultry: 'Put our fowls into their new house in the garden' (perhaps allowing some beneficial pecking and scratching in the orchard).

But they were all concerned about Laura, who was not well. She and Edward had moved into Heath Lodge in Newnham, but it did not entirely suit her, and she felt she must move away. In June she, the children and nurse, went to live in Paris. Poor Edward, doing his utmost to support a restless wife, arranged for the sale of their furniture at Newnham and in July went to join her in Paris.

Lilly spent a fortnight in late autumn with her friends Jane and Percy Lapworth in Hastings. An occasional spell on the south coast seemed to do her good.

At the end of November, 'Mr and Mrs Conder and their daughter Alice came to stay with us'. This entry introduces new friends. Richard's younger son Car was now an undergraduate at St John's College, taking a leisurely course towards a General Degree and eating his dinners at the Inner Temple in London for admission to the Bar. The Conders were a 'good' family, with homes in both Herefordshire and Westmorland, and Miss Conder a thoroughly suitable introduction.

*

Next January, the Widnalls visited the Dixons in their Rectory at Over, and Page 'gave a lecture on Lighthouses'. He loved to branch off into new subjects; but he had recently written on one which was close to his daily life. In February 'Page received £5.5 from Chambers for "A Victim to Modern Inventions"': a small triumph, but one which seems to carry an extra significance, for the publisher's letter was carefully preserved.

What Page had written was a story in which one can recognize S.P.W. laughing at his own propensity to invent clever devices. A young man visits his fortunate friend who, on inheriting money and a large house, had spent the two years since they were last together equipping the place with every kind of ingenious gadget. Each mechanism is explained by the author; and the story is a farcical adventure in which almost every installation produces unintended and disastrous results. Soon after his arrival, Mark Mildmay (the 'I' of the story) has an unhappy encounter with one of Harry Gradient's inventions:

As I was taking off my overcoat in the hall, I exclaimed: 'Why, Harry, what on earth is that extraordinary-looking machine in the corner?' It looked something like a shower-bath without the curtains; attached to the upright supports were a number of crooked iron arms, and on the end of each a brush.

'Oh, that is my automaton brushing-machine. I will explain it to you. You see, at the bottom there is a small platform about a foot high; when you step on this, it gradually descends, and as it does so, sets in motion a train of wheels and levers – you are, in fact, the weight, the motive-power which puts all in motion. All these arms with the brushes begin to revolve, and brush you all over at once. But the most curious and complicated is the hat-brush at the top: you see it is something like a hat-box divided vertically in two parts; you perceive they are now some distance apart, so that you can pass between them; they are lined with bristles, and are fixed on two lever-like jaws. When the machine is set in motion, these jaws come together, and clasping your hat between them, they revolve rapidly; and in a few seconds your hat is brushed, at the same time as your coat, trousers, and boots. When the platform reaches the ground, the hat-brushes again separate, and you step out; then the platform springs up, and is ready for another dusty customer.'

'Well, it is a very curious contrivance. I should like to see it in action,' said I.

'That you shall soon do'; and he stepped on the little platform. All at once the clothes and shoe-brushes began to work vigorously; but the hat-machine did not come into action until the others had about half done their work; it then closed upon his hat, and spun round some fifteen or twenty times, and then flew apart, leaving him free to walk out.

'There!' said Harry. 'What do you think of that? Jump up, and try it.'

'No, thank you; not just now; some other time, perhaps', said I; for I felt too nervous just then to trust myself to such an ordeal.

'Excuse me, then, for one moment, while I just speak to my sister, and then I will go up-stairs with you.'

He had no sooner left me, than, as I stood looking at the curious machine, I made up my mind to try it. Nobody was there to laugh at me if I jumped out suddenly; so I boldly stepped in. The brushes seemed to do their work very well; but I found I must keep in my arms, having got a knock on the funny-bone of my elbow from sticking it out too far. But the hat-brush – oh! Horror! I had forgotten I had no hat on, and that I was a head taller than my friend; the consequence was, the infernal machine suddenly descended, and, seizing me by the head, whirled round at a frightful pace, till I thought no skin would have been left on my nose. I tried to stoop and escape it; but I got such blows behind from the revolving clothes-brushes, that I was glad to stand upright again. Fortunately, it was soon over, and then the hateful thing stopped. I opened my eyes, and saw Harry standing looking at me, convulsed with laughter. I felt very angry at the moment, as I rushed out, with one of my favourite long whiskers brushed across my face, and the other, back over my ear; while my hair was twisted into a vortex on the top of my head...

The letter which came from the editor Robert Chambers so pleased Page that he stuck it in *Uncle Page's Book*, among other special mementoes. One suspects that there may have been in it some significance beyond the promise of a useful five-guinea fee. In sprawling handwriting the Editor wrote:

Edinburgh, 2 Feby 1876
Saml. P. Widnall Esq

Dear Sir,

I have the pleasure of handing you something for your very amusing article *A Victim to Modern Inventions*.

Consistently with your very natural desire, and in fact consistently with fair play to the story, I dealt as sparingly as possible with it, as you will see by referring to last month's Part of Ch.J. in which it appeared.

I have to thank you for the 'Curiosity', so well named. In return, pray accept of one from me, wherein you will see that others besides you have written and printed a book with their own hands. This however detracts in nowise from your merits.

I am, dear Sir,
Faithfully yours
Robt. Chambers.

And the message which accounts for the preservation of this letter must lie in that exchange of home-produced books. The 'Curiosity' for which Chambers thanked Page is most likely to have been *The Miller's Daughter*, which he would have been particularly proud to draw to Chambers' attention since in it he refers to the *Book of Days* compiled by Robert Chambers Snr. And the return gift is very likely to have been *Vestiges of Creation* (written and published by the older Chambers anonymously in

1844 and arousing furious controversy among academics*), a study which followed the publication of Darwin's first observations on his *Beagle* voyages but predates his *Origin of Species*. If so, the mystery of its authorship, still a lively topic of conversation, was revealed to S.P.W.; and it was just the book to stir thoughts about prehistoric creatures and, in due course, influence another novel.

*

Laura's move to Paris had not helped. By March 1876 she was back in Cambridge, staying with Mrs Prettyman (probably the mother of Edward Palmer's intimate friend Pretyman/Prettyman, described by Besant as 'a son of the late Bishop of Lincoln', with whom he used to go off and live for weeks in the Fens, their clothes becoming 'picturesque for rags and mud'). Lally dined with her there, and a month later she, the devoted godmother, 'went to help Laura to pack she and the Children going into Wales'. At first the little girls stayed, with their nurse; and then at the end of September 'Page and Lilly went to fetch the children (Ethel and Maud Palmer) from Ainsworth Street they were very good and full of chatter they call Rachel HL'. A week later 'Rachel took Ethel and Maudie to Aberystwith'.

For 7th November there is a brief but startling entry: 'W.C. made into E.C.' This seems to defy sense, and one looks again. But thus it is written, and later records (*c.*1883) of parish business seem to confirm that it was indeed so: Page, who had installed every modern convenience at the Old Vicarage, was reverting to the old earth closet in place of the water closet.

At the end of that Michaelmas Term, when his exams (the Previous, or 'Littlego') were over, Car brought Alice Conder to stay at Grantchester. Alice Smith was staying too, and so could share a pleasant occasion and meet some of Car's friends: 'Page, Lally, Alice Conder, Alice Smith lunched at Car's rooms St John's Coll. Met Mr Coats, Mr Whitstones, and Mr Piper'.

And on 28th December Page recorded that 'The thermometer was 2° higher than on June 16th and Aug 25th'.

*

Early in the New Year of 1877 Page again gave a lecture at Over, this time on a favourite topic, *Old England*.

*The book's authorship was still, at this time, a mystery: the secret would be revealed generally some six years later.

Grantchester Church, still in its old form, was 'prettily decorated' for a confirmation service in March. A few days later the work of demolition began, removing the roof and the south wall of the nave; then the building of a wide extension supported by pillars, and the replacing of the old low roof and great crossbeams with a steeply-pitched 'gothic' one. Page could scarcely leave the village during the eight months it took to accomplish all this.

Other members of the family were, however, moving about. Laura needed sunshine as well as sea air, and was staying on the south coast of the Isle of Wight; and Lally went to Ventnor to be with her. She was again pregnant, and it must have been evident for some time that her illness was the dread consumption. The choice of Ventnor may have been suggested by the Giles family, who lived at Bonchurch close by. (This name, of later importance, is at this point introduced in the diary with a note of the death, a few days after

Laura Palmer (photo at Ventnor)

Lally's arrival, of the father, George Giles.) After a month Lally, Laura, Rachel and the children left and went to stay with Robinson cousins at Surbiton. While there, Laura 'had her portrait taken by Mr Collier'.*

At midsummer, Richard took his daughters for a great cruise: in July 'Dittin [another of those pet names], Alice, Amy and Dr Taylor returned from their trip of 5 weeks to Norway including the North Cape'. Lally, too, took a short holiday, accompanying Miss Arabella Cowlard to Hunstanton for a week. (The lady, a sister of the Vicar's wife, is said to have had a sharp tongue; but she was now a tenant of Riversdale and relations were amicable.)

Now came one of those 'grand family gatherings' which so pleased them all. Those assembled were Richard, Alice, Amy, Bertie, Car, Mr & Mrs Conder, G. E. Giles, Mrs W. Tennant, Mrs Thompson, Lilly, Page and Lally. On 11th August they all dined in Car's rooms at St John's; and again next day at the Old Vicarage. Of the younger genera-

*The Hon. John Collier

Alice Holme   Amy Giles   Car Smith-Carington

tion, only Bertie was so far married*, but now future in-laws were being welcomed into the family circle. Mr & Mrs Conder and their daughter Alice had already visited, and the delighted Lally may have espied signs of courtship under the chestnuts by the river. Car, with his thick wavy hair and moustache, was a very handsome fellow, and 'Alicie' a perfectly 'suitable' girl.

G. E. Giles was a son of the recently-deceased George Giles of Bonchurch, one of the foremost civil engineers, whose work had included the construction of Southampton Docks besides the development of railway systems in England and the Continent. The father had had residences in Hamburg and Vienna as well as the fine house at Bonchurch, Isle of Wight, where his family of eleven children had grown up. George Giles junior, the second of this impressive man's seven sons, must have seemed well fitted to join the upwardly-mobile Smith family, and indeed an engagement was already settled.

Quite soon after this visit, Amy and George (G. E.) Giles were married from her home, at St Stephen's, Barbourne, Worcester. Richard would have made sure that his daughter's wedding was arranged in style; and the groom, with a taste for extravagance, had his supporting groomsmen fitted out in matching frock coats. The couple then set up home in Nuneaton, where the thirty-year-old George worked as a solicitor.

Late in November Alice, now aged twenty-nine, was also married. The wedding took place in London, from the Langham Hotel; and the groom was Col. Arthur Holme, an army engineer.

*In June 1876 Herbert Smith had married Lizzie Stallard, daughter of a wine merchant (and sister, probably, of the 'J. Stallard' to whom Alice had been briefly engaged). Their first child, Francis, was born in 1877.

While these interesting and hopeful events were taking place, life was growing more difficult for the Palmers. On 20th September their third child, a boy, was born at Aberystwyth. Lally was at home at Grantchester, and joined in a jaunt to Sawston to see the Paper Mills there (a group of eight, including the Boquels). But it was not long before she was summoned for help: '10 Nov I went to Aberystwith to be with Laura who is very ill'. When the patient was a little better Lally accompanied her, with a stop for the night at Hereford, to Bath for treatment at the spa.

On 5th December the transformed Grantchester Church was re-opened by the Bishop, and the event was followed by a celebration lunch (eighty people sitting down to a splendid feast prepared by the Sidney Sussex College cook) in the schoolroom.

And, just in time for Christmas, Page made a twenty-mile journey across to Gazeley, near Newmarket, 'to take some Church Candlesticks I had made for them'.

(When the author searched for these in Gazeley Church in 1999, it seemed at first that no SPW candlesticks had survived. A closer search then revealed two wall-bracket candelabra, one fallen and lying with broken masonry under a pew. A likeness to the Grantchester design was confirmed by traces of similar blue and red paint.)

*

In the New Year they all called on Edward Palmer in his college rooms 'to see Laura's Portrait a lovely picture but very sad'. The artist John Collier was a prolific painter, whose portraits of Edward Palmer, W. K. Clifford, T. H. Huxley, Leslie Stephen and others of their circle are a valuable record. But his reputation was that of a painter 'concerned with accuracy rather than truth in the artistic meaning of the word...' He was a thin, bearded man who gave an 'impression of quiet tenacity and a sort of polite ruthlessness'.* His literal representation of Laura had revealed all too clearly her desperate state. Lally went off once more to comfort her godchild: 'I went to Bournemouth to stay with Annie Creeke and to be near my dear Laura who is very ill'.

Page, meanwhile, was preparing New Year theatricals on a small scale. Mr Banyard, as churchwarden, had provided a supper for the men of the church choir in the Reading Room

*D.N.B., which also tells of Collier's successive marriages to two of Huxley's daughters and subsequent campaigning for the legal right to marry a deceased wife's sister.

... with good old English fare, in his usual hospitable and liberal manner... the junior members being at the same time welcomed by Mrs W. Martin to a substantial tea in the school-room, where both parties afterwards united, and a very beautiful and interesting Christmas entertainment was provided by some kind friends...

This was *Beauty & the Beast*, acted by SPW and his cast.

After nearly a fortnight away, Lally returned from Bournemouth 'leaving Laura very weak and ill'.

Lilly, in February, went to stay with Jane Lapworth in London. The two visited Windsor, where they saw 'the glorious Castle' and the Albert Memorial Chapel – 'beyond words'. But she became unwell and on her return went straight to bed for some weeks.

SPW, in his rôle as model-maker, was busy at this time. A small scale-model of the Manor House was completed on 25th February (only

days after that house, Vine Cottage and Riversdale were all burgled). This model, in its glass case, survives in good condition. There is no chance of seeing inside, yet its construction must have presented a challenge, for the ancient building had over the centuries developed such a complex roof-structure. Still, here it is with its mighty chimneystack, its odd projections and its large conservatory alongside: a fairly small model, the colours still faithfully reproducing that of the old tiles and brickwork. The very next day after its completion Page set to work on his second model of the Church, wanted by its former curate, George Howard; and in ten weeks it, too, was finished.

Now came a notable development in the Smith family. On 28th March 1878 they 'Received a letter from Richd saying he had taken the name of

Carington (by deed poll)'. The antiquarian research in which Page had been assisting was to verify a family pedigree establishing Richard's descent by male line from Hamo, 'Lord of Caryngton, co. Chester, temp. Conquestoris'. There certainly were Caringtons among his forebears and he was entitled to the more dignified name.* So when, a week or two later, 'Richard was married to Patty Leader', she became Mrs Smith-Carington. Richard was now fifty-three and his new wife thirty-seven. She was one of a large family of interesting and energetic people. Her father, Edward Leader Williams, was chief engineer to the Severn Navigation Commission. Her eldest brother followed his father's profession and would become Sir Edward Leader Williams, responsible for the construction of the Manchester Ship Canal. And the next brother was the eminent landscape painter B.W. Leader. Yet another link to engineering, one of the most exciting and profitable developments of the Victorian age, would assist the family fortune. And Patty fitted into her new family with, it seems, perfect harmony.

*

That Easter, Lally spent a week in Essex with her nieces and nephews – Alice and Arthur Holme, Bertie and Lizzie Carington and Car (but not the young Gileses, for Amy was expecting her first child, Phyllis, born in July). And midsummer was spent as it should be, with Bertie and Lizzie bringing 'Nurse and Baby' for a week which must have included fun on the river; for 'Bertie bought us a boat at Rutt's for which he gave £3 and Mrs Tennant £1'. (£4 for a decent skiff; and a few days earlier Page had bought at Huntingdon a carriage – perhaps secondhand – for £5.10.0.)

Lally was off again at the end of August for three weeks of visiting:

Lally went to Barbourn House Worcester thence on 5th Sept to Nuneaton thence on the 9th back to Worcester [where she attended the opening service and the evening performance of the Music Meeting] with George, Amy, and baby thence on the 12th to Manchester with Bertie thence on the 17th to Ackworth to see Alice and Arthur Holme and thence on the 21st home

Someone present in all their thoughts must have been Laura Palmer. Her disease was remorseless. On 20th June Lally had received 'my last birthday present from Dear Laura – a pair of gold spectacles'. On 24th August 'Laura and Edward's baby boy died'. Her own end was only a matter of time.

*He had already incorporated the family coat of arms in his advertisements for the St John's Nursery

At home, meantime, Page was busy with yet another model. This was of Grantchester Mill, made for the miller James Nutter.* It is his largest and most ambitious model and was delivered on 4th October, 1878.

These days, well over a century later, it is displayed in the Cambridge & County Folk Museum, a relic of an important local industry which once employed so many. The Cam had driven a series of watermills since time immemorial, and the one straddling its own stream at Grantchester had been part of the endowment of Merton College, Oxford, in the 13th century. Its long history had included destruction and rebuilding, so the structure in the 1870s was mainly 17th century with later additions, including a high chimney from a furnace driving extra machinery. The whole complex layout was familiar to Page, who not only lived nearby but had grown up with Page Howard, son of an earlier miller. He kept his boat on the millstream and he knew all about the use of the eel trap by which thousands of eels were gathered from the stream. So the model tries to reproduce the stream itself, flowing through and emerging from under the mill, with a wagon standing on the bridge to be loaded with sacks from a high projecting pulley.

Some forty years later A.C. Benson, describing the village, was to give this impression of the mill:

> ...a substantial modern structure of pale yellow brick, high-shouldered and flour-dusted, with an airy projecting pent-house, which swings

*Two further generations of James Nutters were to have charge of Grantchester Mill before its destruction.

down sacks of flour by a well-worn glittering chain; and within, the mill keeps up its homely grumbling and groaning, while the stream spins and gurgles into the deep pool. [*Memories and Friends*]

Farmers from all around were to continue coming with wagons laden with sacks of wheat for grinding until the year 1928. Then the Mill caught fire. The combination of newer oil-fired machinery, dry chaff and a strong wind were disastrous. The huge buildings were full of fuel in the form of grain and flour; and despite the efforts of firemen pumping water from the river, there was total devastation. What remained of the buildings was bought by the Pemberton family, who cleared the site and called the attractive house built as a restoration 'The Old Mill'. Only Page's huge model now shows the extent of what had been, with farming, the village's staple industry.

*

As a change of activity, Page put up 'small shelves ... in the Drawing and Dining rooms over the doors for plates &c' for Lilly's blue-and-white china.

They were seeing a good deal of Car, who early in September had come to stay in order to read more seriously for his degree. He and Page together 'went to lunch with E. H. Palmer at St John's and he began to take their Portraits in water colours': the versatile Edward displaying another of his many talents, and probably glad of the slight yet sympathetic distraction from his almost-crushing anxieties at that time. And Car, as a happy distraction from his own impending exams, in November bought a boat, the *Wild Duck*. A few days later, accompanied by the willing Page, he took it as far as Baitsbite Lock for a trial sail.

The diary records a jumble of events at around this time, some of which may be inaccurately dated. There was an evening when Page, Lilly and Lally, given tickets by George Howard, went to see *The Ticket of Leave Man* at the A.D.C. There is mention of a further model – 'a turnpike house after a snowstorm' – which pleased some friends ('Mr & Mrs Hopkins* and their tall pupil Mr Fisher'). There is a reference to a fuller account, now lost, of 'a daring burglary at Barbourne House' at Worcester in which property to the value of £150 had been stolen. There were Miss Cowlard's 'Hen house Coop &c &c' bought and installed for Page's own poultry. There were further contributions towards the fresh appearance of their drawing-room: 'Received two small oil paintings

*The Rev. E.L. Hopkins, Chaplain of King's College, who lived for a while at Merton Cottage.

long and narrow from Polly Greene one a view at the back of the Mill the other a view on the Ouse'. There was the departure of Lally's pupil Arthur Perowne, off to Peterborough where his father had just been made Dean... And at last 'Car went in for the Special exam in Law for the Ordinary B. A. degree'. (University examinations in those days took place towards the end of the calendar year, with the degree ceremony being held in the New Year.)

As soon as his exams were over, 'Page and Car started on their voyage in the *Wild Duck*'. They were both longing to give the boat a more thorough trial; Page still had a schoolboy zest for adventure. And is it possible, perhaps, that the publication that same year of R. L. Stevenson's *An Inland Voyage* (two canoes venturing through the waterways of Belgium and France) added inspiration? All the details of their adventure are now, alas, lost, except for the terse entry: '13 December Page and Car returned from Worcester leaving the *Wild Duck* in the ice (see Log)'.

To have sailed from Grantchester to Worcester seems, nowadays, scarcely credible; yet an examination of a map of the waterways shows that at that time it was possible – after negotiating countless locks – to make one's way across from the River Ouse to the Nene, and then follow the Grand Union Canal and take a connecting link to the Worcester and Birmingham Canal. The enterprise, dotty in December in any case, turned out to have been undertaken in one of the coldest winters: '18 December About 2000 people skating on Lingay Fen, dancing, cricket, hockey and other games'.

*

But in the meantime, Laura's life came to its end. On 8th December Lally made the arduous journey by train – 'started to go to Bournemouth to dear Laura's funeral (a Sunday) arrived next morning at 8' just in time for the burial. No more is recorded in the diary about that family for some months, but Besant's biography of Edward Palmer tells of the crisis which he now faced: two small girls to look after and 'serious embarrassment' from the enormous debts accumulated because of his wife's endless moves and medical expenses. His great friend Pretyman had assisted with a loan, but had himself died at the end of that year. His only remedy lay in earning whatever fees he might by unstinting work. Having failed to gain the well-paid Chair of Arabic Studies he was left with the paltry stipend of the Almoner's Chair, supplemented by his Fellowship and every fee he could earn to supplement it.

*

At the very end of that eventful year Page started upon what was to become a long labour: 'Began to set up type for the Smith Carington Pedigree book'. Richard himself had made a start, but it would be a slow and tortuous business, tracking through archives to work their way through the dark backward and abysm of time. Verification from documents and tombs was to entail some further years of searching for evidence. In the following May, Page's quest took him to Lincoln, York and Nottingham; in Sept 1881 he would be ranging about the Midlands; and the year after that again going to Leicester to rummage through archives. It was altogether a huge task and, by the end, a wearisome one, although he must have enjoyed its moments of romance. For by the end he had seen for himself the effigy of Sir Francis Smith (d.1606) resting on his elbow in the chantry chapel at Wootten-Wawen, Warwicks, and

the massive family tombs of his descendants – George Smith lying stiffly beside his wife, and his son Sir Francis Smith and wife with their seven sons and five daughters gathered beneath them – in the side-chapel at Ashby Folville. He had found the inscription in Christ Church Cathedral, Oxford, commemorating Sir John Smith (slain at the battle of Cheriton Down, 1644) who had been created Knight-Banneret* at the battle of Edgehill for recovering the King's standard from the Cromwellian side. The volume (over 224 pages) would finally be completed in 1884.

*

As the decade reached its final year, the Old Vicarage trio were able to enjoy contacts with their extended family and its younger generation.

*The highest degree of knighthood, conferred for outstanding service in battle, especially to the sovereign. This was probably the last occasion it was ever awarded.

Lally, on a New Year visit to Worcester, was delighted to be taken to her new sister-in-law Patty's brother's studio. 'My first visit to Whittington, saw a crayon likeness of Mrs Leader when a little girl it was the image of little Maudie Palmer. Saw a sketch of a picture Mr Leader was preparing for the Academy'.

At home, Page was at work on what seems to have been his final scale model; for on 19th February he 'rode to Swaffham Prior with Mr Nutter and took the Model of the Old Church'. Although a dozen miles away to the N.E., this building must have struck him whenever he passed through that village. Unusually, one sees, high upon a mound, two churches standing side by side. One, St Mary's, was a romantic-looking ruin lacking a roof and festooned with ivy; the other, St Cyriac & St Julitta, was entire. Yet the second, a late-Georgian brick edifice added to a Tudor tower, was by that period not much liked. The old church, neglected for more than a century since its steeple had been destroyed by lightning, was now to be restored, and the chosen architect was the one who had enlarged Grantchester Church, Blomfield.* Just as he had done

in his own village, Page wanted to record what was about to undergo change. A very badly-faded photograph survives which shows the church in its old state; and his model must have been intended to preserve its likeness in the round. In November, to raise funds for the building work, the model was raffled, and it was won by Car. Kept for many years by his family, it was eventually discarded.

*

The Old Vicarage garden, down beside the river, was always prone to flooding, and that February a high flood washed right up to the house, bringing down the wall and roof of the conservatory. As spring arrived, 'Lilly found a little Hare in Mrs Nimmo's garden nearly starved. She called it "Bunch" it died [nine days later]'. But the tender-hearted Lilly seems to have lost patience with their surviving peacock, whose harsh cries and scufflings in her flowerbeds could be endured no longer. Page 'took our Peacock "Jacko" to the Duke of Leeds'. A puzzling destination

*later Sir Arthur Blomfield

– his new home was to be at a grand mansion on the Gog Magog hills near Abington. Nothing now remains except the stable-block at Wandlebury, but a panoramic view of Cambridge seen from Madingley hill early in that century shows the residence of the Earl of Godolphin, later Duke of Leeds (a title now extinct), just visible on the skyline.

Alice and Polly Greene, Lally's most devoted former pupils, were visiting – Alice by now aged twenty-one and Polly nineteen – and, with Page and Lally, 'spent a delightful afternoon at Mr Howard's rooms and went to see the carvings in the Library by Grindling [sic] Gibbons he gave each a little vase of Valerie china'. Lally's next treat, a few days later, was to go to a recital with a friend and hear two favourite tenor solos of the time – 'Come into the garden, Maud' and 'Tom Bowling'. And the note of another small event is exactly in period, too: '24 May Tom L. Davis came from London on a Bycicle [sic] and had a bad fall'.

Laura's younger brother Tom was now aged twenty-two and working in a Local Government office in London. Having adopted the new form of transport he was to make many brave journeys on his 'penny-farthing'. Cycling was a challenge which had become popular in the university, where a newly-formed Bicycle Club was organising regular races. The *Cambridge Review*, in its third issue (Michaelmas Term, 1879) reported a 47-mile ride completed by the winner in 3 hrs 8 mins. 'None had had the slightest trouble with shy horses or otherwise', though all but one had needed to dismount for the ascent of Orwell Hill. (As the Bicycle Club flourished, the gymnasium which had provided exercise for Palmer, Clifford and their friends was being closed down.) Tom Davis seems to have been a gentle, agreeable character. Years later the old widows in the Almshouses would still look back fondly on the visits of 'Miss Laura and Master Tom'.

Tom's arrival was followed by a cluster of cousins. First came 'Lizzie Carington and the 2 boys [Bertie's sons Francis and Neville] and Nurse'; then George and Amy Giles with baby Phyllis and her nurse Caroline; and finally Bertie himself. During their fortnight's stay, 'Page, Lally, Amy and Lizzie Carington went to lunch at Mr Howard's room after going to the Senate House to see Honorary degrees conferred on Sir F. Leighton, Rob Browning, Prof Huxley &c &c'. And next day they were in the Senate House again to hear the Rede Lecture, 'subject "The Origin of Life"'.[*]

[*] Four years later, the 1883 lecture was given by T. H. Huxley himself on this subject. The diary's date may therefore be mistaken.

Little indications of family harmony continue with a gift from Patty of a watercolour of blackberries and leaves (probably her own work), and of a black kitten about six weeks old (Pixie) from the Giles family at Nuneaton. A beloved cat, Little Dot, died and 'was buried under the cross'. And Laura's children, Ethel and Maud, were taken by the faithful Rachel down to Cornwall to stay with Captain & Mrs Palmer.

But shortly after that, at the end of June, a letter came from Edward Palmer 'announcing his marriage with Auguste daughter of the Count Von Lange'. It must have seemed rather soon for the widower to be marrying again, especially when he was having such difficulty in maintaining solvency. He had always worked hard to supplement his meagre stipend with individual teaching. Now he turned to journalism and more translation – the Koran, Persian poetry and a revision of Henry Martyn's New Testament in Persian; Hindustani, Urdu; even Danish and Finnish; and a series of papers on 'Arabic Humour'. Having been called to the Bar in 1874 he even took occasional briefs on the Eastern Circuit – but 'chiefly as an amusement and a way of enjoying humanity' [Besant].

The new marriage arose indirectly from all this extended activity. He had been taking German lessons from Auguste von Lange. Her imaginative teaching, including songs and drawings, developed into courtship; and once again Edward had been captivated. This young woman was able to match his love of adventure, and left a description of their return, after marriage, to Aberystwith with the two little girls. One day she and Edward rose early – at 3 or 4 a.m. – and took a rowing boat out to sea. It was crazy, and intensely romantic: 'So early as this there lay a veil over the sea, and only Eddie and I were upon it...' Then a gale sprang up. They came near to drowning in the wild sea, and ended by making a fire from driftwood on the shore to dry themselves.

In November Page and Lally called on the happy couple at their lodgings in Rose Crescent, Cambridge.

*

The Old Vicarage servants, although no doubt hard-pressed at times when the house was full or Lally's small pupils became over-excited, must have found themselves treated very fairly. Their names are found in the diary and in census returns; and it is clear that they had an easy relationship with their master and mistress, and mostly came from local families. When, in 1860, Sophie Papworth left and moved to Miss Fowke's, she had 'been with us nearly 7 years' and was replaced by Ruth Rayner, who must have been related to the Maria Rayner who had been with them before Sophie. In 1865 'Mary Ann Fordham came as servant', and four years later she and Ellis Lewis were married. Mary Ann had bettered herself: we find her, in the 1881 census, with a son and two daughters. Her husband is a 'Corn Merchant, Freeman' and they live in a 'Private House' and themselves employ a servant. They also have one lodger, a student aged 17. In 1879 their son, Owen, came to stay at the Old Vicarage for some days; and he would be mentioned again in the diary ten years later as about to undergo surgery.

In 1876 Emma Plum (previously with the Martins at the Vicarage*) arrived as 'servant', and, soon after, Sarah Clark as 'cook'. Sarah stayed for four years until, on 7th July 1879, she 'left to be married tomorrow to Arthur Baker'. But then, on 23rd August, Charles Muggleton – on whom they had long depended for gardening and the care of their remaining livestock – left. Arthur Baker with his wife, niece and their cat Little Winnie, moved in 'pro tem.' and kept things going until, in October, 'Haddow came'. And Haddow was to occupy the cottage known as Ivy Dene for the next fourteen years. It seems that his rôle was to develop gradually beyond that of mere 'gardener', although that is how he is described in the census.

*

For several years at this period there were some wild variations in the weather. On 3rd August Page recorded 'All night and this morning a fearful tempest causing a tremendous flood so that we could not get out of our front gate nearly 4 inches of rain fell'. The previous winter had been cold, but that of 1879–80 was one of the hardest on record. The *Cambridge Review* of 10th December tells of the frozen river: 'From the mills, almost without a break, the skater could ply his runners down to the "cathedral isle"' … and beyond, with thirty miles of straight run on the Old Bedford River. It was such a great winter for skating that the following month one of the National Championship races was held at Grantchester. For this, Page Widnall must have arranged the opening of sluices to flood his great field, Lingay Fen, which lies between the river and the millstream. This spread of water, frozen, provided a course for the mile race won by a fenman, 'Fish' Smart. Although *Uncle Page's Book* fails to mention any of this, the champion may well be the subject of one

*A letter – 'Dear Mistress' – to Mrs Martin, signed 'Emily Plumb' – concerning apricots and plums in the garden still survives.

or two of those unlabelled photographs – of a burly mustachio'd figure displaying his skating trophy and a painting of himself in action on the ice.

All the diary does record is a disaster caused by violent weather in Scotland: '28 December Tay Bridge accident' – the collapse of a hubristically-conceived and badly-built bridge, nearly two miles long, with the loss of some ninety lives.

The Widnalls and Lally had, despite these dramatic events, been enjoying themselves. They went down to Bishop's Stortford where, just before Christmas, they assisted Page's cousin Mrs Clark and her companion Miss Kelsey with a theatrical performance in the Assembly Rooms of *Blue-beard*. Perhaps Mrs Clark had remembered it from the Castle Theatre production of 1868. Not so lurid as its title might suggest, the little play was written by Bishop Heber, Bishop of Calcutta and author of 'From Greenland's icy mountains' – and so was a perfectly suitable choice for Bishop's Stortford Ladies' College. S. P. W. himself played Abou Malek (Blue beard), a magnificent presence complete with huge turban and cummerbund. Judging by photographs, he was also responsible for the elaborate scenery. And he had probably borrowed one 'prop' for this performance, his hookah, from Edward Palmer.

CHAPTER 20

Into the 1880s

AT THE END OF JANUARY 1880 Car married his 'Alicie' (Alice Conder) and set up home in Malvern. Having no other plans for a career, he chose to take over responsibility for the St John's Nursery – without great success, as it would turn out.

The diary records a mixture of events at Grantchester. First, there was the sale by auction of Merton House. George Howard was now, as college chaplain, living in Trinity and so had decided to end the family's last link with that house.

Then comes a sad entry: 'The Atalanta set sail from Bermuda and was never heard of after'. A black slab set in the church wall by the font tells more of the story. Robert Nimmo, the only son of the large family who lived next door to the Widnalls, at the Mill House, had been a naval chaplain serving on this ship. At the Old Vicarage they would remember him, as 'Mr N. O. Nayme', acting in their theatricals; and his mother is said to have been ever after gazing along the road towards Trumpington, longing for his return.

There was a small triumph for Lally: one of her former pupils, Alice Greene, had won a prize (£1) 'for writing the lines on the Battle of Semprach' – a spirited poem of heroism on the battlefield.

Page, meanwhile, had been planting gooseberry bushes among the fruit trees in the orchard. And he was busy at his carpenter's bench, too. On 23rd March he once again made the twenty-mile journey eastwards, this time to Kentford, to set up a pulpit he had made. There, in this ancient small church, his oak pulpit stands still, with its simple open carved work. If it seems strange to have gone so far, an explanation is found in a framed document lying amongst discarded volumes in the vestry there. There had been at that time a Church Restoration Appeal, and the list of donors includes several Grantchester names (F. G. Howard, F. Lilley, etc.). The name of Widnall is missing, but he must have been moved to make his own gift 'in kind', as he had previously done at Gazeley; for the Vicar of those two parishes was the Rev. Mr Tearle, husband of Lucy Lilley.

*

For the past fifteen years the Bensley family had been living at Vine Cottage, and now they were leaving. As was usual with the Widnalls, neighbours had become friends – especially close since their children had received their early schooling from Lally. Mrs Bensley was from an aristocratic German family, her husband a scholar who had for years been Lecturer in Hebrew at Gonville & Caius College. Then, as Under-Librarian of the University Library, he had been made a Fellow; and some years hence he would become Lord Almoner's Professor of Arabic. There were similarities with Edward Palmer's career; and his work on biblical translation and marriage to a German lady would be echoed again in the new arrival in the village of his exact contemporary, Professor Lumby.

For in the same month, March, of the Bensleys' departure, Joseph Lumby and his large family came to Merton House.

Lumby, Norrisian Professor of Divinity, was a mighty man, a Yorkshireman, Dean of St Catharine's College. 'Lumby is omniscient and omnipotent, but (thank Heaven) not omnipresent' was one epigram. And a parody current at St Catharine's went:

> I heard the voice of Lumby say
> 'My height is six foot one;
> I'm forty inches round the chest,
> My weight is twenty stun.'
>
> I heard the voice of Lumby say
> 'I know six hundred creeds;
> I don't believe in one of them
> (We never did at Leeds).'
>
> I heard the voice of Lumby say
> 'Sense I postpone to sound;
> Let others argue to the point;
> I argue round and round.'

It had been the death of his first wife, Susanna, in 1873, which had made possible Lumby's election to a college fellowship. But he had been left with five children, and a governess was attending to the education of the younger ones. She was Luise Dahlmann, daughter of a German lawyer. On 15th July 1880 'Dr Lumby brought home his young bride to Merton House'. She, the same Luise, was indeed young, only twenty-three and barely older than Amy, Constance and Helen. But it was to be a successful marriage, with the birth of seven more children.

Lumby, formidable as he was, had had his academic career impeded by the University's strict regulations concerning marriage. An early fellowship at Magdalene had been relinquished because of his first marriage. As a widower in the 1870s he obtained a fellowship at St Catherine's; and on becoming a professor at the end of the decade had been permitted, while keeping his fellowship, to marry again. This rule of celibacy for all dons except those with church livings, university offices or professorial chairs affected many able men who found themselves reaching old age comfortless and without progeny. Their frustration was expressed in a parody of *The Lady of Shallot* published in the *Cambridge Review* of 26th October 1881:

> They hobbled o'er the grassplot,
>   For they were aging one and all,
> They mumbled at their wretched lot
>   When they were carried into hall.
> Their wanting teeth looked sad and strange,
>   Their eye had lost its youthful fire,
> Weak hand, mis-tended their attire,
>   But found no hair to disarrange.
> They only said, "Our life is dreary",
>   "They'll never pass," they said;
> They said, "We are aweary, aweary,
>   We would that we were wed!"

But the following year the Royal Commission did 'pass' and the statutes were at last changed. (At Jesus College, despite the Master's disapproval, all but one of the fellows married – or revealed their clandestine marriages – forthwith. And the enlargement of the town with large late-Victorian houses dates from that moment.)

It is likely that the Lumby family were already known to the Old Vicarage ménage before their arrival in the village. There were those who found them – the great theologian, his tall German wife and their brood – rather forbidding. But with Lally especially, the relationship would become a warm one.

*

With the spring came a terrible event: the 'Sad accident on the river Mr Eddy of Pembroke Col. and his brother both drowned'. The river as it flowed beside the meadows had always been a dangerous playground; and this latest tragedy had especially disturbed Page (so regularly afloat with his fishing rod, so familiar with the wildlife along its banks). Two mementoes were chosen and pasted into the back of Uncle Page's Book. The first is an example of his own printing, by now expertly laid out: an *In Memoriam* sheet set in Gothic type, giving extracts from the *Clifton College Magazine* (the school attended by both brothers), the *Cambridge Review*, and *The Guardian*. From these we read details of the accident and of the funeral service at Pembroke College Chapel, and then of the burial up in Yorkshire, where 'long before the hour the pretty Village Church was crowded with those who from the village and surrounding neighbourhood had come to pay their last tributes of respect and affection…' That village was Carleton, near Skipton. Mr and Mrs Eddy had lost their only two children.

The other item, a dignified letter of thanks from the father to 'Miss Smith', shows that Lally, too, had made an imaginative response to the tragedy. It had happened in late April, when the Meadows were bright with springtime blossom. Lally, meeting the parents, had thought to comfort them with 'tiny flowers and sprigs of hawthorn' from the riverside (later preserved by a member of the bereaved family); and afterwards from the Old Vicarage a painting was sent, one of Polly Greene's small landscapes, 'a representation of what they last looked on'.

*

By contrast, the next diary entry records an interesting venture: '13 May 1880 Page & Lally went to the Vegetarian Banquet in the Town Hall'. This, for those carnivorous Victorians, was a novelty.

The *Fruit Banquet at Cambridge* was fully reported in the *Cambridge Review*. It was given in the lecture room of the Young Men's Christian Association by the Rev. Professor Mayor, Fellow of St John's College.

> The fare consisted of vegetables, fruit, eggs and milk. Salad oil was employed for frying the croquettes, fritters, &c. The beverages provided consisted of new milk, Wright's unfermented wine, and home-made lemonade.

And the menu certainly reads like a banquet. It was followed by several speeches advocating vegetarianism. The first, for instance, was from a man who had suffered very poor health and was 'full of gout'. His physician's opinion was that 'he would never be better till he had had an acute attack, which would drive it out of his fingers and toes'. The alternative was 'abstinence from all flesh food and alcoholic drinks, and other stimulants'. This he had adopted, with great benefit. The various other speakers had lived on this diet while living in India, Madagascar, and 'the north of Scotland, eleven miles from a butcher's shop'. The occasion ended with a number of diners signing up as members of the Vegetarian Society. One wonders whether the régime at the Old Vicarage was altered after this: they may well have favoured vegetables and fruit even more than before, especially with Lilly's health in mind.

Lilly herself was mostly staying at home, it seems, content with her gardening, embroidering and the making of preserves. There may have been a link with her mother's family in this last occupation: an expertise with fruits, seeds and herbs deriving from the Hanbury background. The great pharmaceutical firm of Allen & Hanbury owed a great deal to Daniel Hanbury (1825–1875), an expert botanist who was very likely descended from Lilly & Lally's great-grandfather Daniel Hanbury of Bridgenorth (1712–1785).

But poor Lilly, in spite of having had that protracted spell of 'rheumatic gout', had not found that it emerged from her fingers and toes. She was still susceptible to illness and seems to have borne her troubles bravely while her husband and her sister enjoyed their companionship further afield. And it was those two who were able to accept Mrs Bensley's invitation to watch the May Races that year with a party gathered on a houseboat on the lower river by Fen Ditton.

*

Lally spent a few weeks in London with Jane Lapworth . She 'spent a most delightful day at the Academy met the Greenes there'. Her young protegée Polly was now an art student at the Academy Schools, and probably surveying the crowded walls of the Summer Exhibition intently. In a few years she would herself be exhibiting there.

While in London, Lally also paid three visits to the new Palmer household, to see her little great-nieces Ethel and Maud: it was important to keep the children in touch with their maternal relatives, and perhaps reassuring for them at a time when the new Mrs Palmer was about to give birth to her own first child, Carl. They were established now in Bloomsbury, and Edward, having 'chucked teaching', was 'happier than he had ever been before' [Besant].

That year, as usual, summer visitors came and went; and the Old Vicarage was more than usually crowded in August when Mr Howgrave Graham brought his wife, with 'Bertie (5 years), George (3), Baby &

Nurse' to stay. In addition, those two from Bishop's Stortford, Mrs Clark and Miss Kelsey, were somehow accommodated.

Howgrave Graham had come to attend the annual gathering of the British Medical Association, which this year was being held in Cambridge. For several days in succession its members heard addresses on the latest developments in medicine (with particular attention to matters of public health and hygiene, and suggestions that it was high time for the University of Cambridge to introduce a Medical Tripos). And as is the way with conferences, their hosts provided some lavish social events. The Widnalls and Lally were fortunate:

> Mrs Graham got us tickets for Soiree at the Fitzwilliam Museum, the Garden Party at Kings Col. and the Converzatione [sic] at St Johns Col. the grounds illuminated

The soirée, held both in the gardens of Peterhouse and the Museum, 'brilliantly illuminated with the electric light', was judged by the *Cambridge Chronicle* to be 'pre-eminently the *piece de resistance* of the many meetings'.

*

After this diversion the diary returns to practical matters. A good auction sale was always hard to resist, and so the trio went with Haddow to Abington Hall, where they bought a cow for £15 (and Lally was 'struck with the carpet gardening'). A few days later they bought another cow, 'Nancy'; and then 'Mr Pemberton* gave me the old ruined Boathouse the tiles were used for a new roof to the Cow shed (P)'.

It was a remarkably mild autumn. Lally, visiting the Greenes at Bedford, had a happy outing to Turvey – 'the prettiest village she ever saw'. And on 2nd November, 'Lilly saw 5 swallows and gathered a sprig of apple blossom'.

Just before Christmas, Amy Giles' second child, Humphrey, was born at their home at Nuneaton.

For Page and Lally the New Year of 1881 brought theatricals. It was like old times, though this year not in the Castle Theatre at Grantchester but with the Greene family. They themselves could muster a large cast, and the vast drawing room in their home there, though chilly, invited such activities.

12 *Jan*   Theatricals at East Lodge Bedford they acted "The Sheep in Wolf's Clothing" & "Only a Halfpenny" all went splendidly

*Head of the great land-owning family of Trumpington Hall

18 *Jan*   Page & Lally at Bedford went to the Grammar School
Theatricals "The Rivals" and "Diamond cut Diamond".
Fearfully cold wind with snow, a perfect Blizzard said to have
been the coldest day ever known in England

19 Jan   Page & Lally returned from Bedford had great difficulty in
getting home on account of the snow, trains could not run till
after mid-day. Our horse could not get out so I had to walk
from the station through the deep snow Lally went to the
Boquels' Haddow went for her walking, she got home at 9.30

21 *Jan*   Thermometer went down to 4 degrees – 28 below freezing
[Farenheit]

The severe weather was too much for part of the Castle Ruin:

11 *Feb*   The wall and chimney of the Tapestry Chamber fell with a
fearful crash about one o'clock in the morning

Amateur building has its limitations, and the materials used, which
seem to be a mixture of clunch – the local soft limestone – and clay batts
– the local unbaked bricks – both porous, could easily become unstable
on a site prone to flooding. But the damage was repaired, and the Tapestry Chamber* lasted awhile longer.

And back went Page to Bedford, this time to assist with a performance at Barford, nearby. It was by 'a party of ladies and gentlemen' in
aid of a children's clothing club. Page took parts in two of three playlets.
It was reported afterwards that the 'mingled humour and pathos...were
admirably brought out' in *The Sheep in Wolf's Clothing*; and 'special
applause was earned' by many of the cast, including Mr Widnall as
Baron de Gortz in *The Victor Vanquished*. The local paper went on to say
that 'the stage and scenery were prepared and arranged in a most convenient and effective manner by the last named gentleman, to whose energy
and ingenuity the success of the evening was greatly due'.

The ingenious Mr Widnall had also been making a third model of
Grantchester Church, and this he took to Mrs H. Lapworth (Matilda,
née Stroud) in March. But a few days later 'Dear Lilly fainted away in
Church and frightened us all' (13 March, when the diary entry adds 'The
Czar of Russia murdered').

---

*The long upper room of the Castle Ruin, formerly used as SPW's photographic studio, was now
hung with tapestries which he had acquired in a sale.

A month after this episode all seems well: the three of them shared an excursion to Bourn with the Lumbys and Alice Greene; and visitors came as usual. 'Poor old Puck', a favourite cat (whose successor, Puck II was born in September), died aged seventeen. In June 'Lilly and Lally recd two pretty Satine dresses from Madame B.' – Mme Boquel being by now a close friend.

In June that year their nephew Tom Davis came to stay, introducing his friend, Miss Theobald. Their visit is commemorated in one of those photographs taken in the garden. Page's arrangement of this group conveys a good deal about his subjects. He himself is by now a bulky figure; Lilly and Lally sit on the grass, no longer with quite the ease of former days. With them are the two Greene sisters, Alice and Polly, in characteristic poses: Alice, a future headmistress, is consulting a book with her own former teacher, and Polly, well on the way to becoming the established artist Mary Greene, displays work in progress on her easel. With them are the visiting couple – Tom, dressed informally as for cycling; and Dolly Theobald a shy girl of seventeen. (Tom and Dolly stayed for twelve days. Once more the garden, the river walk, the boating worked their enchantment ... and in November 1884, the moment she reached the age of twenty-one, Dolly would become his wife.)

Tom Davis, Polly Greene, Dolly Theobold, Page Widnall,
(*seated on grass*) Alice Greene, Lally and Lilly

*

In the following month the diary records, not a succession of visitors but a startling new enterprise: 'Page & Lilly went to Willingham and Rampton to paint letterboxes with luminous paint'. Whose idea could that have been? Was it perhaps Lilly, who was so handy with a decorator's brush? Or was it the 'capital contriver' himself? After all, Page, from that moment in his boyhood when he had watched his father dispatch 193 letters on the first day of the Penny Post, had been fascinated by systems of communication.

Passers-by must have thought their activities a little odd. A couple of months later, travelling northwards and westwards on his own, Page may himself have attracted attention when conducting his genealogical research; for on his way to visit the young Giles family, he was to call at Ashby Folville and 'other places' (Wootten Wawen in Warwickshire particularly), taking photographs and plaster casts from the Smith Carington tombs. After that, another of his proposed experiments with phosphorescence entailed a diversion:

27 *Sept*   On my way from Nuneaton went to Nottingham to see Messrs
Jacoby about luminous lace which they had promised to try
but now say it is too much trouble

But in spite of that rejection, the postbox project continued:

20 *Oct*   Page & Lilly to Quy Bottisham Lode & Reach Slept at
Burwell wet day could not finish painting the letter box

8 *Nov*   Page & Lally to Wilbraham to paint letter box, the last.
Have painted them at Willingham, Rampton, Cottenham,
Impington, Madingley, Hardwick, Cherryhinton, Gt. Shelford,
Newton, Haslingfield, Ditton, Horningsea, Hadstock,
Pampisford, Bartlow, C. Camps, Streatly End, Quy, Bottisham,
Lode, Reach, Burwell, Swaffham Bulbeck and Little Wilbraham

One can only wonder whether the twenty-four villages were grateful for these attentions. Did the letterboxes, beaming in the darkness, frighten the horses? And why was this particular good wheeze not inflicted on Grantchester? Or was, perhaps, the small Victorian letterbox which is still set in the Old Vicarage garden wall itself once aglow too? The local newspapers make no mention of the enterprise.

And the really astonishing thing is to find that it was not just the product of a village eccentric's mind, but appears to have been a general obsession at the time. Gerald du Maurier, whose *Punch* drawings mocked

society's sillier fashions, was at
that very moment laughing at the
craze. (His 'Brown' family exem-
plified every current trend – Mrs
Cimabue Brown gushing over the
excesses of the Aesthetic Movement, and now the younger and
livelier Browns dancing and hold-
ing river parties after dark, all
themselves covered in luminous paint.) It must have soon passed away,
as such things do. But it cannot have been good for Lilly's health.

*

Winter was drawing on, and it was time for indoor diversions. A new
Shakespeare reading society was formed with the Lumbys at Merton
House, and took *As You Like It* as their first play.

There was concern about Lilly and Lally's sister, 'dear Annie'. Her
husband, T. A. Davis, had died at Malvern in September, and the widow
was not in good health. Page and Lilly fetched her from Colney Hatch
to stay with them at the Old Vicarage; and next February Page, assisted
by Haddow, took her to Peckham to be with young Tom.

Their niece Alice, happily married to Arthur Holme but childless,
was experiencing troubles similar to Lilly Widnall's; for she, too, needed
an operation in April for the removal of a tumour.

But Lilly, at present, was well, and busy decorating again: 'Lilly papered
the—with the stork paper'. As an aesthetic lady, she evidently favoured the
Japanese taste, even in the lavatory (for the '—' was a euphemism for *loo*).

In April 1882 they received two young visitors who arrived on a
strange vehicle: 'Charley Greene and Emeric Beamon arrived on a double tricycle and stayed for three days.' SPW, Photographer, must surely
have recorded this contraption to add to his collection of vehicles, but no
picture survives. (The Smith-Carington photo album does, however,
contain one of Bertie's elder son Francis, aged about six, perched on an
unwieldy machine with two huge wheels and one small one.)

Charley Greene was at this time seventeen. His father, after years of
semi-invalidism, had finally sought comfort in that island which in his
boyhood had seemed such a paradise. He went back to St Lucia, and
there died in 1881. Mrs Greene and her large family, with a declining
income, battled courageously on. Charley and his friend would have

found the thirty mile ride from Bedford moderately strenuous, and at least their tricycle was far safer than the lofty 'ordinary' bicycle of the time, the penny-farthing, or the bone-shaker. (Some idea of their conveyance and its attractions can be found in an article which appeared in the *Cambridge Review* of Nov 1884. *France Seen From a Double Tricycle* describes a tour taken by two young university men who were pleased with their machine, enjoying the companionship of riding side-by-side and its steady pace. Their luggage went ahead by train, and so they had the freedom to exchange greetings as they passed by or to linger in churches and cathedrals. While they appreciated the tourist sights, they themselves provided a spectacle which fascinated villagers and townspeople on their way. On their first day, in a picturesque little hill-town, a procession of the Host had broken away from its devotions to gawp at their arrival. Closer inspection prompted questions –the space between the seats with the brake-handle suggested 'Il y a de place pour Mademoiselle, n'est pas?' The tyres of rubber were a marvel; the machine was 'bien solide', 'ça coute cher?', 'c'est très difficile pour les jambes, c'est fatigant' were other frequent comments. The first 'safety' bicycle was to appear in 1885, and pneumatic tyres – at last – in 1888.)

*

There were changes in the village. On 5th July 1882 the Rev. William Martin, 'our dear Vicar for 32 years', died. Next day his sister-in-law, Miss Arabella Cowlard, tenant of Riversdale, died too. There was an emptying of the Vicarage, with a sale of furniture; and Mrs Martin went away to live in Bournemouth.

Page, that summer, spent some days in Bedford, where a bazaar was being held, together with tableaux of *Sleeping Beauty* and *Historical Portraits*. And he noted a remarkable occurrence:

> At Bedford went to see Mr Phillips at the County School he told us of a boy who the night before had in his sleep jumped from a window 17 feet without injury.

That September, Lilly went off for a short holiday in Derbyshire with Amy Lumby. Amy, in her early twenties, was the eldest of that family, a pleasant companion with whom to explore the country around Baslow, on the edge of the Peak District. Lally too was enjoying that friendship, for she at that time went on a rather shorter excursion with Dr Lumby and his wife to the village of Tadlow.

Once again Page set off on his pedigree research, going first to Nuneaton to take Car his model of Swaffham Church and then on to Leicester 'to look over Register transcripts to try and find marriage of Thos Smith & Powtell'. But his plans were cut short. 'Dear Lilly sprained her ankle badly in the woods at Chatsworth'; and so he soon travelled there to join her. His few days spent at Baslow must account for a small collection of Peak District photographs. It would seem that he was able to take a few walks around Eyam and Monsal Dale before escorting the limping Lilly and Amy Lumby home.

They were back in time for the induction of the new Vicar of Grantchester, the Rev. Edmund Godfray. And that same month, October 1882, Lally 'Saw the Comet. A splendid one such a long tail'.

*

Lally then made one of her journeys to visit members of her family, moving from one home to another. In those days of constant letter-writing she never lost touch with Richard's family; yet now, visiting first Nuneaton (11 days), Blea Beck, Malvern (6), and then St Cloud, Worcester (18), she was able to immerse herself thoroughly in their affairs.

First, at Nuneaton, she was visiting Amy and George Giles at their pleasant house (said to have associations with the novelist George Eliot). George was a solicitor, and the small family, with its two fair-haired children, Phyllis and Humphrey, must – should – have seemed very comfortably settled.

Lally's next call was at Blea Beck, to stay with Car and his wife Alicie, and to get to know little Enid, their first child. Car, although qualified, was not practising at the Bar. He had elected to take on his father's nursery business. But it was not to prosper indefinitely: the export of decorative trees and shrubs to the United States was halted by an embargo, and after some years the business collapsed. A more energetic man might have taken the enterprise in a more profitable direction; but Car seems never to have exerted himself very much except in his enthusiasm for field sports: he was an excellent shot, and at the outbreak of the First World War would volunteer at once for a sort of 'Dads' Army'. (He never quite lost his love for sailing craft, and even for a journey from London to Bristol preferred to travel by one of the ships regularly taking passengers around the south coast. The device he invented for launching lifeboats at sea was to be a minor success.) Alicie would have two more children, Michael and Arthur; but much of Car's time was spent among old friends in London.

Finally, Lally stayed with her brother at St Cloud, his and Patty's new home. Again there was plenty to talk about – all the family joys and worries. And in that autumn of 1882 there was a development to shock them all: news must have come through about Edward Palmer, who in August had died in the most dramatic way imaginable.

Palmer had undertaken a secret mission for the British Foreign Office, one for which he was uniquely qualified. Presenting himself again as 'Abdullah Effendi', in the robes of the desert, he travelled about Sinai making contact with the sheikhs to enlist their cooperation in order to secure the immunity of the Suez Canal from Arab attack. He had been provided with a quantity of gold coins for the purpose, and all at first seemed to be going well. But he and the military officers on this final mission were betrayed by

Prof. Edward Palmer.

their guide, who led them into an ambush. At the Wady Sudr the delegation were lined up above a precipice with a 60ft drop, and shot in the back. The remains were found later by an expedition and returned home for burial in the crypt of St Paul's Cathedral. There, a plaque honours the men and records their fate.

*

The Old Vicarage trio spent Christmas together, after which Page left the two sisters and took himself off to watch theatricals at Barford – *She Stoops to Conquer* and *Cut off with a Shilling*. Meanwhile, on the 29th December, 'Lilly and Lally <u>walked</u> into Cambridge!!'

Page must have stayed on with the Greenes to help them prepare for their next effort, which took place in the Assembly Rooms at Bedford. Eight members of the family were taking part in Tableaux Vivants in aid of church restoration funds. In the long programme (Price One Penny) for the twelve scenes from the popular *Waverley Novels*, Page's own contribution is indicated by pencil scribbles beside each scene: properties such as table, chair, inkstand, pens, lanthorn, greenery shrub, sacking, tent & pole, spear, stalactites, turret window and so on all seem to have been supplied by him. Had the family chaise made the journey, heavily laden? Or did he travel by train, relying on his famous 'ingenuity' to conjure up the necessary items after arrival?

In February he had a more serious errand. Following Edward Palmer's death there was concern about those two great-nieces Ethel and Maud, Laura's children. Page went up to London and, with Tom Davis, called at the Admiralty to procure financial help for them. Edward's widow would soon marry again, a Dr Donkin; and perhaps for Maud, the younger sister, the step-parents' home would seem an adequate substitute for her real parents. Besant's biography of their father says that 'the two little girls [were] sent to Germany, where they were comfortably and happily bestowed and well taught...' But their whole childhood, first with the loss of beloved, restless, ailing Laura; their father then besotted with a German bride; the birth of a half-brother; the disappearance of Edward on his secret mission and the late revelation of his grisly death – year after year had produced unsettling events in their lives. The effects would show later, especially with poor disturbed Ethel.

A month later an alarming event is noted: 'Explosion at the Local Gov. Board providential escape of Tom Davis'. Tom (perhaps a little shaken) and Dolly spent Easter at Grantchester, sharing with the trio 'A pleasant evening – the Lumbys, Alice Greene, Tom & Dolly – Writing games – a question and a word': typical cosy Victorian home-entertainment.

As time went on there were more and more deaths to record – of cousins (Alfred Robinson drowned, the Rev. Edward Robinson), and friends (Mrs Dixon, née Hawke, and Mr Lilley). And not least lamented, 'Poor Old Dapple found dead in the stable'. That was in January; and his replacement, Kitty, was bought for £12 in May.

*

Riversdale had been standing empty since the death of Miss Cowlard. Now, in the spring of 1883, new and very different tenants arrived. Dr Alexander Hill, a neurologist, was quite young but already a distinguished Fellow of Downing. He was outgoing and energetic, and he and his wife were soon on warm terms with their neighbours across the road. Their stay in Grantchester would end after five years, but during that time they were liked by everyone.

'Amy and George removed from Nuneaton to 7 Wellesley Terrace, Princes Park, Liverpool' in April. A month later, George Giles was visiting the Old Vicarage together with Arthur and Alice Holme. In addition there were Mr & Mrs Howgrave Graham, Mrs Graham senior, Jane and Percy Lapworth there for at least one day. They all, on top of 'Miss Adcock and ourselves made a house full'. That is all the diary reports – a large gathering of family and friends.

For the rest of the year little is set down except for visitors (the whole Howgrave Graham entourage for a while, and a Miss Hickey). But Lally herself made a visit, spending a few days only three miles away 'with Mr & Mrs Howard at Harvey Road'. George Howard had the previous year called to announce his engagement to a Miss Cureton.

Rev F. G. Howard

Now married, they were settled in one of the newly-built large houses in Harvey Road, between Hills Road and Fenner's. George had been made, first Chaplain to Non-Collegiate Students, and then Censor. The University had recently extended opportunities to students unattached to the endowed colleges. Although they lived in lodgings, hostels or the theological colleges, through membership of Fitzwilliam Hall,* as this institution was known, they were able to share the teaching and examination system of the rest of the university. To be made Censor (Head) was a challenge, and one for which George Howard was well suited. Nevertheless, an allegiance to the village of Grantchester was maintained still, for his name appears as Parish Clerk at about this time.

A final note for 1883 shows that Lally's most devoted pupil was hard at work, for in the autumn the trio received 'two little pictures from Polly Greene one was Newnham Mill Bedford the other the Fish Pier Whitby'.

*

*Changed to Fitzwilliam House in 1922; and finally established as Fitzwilliam College in 1966.

At the New Year 1884 Lally paid her last visit to East Lodge, Bedford. The Greenes had spent twelve years there, and by now all the children's education was complete. For Polly it had been a period with little of significance. Although the house and its garden, full of trees and with a millstream running by, were pleasant enough, 'I did not care for it' she was to declare. Her real feeling was for Grantchester and the countryside nearby.

That January Page and Lilly made a journey together to Liverpool, to see Alice and Amy's homes for themselves and to take a wonderful present for little Phyllis. The five-year-old was the first child to receive one of Uncle Page's doll's houses. For years he had been making scale models of actual buildings, full of details which might tempt little fingers. But they were of course strictly to be admired and not touched. Now he had made a house filled with people and gadgets which might actually be set to work by a child: the figures who moved, the pump which poured water. Such toys tend to become loved to pieces, but Phyllis saved hers for some sixty years. (A nephew made a careful restoration; but eventually, with a house removal, it was sent off to a saleroom.)

The Widnalls' visit, first to the two homes at Liverpool and then to Bertie at Whaley Bridge, prevented them from attending the funeral of their 'dear sister Annie Davis' who died at Peckham while they were away. Lally and their brother Richard joined Tom and Dolly there; and – a characteristically consolatory swerve in mood – the diary reports, 'Lally returned the same day and found little Puck had come back after being lost for a whole week'.

*

'My first morning with Jack and Katie at Dr Gaskell's' noted Lally in February. She was to teach the little brother and sister whose parents had come to Grove Cottage some five years earlier. Dr W.H. Gaskell was University Lecturer in Physiology and a Fellow of Trinity Hall; and, like the newer arrival, Dr Hill, he took an interest in the welfare of the village.

It must have been at about this time that a report was presented to the Chesterton Union Sanitary Authority by Grantchester Parochial Committee on the *Disposal of Sewage*. Under the chairmanship of Dr Alex Hill an impressive committee, composed of the new Vicar, Dr Gaskell, the Rev J. Rawson Lumby, the principal farmers, the miller and four other principal residents, had examined the problem very thoroughly. 'In Grantchester pure water is obtainable in unlimited quantity by means of artesian wells', they said. 'The difficulty is to keep it pure, since the greater part of the village is above the level to which water will rise without pumping…' There follow several pages of detailed argument, describing the geological strata and the various premises with cesspits which might contaminate nearby wells. It was an unpleasnt subject yet of great importance to the health of inhabitants and avoidance of river pollution. It concludes,

> The very objectionable condition of the ditch running by Mr Widnall's garden would appear to depend principally upon the overflow from the w.c. at Dr Hill's house. Arrangements have been made for substituting an earth closet for this w.c. …

And it vindicates Page's decision some years earlier to alter his own water closet to earth closet.

*

Another alteration took place in June that year: 'Page's work room turned into a bedroom'. The extra accommodation was used soon after, when Amy, with her two children and their nurse came to stay for a fortnight. After a month, on 28th July 1884, the diary records 'Amy's sad trouble, home broken up'. No further explanation of the 'sad trouble' is given, and no mention made of Amy Giles for the next three months.

*

It was the time for Page's customary summer recreations on the river. This year 'Page, Fred and Ben Greene went to Wicken Fen in a boat'. Fred Greene was a young man of twenty-two. After rather unprofitable years at Bedford School, he was now, by getting some training in farm work and learning languages on the continent, equipping himself for what would turn out to be a tough but successful business career as a coffee merchant in Brazil. His brother Ben was only fifteen at this time, and had been left slightly lame from childhood polio; but he, too, was going to overcome difficulties and would join in a farming enterprise in Canada.

Although it was a minor jaunt compared with Page's voyage with Car in his *Wild Duck*, their trip to Wicken Fen called for some stamina if they were to get there and back in one day, the distance being some thirteen miles in all, down the Cam and along the New River; so by the time they arrived at Adventurers' Fen there would indeed have been a sense of adventure.

It was a good way to approach this wild place. Taking their craft – Page's 'big boat' probably with a small mast and sail which could be lowered under bridges – down the familiar stream winding below Grantchester Meadows, they would negotiate their first lock beside the great mills which then stood near the Anchor Inn; then proceed along 'the Backs', that famous stretch beside the Cambridge colleges – Queens', King's, Clare, Trinity Hall, Trinity, St John's, Magdalene – with their gardens, pasture and huge trees. The sight of King's College Chapel looming above the riverbank was then just as it is now; but the river itself, narrow and undramatic, still to some extent fulfilled its agelong purpose as a thoroughfare for trade and carried a greater variety of traffic in those days. Some grain was still being brought up to the mills at Newnham by barges; coal and other goods (wicker baskets made from fen osiers and such) arrived at the wharf by Magdalene Bridge. Below the lock at Jesus Green there were steam-powered vessels with high funnels, dirty ones carrying 'gas water' from the gas works for conversion into fertilizer, and a few elegant ones carrying groups on pleasure trips. There were riverside inns where crossings could be made by ferry. For a long stretch their way would be featureless apart from such excitements. But then interest would sharpen as they entered the Wicken Fen area; for here, around them, was the last true fen, undrained and uncultivated. Today one can visit a section of the old fen, preserved by the National Trust, riding high above the flat fields around – a tidied-up version of what they must have seen in 1884. Even in 1910, Coneybeare could still describe its primitive state:

> …a morass hopelessly impenetrable, covered with a dense growth of tall reeds rising high above your head, through which you push your way blindly, to be constantly checked by some sluggish watercourse, too wide to jump, too shallow to swim, and impossible to wade, for the bottom is a fathomless stratum of soft turf and ooze giving no foothold…

yet a sanctuary for rare plants and insects, especially the swallowtail butterfly 'which flits about, dashing with bright touches of colour the weird and sombre beauty of the silent scene'. A wonderful place for SPW the naturalist.

*

Small items of domestic news follow. There was the harvest thanksgiving, when the 'Dossel cloth' was hung up (evidently an embroidered hanging behind the altar). Lally paid the dentist £9, and shortly afterwards Page spent £3.5.0. on new type. (Dentists' fees, as always, seemed exorbitant; but a new font for the printing press might, perhaps, eventually pay for itself.)

On 23rd October the trio went to *Patience*. The D'Oyly Carte Company had revived their original production (with 'costumes designed by the author') of three years before. Although the fifth of the Gilbert & Sullivan operas, it was for the Widnalls and Lally their first. Nothing could have delighted the three of them more – they, who for years had performed their own burlesques with such zest, might even recognize in themselves a touch of the 'sentimental passion of a vegetable fashion' displayed by the swooning ladies and earnest gentlemen on the stage. Page would have loved Gilbert's energetic wordplay; and Lally could appreciate Sullivan's musical wit.

*

During the three months which had followed 'Amy's sad trouble', her sympathetic aunts and uncle had planned how best to help her. First they took their ageing lodger-cum-teaching-assistant, Miss Adcock, to suitable accommodation in London. And then, on 31st October, 'Amy children and nurse came to live with us'. When, some sixty or seventy years later, Humphrey was asked what had happened to his father, he was evasive – 'Oh, he died when I was a baby'. But the truth is that George Giles lived until 1888, and that the family home at Liverpool had been 'broken up' by the seizure of his property. His habit of living beyond his means had gone too far and had culminated in bankruptcy*. A photo-

Humphrey and Phyllis Giles

graph of the two children taken in Liverpool expresses the sense of desolation which must have overwhelmed their family at this time.

But on both sides – the Gileses and the Smiths – their relatives were to be wonderfully supportive. (Amy's own loyalty to the Giles family would appear at her death, when her wish to be buried beside her late

---

*The Bankruptcy laws had been made more stringent the previous year. Fortunately for Amy, the Married Woman's Property Act of 1882 protected her own property and allowed independence for herself and the children.

husband was carried out.) Old Vicarage life carried on cheerfully, and over the following years Phyllis and Humphrey's early childhood was scarcely doleful. They would look back on their Grantchester life with some nostalgia.

*

Patience having been so enjoyable, Lally must have been delighted to be taken to another Savoy Opera three weeks later. 'Dined at Dr Gaskell's and then to see "Princess Ida" Helen Lumby with us' she wrote in her diary. Though rarely performed nowadays, *Princess Ida* was the latest in the series, and highly topical, since it concerns the admission of women to higher education. W. S. Gilbert had based his libretto this time on a poem by Tennyson which was sure to be familiar to his audience. *The Princess*, a strange 'medley' unlike anything the Poet Laureate had produced since, had been written in 1847 when there was a strong sense of Progress in the air – the scientific thrills of electric telegraph, railways, hot-air balloons, and all those inventions soon to be celebrated in the Great Exhibition. Tennyson was dissatisfied with the English universities' failure to recognize the beckoning intellectual challenge. Already, years earlier, he as an undergraduate at Trinity had protested that for all the grandeur of college traditions, '… your manner sorts / Not with this age'. So, in *The Princess*, he was proposing that dons, rather than confining themselves to the dry old disciplines, should address the new learning and examine the latest ideas on 'whatever is'. And in his fantasy he even suggested a breathtaking innovation: a severely feminine university, secluded in its Castle Adamant.

> Pretty were the sight
> If our old halls could change their sex, and flaunt
> With prudes for proctors, dowagers for deans,
> And sweet girl-graduates in their golden hair.

Gilbert, realizing that such a manifestation was almost upon them (for both Girton and Newnham Colleges were by now receiving students), took up Tennyson's poem and made a rather heavy comedy of it. His topical jokes included a song about Man's descent from the Ape:

> While Darwinian Man, though well-behaved,
> At best is only a monkey shaved!

Lally was well able to appreciate all this, for she had long been eager to attend what lectures were available to women on the fringe of Cambridge's academic life. Many of her friends were university men and their not-unintelligent wives, and Page's daily readings from the *Morning Post* kept their own household in touch with the debates of the day. They had even seen and heard T. H. Huxley, popularly caricatured as the 'ape-man', himself the previous summer, when he had delivered his Rede Lecture on 'The Origin of Life'. (And how pleased they would have been to know that his grandson, Sir Andrew Huxley, O. M., would in the following century make his home in the village.)

CHAPTER 21

Family events

———·—·———

TOWARDS THE END OF 1884, after their long engagement, Tom Davis and Dolly (Mary Theobald) were married. She had just passed her twenty-first birthday.

Page and Lilly spent Christmas on their own this year, while Lally accompanied Amy, with the children and nurse, to spend Christmas with Richard and Patty at St Cloud. There they were joined by Alice and Arthur, and enjoyed 'a pleasant family party'. The womenfolk later drove to Whittington and saw the new studio in which Patty's artist brother B.W. Leader worked. After three weeks Lally made a slow return journey, meeting Page at Oxford and going with him to Salisbury, where they joined his cousin Mrs Clark and her companion Miss Kelsey. There, they 'went to Wilton and saw the carpet manufactory and Wilton House the seat of the Earl of Pembroke'. They wandered about the city, seeing its museum and noting 'a curious fresco at St Thomas's Church Salisbury subject the Last Judgment'. Then they stopped in London to see Tom and Dolly (and also Miss Adcock, frail and failing) before getting home.

An event was noted on 4th February, 1885 – small but significant: 'Lally's Botany book bought'. This was *Bentham's Hand Book*, with its illustrated Companion Book giving the outlines of 1306 flowers, ferns and grasses. Lally, who had always been good with watercolours, decided to colour in each of these illustrations when she had herself actually seen a specimen of each plant. Humphrey Giles, writing in old age, would recall how 'every member of the family and friends were always looking out for "a flower for Aunt Lally's Book"' and how 'one of the Great Days in my life [was] when in 1887 I found No.0006 the Man Orchid at Haslingfield!' The precious book was rebound by Uncle Page, who 'carved a v. good wooden exterior for it'. Humphrey, writing in 1962, wondered about the volume's current value:

> In many cases she wrote (alongside the illustration) the date and place found, and the common name for the flower. There is really no blemish in the whole Book which is perfectly clean. And I suppose it really must be unique...

With the young Gileses still away, Lilly embarked on some home decorating, first papering the passage 'with the sunflower paper' (likely to be a William Morris design), and then 'papering the Drawing room staining the beams &c'. At last, on 10th April, when an overmantel had been added to the drawingroom fireplace, Amy and her family were welcomed back.

The summer began much as usual. Their old friend Jane Lapworth came, and the Widnalls took her with them to Linton, where they 'bought some chicks at the little mill'. Some days later they all 'went to the boatrace' – which must have been the 'Bumps', the May Races which take place on the lower stretch of the Cam. There, the river being narrow, it is only possible for college 'eights' to race each other in line, winning a higher place by colliding with the boat ahead. For those not familiar, this sounds destructive; but there are rules – the coxswain of the boat in front raises his hand the moment he senses that he has been bumped, and so accidents are few. (There were in 1885 two 'divisions', with fifteen crews rowing in each. Jesus College came Head of the River, with its most celebrated oarsman, Steve Fairbairn, in the boat. Fairbairn, an Australian, was to dominate the college's boat club as coach until his death in 1938.) For our group of spectators the event would have offered many delights. There was the suspense of the chase, as one crew closed on another; a delicious tea eaten on the river bank or perhaps on a launch during the interval between Divisions; and the brilliant fluttering of ladies in summer dresses and men with boaters and college blazers.

Then they had a crowd of visitors, Car's wife and little daughter Enid ('quaintly dressed in Kate Greenaway style'), and his in-laws, the Conders. The drawingroom was now even more elegant, with the addition of 'the China set out in the niches'. Car Smith-Carington was himself at this time travelling in the U.S.A. He stayed in Philadelphia, and also made contact with people named Carrington at Richmond, Virginia, whose coat of arms made clear their common ancestry. This branch of the family had settled in Barbados in the sixteenth century – news to add interest to that complex pedigree which his father Richard, with Page's help, was drawing up. (Car would be off westwards again the following year, to Salt Lake City, Yosemite and Yellowstone.)

More visitors came. But this summer, amid the normal busyness, it became clear that Lilly was not at all well; and on 21st July 'Lilly went to consult Dr Bradbury'.

The usual restorative was tried. On 2nd September 'Page & Lilly went to Worthing to see Mrs Clark & Miss Kelsey'. They returned on the 14th, 'Lilly better but far from well'. Three days later 'Page, Lilly & Lally went to tea at H. Ellis's Lilly's last visit out'.

Lilly must already have been losing weight, for by the 24th she weighed 6st 7lb. (Page had also been on the scales: a solid 14st 9lb.) The diary notes that next day 'Haddow bought "Bessie" at the fair 2 years old'; but thereafter each entry records Lilly's decline, and the few contacts with old friends.

Mrs Martin, widow of the former Vicar, called while visiting from Bournemouth. On 17th October 'Page Lilly & Lally drove into Cambridge dear Lilly's last time, to have coffee with Madme B'. And on 6th November Lilly

	…went to see Dr Bradbury he found a lump in her stomach
17 *Nov*	Letter from Dr Bradbury saying dear Lilly had cancer
26 *Nov*	Jane Lapworth came for the day to see dear Lilly for the last time
8 *Dec*	Lilly weighed 5st 12lb
13 *Dec*	Dr Sturges came to see dear Lilly there is no hope
15 *Dec*	Dear Lilly asked what Dr Sturges said and when told bore it very bravely and went out the same day in a Bath chair
23 *Dec*	Mr Godfray came and administered Holy Communion to dear Lilly
1886	
1 *Jan*	M. & Madame Boquel came to see Lilly who had not expected to see this new year's day
2 *Jan*	Dear Lilly died this morning almost her last words were "I am very happy I've had a happy life, love to all"
7 *Jan*	Dear Lilly buried Page, Lally, Car, Amy, Tom Davis, H. Ellis, Dr & Mrs Lumby, Amy L., Dr & Mrs Hill, Anne & Mary Nimmo, and our 2 servants Julia Cox & Amy Docwra followed

CHAPTER 22

Uncle Page & Aunt Lally

—•-•-•—

Now PAGE AND LALLY had to resume their lives, with Lally in charge of the housekeeping. The two companions had already shared more than thirty years, and they both had plenty still to do.

Uncle Page's Book maintains a bleak silence until March, when Mrs Conder came to collect the doll's house which Page had made for Enid's fourth birthday.

There were visitors, two spinster ladies, for Easter. Then in mid-June 'Our 2 servants Julia & Amy left'. Was the reason for their departure perhaps because of the need for economy? Or had they been intending to leave but hanging on out of loyalty to Lilly? Her illness must have entailed extra expense, with a resident nurse (a pleasant-looking woman, photographed by Page) and doctors' and funeral fees. When Humphrey set down some recollections in his old age, he described the burly genial figure of his uncle, in frock-coat and flat parsonical hat ('A wonderful old chap. His Christian name was PAGE and nearly everyone called him "Uncle Page"'). Aunt Lally, herself by this time beginning to grow a little stout, was still taking pupils. But to conjure up a little extra money at this time, Uncle Page sold some pieces of land and toyed with far-fetched schemes, such as the marketing of bottled water. His artesian well, which had been drilled so deep that it supplied the fountain by its own natural force, certainly produced water in abundance … but Humphrey doubted its health-giving properties, since it tasted, he said, of rotten eggs; and nothing came of the idea. Hopes of patenting more of Page's inventions were dashed, too. Modest farming activities were left in the hands of Haddow, who on 4th July 'brought home a carriage he had bought at a sale at Willingham Vicarage £7.10.0'.

Lally's canary died, thirteen years old. Other old friends were dying, more and more. But as summer wore on one has the impression of a return of energy. At the end of August they took a short holiday at Worthing and stayed awhile in London on the way back.

In September Lally received little Mab Gaskell as a pupil, and noted that her brother had now moved on to the Perse School. Phyllis and

Humphrey Giles were still at the Old Vicarage, and in November their mother went to London to collect a German nurse, Martha Eddelbüttel, for them. (Increasingly, until brought to an abrupt end by the Kaiser, the English view of German culture was favourable, and the system of education in that country particularly admired.)

When it came to Christmas this year, Page (who had spent his sixtieth-birthday-Christmas watching the remorseless progress of his wife's illness) and Lally dined at Riversdale, with Dr Hill's family.

*

Whether the Hill family included a boy of about 8–12 years old or not, there were certainly some boys of that age who received a treat that year. Bertie's two eldest, Francis (Frank), nine, and Neville, eight, would qualify, especially as Neville's birthday was on Christmas Eve; and perhaps even Humphrey, at six, could enjoy what Uncle Page had produced. This was a schoolboy story.

How Lord Engledown kept Christmas in his Castle (1886) must surely have been intended as a Christmas present. It seems to have been quite a private production, with few copies printed; for the pages are cut and folded rather roughly, and held together with glue. It is a yarn about the usual schoolboy fantasy of getting away from the grown-ups and escaping to a place of romance. In it a boy called Engledown is the ringleader, enticing a group of schoolfriends to spend Christmas with him in a secret hideaway, a ruined castle tower. It was the stuff of which Page's dreams had always been made. The 'child-man' of Polly Greene's poem dwelt, or at least a part of him dwelt, in the world of medieval castles and knights in armour: it all came out in his own Castle Ruin and its carvings, in the scenery and costumes for theatricals, the tale of *The Miller's Daughter*, and the recent task of tracking down noble lineage.

Now he tells how the schoolboys arrange their 'jolly lark' with schoolboy discipline – the solemn swearing, on a Latin dictionary, of an oath of secrecy and the adoption of titles and ranks. 'Lord' Engledown, whose father farms the land close to the castle ruin, is in command. Their plan succeeds: a letter is left to reassure the parents, and the boys disappear into the castle's underground vault. There they find ancient swords and pikes, and his lordship struts about in an old gown and embroidered cap. Cooking their stolen provisions is not at first very successful, but they eventually manage a pretty good Christmas feast (after first reading Morning Service in the ruined chapel). By next morning there is no food left, and Engledown must go down the hill and face his parents. But in their underground chamber the boys had made efforts to prise open an ancient chest; and at last Engledown has gouged a hole in its side large enough for him to spy parchments and to draw out one of the documents. This, of course, turns out to be an ancient Will, proving father Engledown's entitlement to the castle and estates.

One source for the setting of all this nonsense may have been nearby. The ruined castle on a chalk hill resembles the spectacular 18th century folly at Wimpole Hall, only a few miles from Grantchester. And Page's habitual dream-world accorded  with the collective dream-world of his period; for Queen Victoria and Prince Albert had themselves dressed as fairytale royalty for fancy-dress balls, and Academy paintings of the time share this fantasy medievalism. Mrs Julia Margaret Cameron harked back to this imagined realm in her photographs; and even the artist who had produced the great series of stained-glass windows for Trinity College Chapel and those in the south aisle of Grantchester Church, Henry Holliday, posed for a photograph wearing chain-mail (and looking very, very Victorian).

Those Victorians had an intense interest in antiquity: in excavations, in the recovery of ancient documents, and in making sense of history by the retelling of legends. It combined with that passion for the 'picturesque' which so often included gothic ruins (Gothic good, Classical bad: the chapel of King's College was praised, while its Fellows' Building was declared 'hideous'). Some fine illustrated books were published, and it is very likely that SPW had the volumes of *Old England*, 'A Pictorial Museum of National Antiquities' (1844) which combine scholarly details of ancient buildings with more fanciful reconstructions of exciting moments in real or legendary history. Volumes such as these he would have found engrossing, and from them gained a valuable framework for an appreciation of architectural styles and period costumes. Those pictures of kings and queens were, however, necessarily drawn from imagination, and the artists who depicted successive kings gave them all much the same appearance, their bearded faces staring from beneath gold crowns. The ladies have an even more uniform look, their heavy cheeks and small pursed mouths reminding one of Queen Victoria herself; and the nobility are of course heroic figures clad in armour or velvet and ermine cloaks. It is these images, just like those by the popular painter and engraver Daniel Maclise, which had become set in the Victorian imagination. Page had adopted figures such as these for his illustrations to *The Miller's Daughter*; he carved the heads of these kings and queens for the archways of his Ruin; and another pair, in wood, large and mysterious, were left in the Ruin after his death.

*

For the New Year, 1887, a Minstrel Entertainment was put on in the village schoolroom 'by the six Miss Nimmos and friends'. The programme, giving their stage names as 'Topsy', 'Sukey', 'Pompey' and the like, suggests a possible cast of 'darkies' singing to banjoes. The following month an audience gathered again to hear Page Widnall talk on the History of Grantchester.

The family was enlarged by the birth of another little great-nephew, Car's son Michael, that February. And Bertie, heir-apparent to the Manorship of Ashby Folville and the family's recovered glory, was made a Director of Whitworth Co.

It seems that Mrs Conder had been so pleased with the doll's house Page had made for her grandchild Enid that she wanted one for herself. This time he produced something less like a toy: in March 'Amy took the Doll's House (the Elizabethan Mansion) to Mrs Conder'. There were to be four – possibly as many as seven – doll's houses created over the years, each with its own tiny figures and mechanical gadgets. One, kept in the Castle Ruin, was

> ... a wonderful delight to us children – and full of mechanical devices.
> If you rang the bell – a maid opened the door and in one bedroom a little
> lady was in bed and was later found very discreetly and demurely sitting
> in her bath!   [Remembered by Mrs Morland (née Pearce, of Cedar Lodge)]

and another is described by Polly Greene:

> ...The front door had a bell, a lock and a real little key. In the drawing
> room was a piano with a lady sitting at it. The piano could play two tunes
> – 'Home sweet home' and 'Auld langsyne'. The dining room and kitchen
> had everything that a dining room and kitchen should have. A real fire
> could be lit in the kitchen range and out of the spout of the pump could
> be pumped real water.

*

Life at the Old Vicarage, for all the delights it offered to eight-year-old Phyllis and six-year-old Humphrey, had its drawbacks. Down there by the river, the damp that pervaded the place in winter encouraged colds and coughs. On 22nd April, Page and Lally 'heard from Amy saying her doctor Mr Whitehead declares she must leave us as the children require bracing sea air'. This may have come as a shock and a disappointment to her aunt and uncle, but the decision was a wise one, and perhaps even a relief to the elderly pair. For the little Giles family would reappear, joyfully, for many future visits.

It was three months before they actually left, and in the meantime there were summer diversions. In May Week, Amy was able to go with Page and Lally to Christ's College Private Theatricals, invited by Mr Paul England. The show was *The Mikado*, which matched their own sense of fun perfectly.

By 20th June 1887 Queen Victoria had been on the throne for fifty years; and in London her Golden Jubilee was celebrated next day with a great Thanksgiving Service in Westminster Abbey, attended by more than fifty Royal and Serene Highnesses (for Her Majesty, a supreme family gathering), and by later festivities in Hyde Park. In Cambridge, the Mayor and Corporation processed to a service in Great St Mary's Church, which was followed by sports on Midsummer Common and a Promenade Concert and Fireworks on Parker's Piece.

Grantchester marked the occasion in its own way. It held a Thanksgiving Service on the great day, with the choir processing from the school to the church. Then, never-to-be-forgotten, came the festivities three days later when four hundred parishioners assembled for a great meal in the barn at Lacies, with the Trumpington Brass Band playing throughout. The Queen's health was proposed and 'responded to most heartily, cheer after cheer ringing through the barn'; and then, after the National Anthem, everyone trooped down to the meadows for sports. Dr Gaskell had played a great part in organizing the sports and had set a Greasy Bowsprit across the river. This was

> a great success, one after another trying in vain to reach the flag at the other end. Nearly 20 fell into the river. A tub race should have followed this, but one of the tubs could not be made to keep its equilibrium, so a swimming race had to take its place ...

(One of the elderly Humphrey's treasures would be the 'Jubilee photo of 1887 ... won at the Grantchester Sports "for boys under 8"'.)

The Grantchester & Trumpington Flower Show a day or two later gave an opportunity for more festivities: the river and boats were illuminated all night, and Dr Hill invited his neighbours in to supper at Riversdale, where the garden was filled with fairy lights.

The Giles family left next day to settle into a new stage in their lives. Arrangements had been carefully discussed beforehand. First, Miss G. Giles (from their father's family) had visited the Old Vicarage for a week, then a Miss Bindloss, who seems likely to have been a governess anxious to learn about the children's progress from Lally before starting her own work. Now at their new home, on the Wirral peninsula close to Liverpool, there were both bracing sea air and fine views. Even more important was the presence nearby of Alice and her husband Arthur Holme. He, retired from the Army but still active as an engineer, was to provide valuable support as the children's guardian.

*

As soon as Amy left, Page and Lally gave themselves a holiday. Page took his camera, by now a less cumbersome piece of equipment than in the early days. A faint photographic record of this holiday survives; but it really is faint, just a few faded prints in a tattered album. Three weeks were spent on the Norfolk coast at Overstrand, close to Cromer. At the end, on 23rd August, they spent a day seeing Wroxham Broad. That is all the terse diary entries tell us; but from pictures of Potter Heigham and Horning Ferry and sailing craft on the Broads we can see that Page was attracted still by those subjects – the ancient buildings and shipping – which he had photographed in Dorset twenty-five years before. Now, though, the late-Victorian holidaymakers in his pictures were wearing comfortable boating gear rather than the dark frock coats and top hats of yore. (This very summer an article in the *Cambridge Review* commented on the tendency to informality in hats, the 'stovepipe' having given way to the 'billycock', and now even to the more comfortable cap.)

Photography had become easier with the use of dry plates which could be processed at home, but it was still a demanding craft; and one of

those faint Norfolk images has a self-critical note on the back, 'much over exposed'. In that same album are scenes taken on the Cam, showing the Backs, Old Chesterton and Fen Ditton.

*

Old friendships, and the cultivation of new ones, continued. There were visitors, among them young Edward Howard, son of George Howard's elder brother Charles, who had arrived from New Zealand. Lally and a Miss Jones went together to see *Ruddigore*; and the intellectual Miss Hickey 'came to see the Greek play'.

It was the Gaskell family who invited them for Christmas dinner this year. And, as so often before, they went away for the turn of the year. This time it was to stay with Page's cousin Mrs Elizabeth Clark at Bishop's Stortford. While there, they went one day with Miss Kelsey to see 'Miss Miller's pictures', and another to be shown around the church, where there was a good deal of medieval carving to be admired.

Another treat for Lally was noted in February – 'Kind Mrs Hill sent Elsie and me to hear Mr Ap Thomas the Welsh Harper'. Lally would take good care of small Elsie, and would delight in the renowned composer-performer's melodies on his harp. In May she and the less musical Page went together to see *Pinafore* in Cambridge, another rumbustious Savoy Opera to add to their tally.

When the diary notes, on 16th April, that 'Helen Lumby went to Addenbrookes Hospital to learn nursing' it was a sign of the times. Brainy young ladies had by now, thanks to Emily Davies, Henry Sidgwick and Anne Jemima Clough, earned the right to sit the Cambridge Tripos exams (though only to be rewarded with a certificate, not a degree); and it had also become possible, thanks to Florence Nightingale, for the daughter of a Professor of Divinity to train as a nurse. Helen was probably a 'paying probationer', provided with a great deal more comfort and free time than the poorer probationers and with much brighter prospects of promotion; for there was a cruel class distinction in the training of hospital nurses at that time. Still, although her family were regarded by some as intellectual snobs, perhaps they understood that nursing demanded high intelligence as well as dedication if it was to become a proper profession.

*

In early summer 1888 they visited Amy at Hoylake, and while there the ladies – Lally, Amy and Miss Bindloss – went off to Liverpool 'to see Mad. Marie Rose in "Marriage of Figaro"', an opera rarely performed in those days. Their three-week stay was completed with a visit to Alice and Arthur Holme.

Back in Cambridge it was May Week again. 'Lally went with Mrs Hill &c to the University Concert (Golden Legend) then to the Boat race with the Gaskells and finally to the concert at Queens.'

It was wonderful to have these opportunities to share in some of the university treats. And now another friend, Mr Paul England, who the previous year had invited them to the performance of *The Mikado* at Christ's, called at the Old Vicarage for a purpose which must have thrilled the two companions. He had moved from college to a post in the Department of Printed Books at the British Museum, and took from them copies of two books, *The Miller's Daughter (The Legend of the Granta)* and *Aunt Lally's Poetry Book*, to be placed in the library there. (After his few years at the British Museum, Paul England went on to make better use of his talents, musical and literary, in Germany, where he both sang and produced translations into English of musical texts – of Wagner, Berlioz and Bach cantatas.)

Aunt Lally's Poetry Book is not mentioned elsewhere in the diary, but must have been recently compiled, and was printed by Page as another octavo volume, matching his earlier ones in appearance. The rare surviving copies of this anthology show all the signs of having been well loved. Evidently those children taught by Lally had been introduced to poetry of every kind – from the usual Victorian children's fare of sentimental piety to far stronger stuff: passages from Chaucer and Shakespeare (John O'Gaunt's patriotic speech from *Richard II*) and the rousing *Battle of Semprach* written by Alice Greene, among others. The selection is original, encouraging a sense of history as well as an appreciation of different forms of poetry.

*

On 16th June they heard that the Hills would soon be leaving Riversdale, but for the very best of reasons. Dr Alex Hill had been elected Master of Downing College, and so the family would move into its grand Lodge. In due course he would become University Vice-Chancellor. For all his undoubted distinction as neurologist and administrator, he was never to lose the common touch, and the energetic contribution he had made to Grantchester life was recognized by a farewell presentation later that summer.

The village's other medical don, Dr Gaskell of Grove Lodge, and his wife, were still close by, and among that summer's diversions was a 'delightful excursion' with the whole Gaskell family. The children, Jack, Katy and Mab, were all pupils of Lally's; and like others, they found it easy to love a teacher who was herself so tiny and so childlike in her enthusiasm.

On 1st August 'Page and Lally went to the marriage of Florence Greene and Mr Phillips'. Florence was the only one of the Greene daughters to marry: she and her husband would go out to British Columbia to assist her younger brother Ben with a farm there – an enterprise which evidently failed to thrive, for they all later returned to England.

Presently some days were spent in London, where as usual contacts were renewed: dinner with the Howgrave Grahams, a stay with Tom and Dolly ('went to see "Niagara" then to the Grand Hotel to see Richd & Patty then to the Academy'), after which Lally accompanied Mrs Gaskell to Hindhead for a further few days.

Next month they were receiving friends at home, Mr & Mrs Wagenrieder (Dolly's parents) and Polly Greene; and then in addition, Amy and the children, with Martha. Clearly it was time for more help to be found with Lally's housekeeping. So on 11th September they 'drove to Duxford in search of a servant and engaged Mary Stigwood she came on the 15th' (and was with them still at the time of the census three years later).

The Old Vicarage ménage had always been fairly modest. Visitors, warmly welcomed, would have found no pretensions to anything beyond simple homely comfort. The servants are mentioned by name in the diary, given as much prominence as the arrival of new pupils or kittens or professors or the death of a canary. Their presence was certainly needed, for there was endless work to be done – the lighting and fuelling of stoves, fires and lamps, the laundering and cleaning and cooking, all with primitive implements. Decent board and lodging was provided, but probably not more than £20 a year in wages. In some houses discipline might be harsh; but the Old Vicarage, especially in the days when there were so many young people about, must have been more fun than most.

The labour of preparing a meal became even more difficult than usual on 6th November 1888. The Misses Howard came, but since

> we could have no fire in the kitchen as the chimney was being repaired, we cooked a beefsteak pudding in the Tapestry room

Not every Victorian household would have shown such good-humoured resourcefulness! They had crossed the garden to the Castle Ruin and mounted its narrow winding staircase to find themselves in

> ...a long, well proportioned room hung with old tapestry. The mantelpiece was an ancient carved oak one. Chippendale chairs stood round the walls. Mr Widnall had bought the tapestry, chairs and mantelpiece for a pound or two. They were regarded as old fashioned rubbish.*

So they cooked, and probably ate, their improvised meal in splendid surroundings.

*Polly Greene

The tapestries showed five biblical scenes: Isaac & Jacob, Esau hunting, Jacob's Dream, Jacob meeting Rachel, and Jacob wrestling with the angel. As good churchgoers the diners would have had no difficulty in identifying these scenes – or, indeed, in empathizing with the characters. Years later, after Page's death, Lally wrote a detailed description of each picture. In the first is

> … poor old Isaac sitting up on a couch overhung with shaded blue drapery which is decorated with scollops and fringe. Jacob, apparently not fully grown up, timidly presents a dish with what looks like a scrag of mutton, urged on by his Mother

At the end of the five descriptions she commented: 'All the houses look like Italian Villas'.

A few days after this the village had an entertainment in the Schoolroom unlike any before: it was 'Mr Brown a liberated slave negro songs &c'. People in the village must have known about the freeing of slaves in America, read *Uncle Tom's Cabin*, sung 'Mine eyes have seen the glory', seen pictures of 'darkies' with their 'piccaninies' toiling in the cotton-fields. But how many, in 1888, had actually seen a black man? It must have been an enthralling evening.

*

Towards the end of the year, on 21st December, Page and Lally travelled over to Worcester to St Cloud, Richard's home. Richard Smith-Carington had become a greatly respected figure. There is an air of genial self-assurance in photographs of him at this time: his marriage to Patty Leader-Williams, and the children and grandchildren of his first marriage, none living too far away, were all a source of contentment. On Christmas Day itself the visitors 'went with Richd & Patty to dine with Mr Leader at Whittington lots of presents for the children we too were not forgotten'. A few days later they went to lunch with Car and Alicie at Southbury House, Malvern, where they met Mr & Mrs Conder

and Ned (Alicie's brother), and 'little Enid quaintly dressed played and sang to her guitar'. Still at St Cloud, Page noted on 7th January, 'The wonderful Hoar Frost which began on the 3rd has continued increasing in beauty and this day the most beautiful of all'. Finally, on the 9th, 'Page and Lally left St Cloud went with Richd in his Carriage to Malvern he met Mr & Mrs Hanbury at the station there and took them back with him we stayed with Car at Southbury House'.

It had been a Christmas filled with delights: the great day with Patty's admired artist-brother, sparkling seasonal weather, and reunions with both Smith and Hanbury relations. That enchanting child, little Enid, would continue to charm although not with her music. When she was a little older a local church organist, newly-married and impecunious, was engaged to give her piano lessons. One day Alicie could not resist peeping round the door to see how things were going. There was Enid labouring at the piano; and there was her teacher, Mr Edward Elgar, with head bowed and hands clapped over both ears.

*

'A pleasant evening, had tea with Mr Ashworth in his rooms at Christ's Col.' The bare diary entry, for 19th January 1889, tells nothing more; yet this particular young man was to become an engineer, building railways in S. America, S. Africa and Siberia. There must surely have been talk, over their tea, about the Smith-Carington family's own connections with some notable engineering enterprises – such as the work of Amy's father-in-law George Giles, Alice's husband Arthur Holme, Richard's in-law relatives the Leader-Williamses, and with Bertie's great precision engineering firm, Whitworths.

The next entry, 'Mrs Clark and Miss Kelsey came' (6th Feb.), is an intriguing one, followed as it is by 'Bought afternoon tea set for Miss Kelsey as a wedding present' (9th) and 'Miss Kelsey married to Mr Beard Bish Stortford' (16th).

What later became of Mr Beard is never mentioned in the diary; but after a year or so Mrs Clark would once more be regularly accompanied by Mrs Beard alone.

Mrs Clark was by now in her late seventies, and must herself have been widowed some time before, for there is no mention of Mr Clark* in

---

*Two mystifying photographs in Page's family album, of a man and a woman, both aged about 30, bear such a strong resemblance to SPW himself that they might well be a son and daughter of Elizabeth Clark. Might they live at Worthing? The studio portraits were taken at Hastings.

these years when the cousins frequently met. Miss Kelsey may earlier have assisted Lally with her pupils for a while before joining Mrs Clark. And there may, with her marriage, have come an additional relationship between those female companions and the Old Vicarage pair. Could Mr Beard have been a remote cousin of Lilly and Lally? It is possible, for a cousin of their mother's had married a Mr Jeremiah Beard of Bishop's Stortford. In one of the more tattered albums a series of photographs seems to portray the extended family of Beards. The elderly father who looks gentle and distinguished could well be related to Lally. One young man with a lush moustache is elsewhere shown as a champion skater; another poses, all arrogance, with his enormous bicycle; a lad of about 13 scowls at the camera; a young woman in a shawl darts behind a tree and so appears in the picture as a ghostly blur... There are photographs of the group taken (perhaps during that visit to Bishop's Stortford the year before) in the wintry garden, in which one of the ladies shows that she has had quite enough of standing about in the cold; and in another Miss Kelsey and her 'intended', probably on the day of their engagement, stand shyly together and are labelled 'The Bill-doves'. Finally, there is the wedding group.

*

Edward Palmer's widow was now married to a Dr Donkin and living in Harley Street. For her stepchildren Ethel and Maud – Ethel especially – attachment to the Donkin family was uneasy.

While Tom and Dolly were visiting Grantchester that year, a diary entry, 30th April 1889, announces: 'Letter from Mr Besant saying the children might come and visit us', followed on 2nd May by a triumphant 'Ethel and Maud Palmer came to see us!!' And at last, thanks to the intercession of Walter Besant, the Old Vicarage could welcome these children again. As much as possible was done for them

> 4 *May* Took Ethel & Maud P. to see Mrs Bensley, Mrs Cowell, and
> Madm Boquel. To the Fitzwilliam Mus. And St John's Col.
> to see their Father's Portrait We found Dolly and little
> Harold at home when we returned
> 6 *May* Took Ethel & Maud for a long drive they and Dolly returned
> to London the same evening

Three generations of family; old friends; a portrait of their father in ori-ental robes given an honourable place in his college hall – their reception on those few days, if rather overwhelming, must have conveyed the warmth of feeling for them.

CHAPTER 23

More Books

1889 WAS ALSO the year when two more of Page's books came out. Only one is mentioned in the diary, and that is *Reminiscences of Trumpington Fifty Years Ago*, which he finished printing on 1st August. This little publication (25 pages) is bound with two staples and enclosed in a cover of pink embossed paper. He probably printed 200 or so, for it sold 'Price sixpence. May be obtained at the Post Office Trumpington. Or post free from the Author'. It includes one lithograph illustration, his drawing from memory of the old Blacksmith's Shop (a little thatched building with the village stocks alongside) which had been demolished in about 1855.

Some of the contents of this booklet have been quoted earlier, for in going back fifty years Page recalled his time at Mr Cumming's school, the place where his sense of independence and love of experiment had been encouraged. It is here, too, that he described the traffic which regularly passed along the main road in those days, and his memory of driving with his father to one of the ancient London inns with galleries above its stableyard. He talked of the roads and trackways, with characteristic speculation about a Roman road and Roman fort. For him, even his own reminiscences carried the romance of history.

*

A larger undertaking was his second novel, of 195 pages. It looks as though he had real hopes of this as a money-spinner, for it has a dust-jacket advertising it as

A NOVELTY !!

A MYSTERY OF SIXTY CENTURIES

THIS BOOK (with the exception of the binding)
IS THE WORK OF ONE PAIR OF HANDS,
BEING WRITTEN, PRINTED, ILLUSTRATED,
AND PUBLISHED, BY AN AMATEUR.

PRICE 2/6 net

The actual binding, surely by Grays, matches his other two octavo volumes, *The Miller's Daughter* and the *History of Grantchester*. His illustrations are again done in lithograph – except for the frontispiece, 'The Dragon's Head', which is meant to have a grisly realism. To achieve this, Page actually made a 'dragon's head' of *papier maché* laid on a light framework, with shiny large eyes and spiky teeth embedded; and then photographed this trophy. Afterwards it was kept beside the steep staircase of the Castle Ruin, a thrill to children who clambered up in the dim light.

The story, this time, was science fiction, plunging back into prehistory. It is of a 'Lost World' which predates Conan Doyle by some twenty years and displays yet more byways of SPW's fertile mind.

The *Cambridge Chronicle* gave it a short review (13 Sept '89), commenting first on the extraordinary labour of its production. Then:

> For the story we may say without giving us the terrible conceptions of the interior of Africa, in which Rider Haggard indulges, Mr Widnall has concocted a stirring tale, full of adventure, mishap and strange encounter, in which any boy would revel, and he has also skilfully introduced some account of the phenomena of Nature, and the triumph of science. The second title of the book, *A Modern St George and the Dragon*, forms some key to the *Mystery of Sixty Centuries*. We feel as disappointed as Max at Jack's discovery that the monster they had met with "was not a dragon at all, but Pterodactyle, saurian reptile, supposed to have been extinct for thousands of years". The mode of warfare too – dynamite – was somewhat novel: scarcely chivalrous enough for the days of St George°.

The story concerns two young men, Maxwell George and Jack Engledown – already encountered in the short Christmas story – who decide to venture together into darkest Africa in search of elephants to shoot for ivory. (Although this aspect of a late-Victorian story may be abhorrent to late-Elizabethan society, its outlook on the people of various tribes is remarkably humane.) This time the dream-world of Page Widnall pours out new themes recognisable from his more recent preoccupations. He, like so many about him, had been reading of the gradual penetration of Africa by white explorers – Stanley's dispatches and his *Through the Dark Continent*, and the earlier accounts of Burton and Grant, besides his vivid memory of Livingstone himself lecturing in Cambridge. A tumult of ideas garnered through a lifetime of self-education are stirred into this confection, his *Modern St George & the Dragon*.

Max, who recounts the story, has the family name George (derived, as is proved by genealogical research, from St George); and so in the long preamble to the great adventure tale, we hear how as a child he

> ...used to engage in mimic warfare with a toy spear, and after a terrific combat with a huge Dragon (the part of Dragon being kindly taken by Nero, our black Newfoundland dog) and having slain the monster, I would rush to release from confinement a young lady, who had viewed the combat from between the bars of her dungeon window, formed by the backs of two chairs, set on the seat of the old nursery sofa, behind which she was imprisoned.

He and his friend Jack Engledown first gain some years of experience, Jack for a while down at the Cape, Max in Egypt, where 'I had not been in the country long before I began to pick up some Arabic, and made friends with some Bedouin Sheiks, and donning their costume, went off on expeditions with them'. Already in this introductory chapter there are echoes – of SPW's own childhood, of Edward Palmer's romantic wanderings, and of the emigration of his friend Mr Jackson.

Max and Jack together plan an expedition to a mysterious river on the East Coast whose lower reach had been discovered but never explored further. This, they hope, promises good game-hunting. But first they recruit Charley Day, a gamekeeper's son with strong physique, and equip themselves for all possible situations.

> Of course we had tents, rifles, revolvers and ammunition, but we also provided ourselves with:
> Rockets, of several kinds
> Roman candles
> Bengal lights
> Red fire
> Magnesian ribbon
> Dynamite cartridges
> A Galvanic battery
> An Induction coil
> Fire balloons in the shape of men and animals
> Luminous paint
> Some steel flasks containing Carbonic-acid gas under great pressure
> Telephones and covered wire
> A Magic lanthorn, made like a bellows camera
> Two good Field-glasses

> A small steam cooking apparatus
> An India-rubber boat to be inflated with air
> We also decided upon having a boat made in sections, so that we could
> take it in pieces for transport.

And so, like the great missionary-explorer David Livingstone, they venture into the dark continent by way of Zanzibar and progress up a river in a collapsible boat. Some of those gadgets and chemicals with which they 'astonish the natives' and subdue monsters during the course of their subsequent adventures seem strangely familiar. *Luminous paint* we have already come across. *Magnesian ribbon* and perhaps the *Galvanic battery* are very probably associated with a recent friendship – for a distant cousin of Lally's, Mary Sonstadt, had begun to visit the Old Vicarage, and her Swedish husband was a scientist whose inventions included the use of magnesium for its brilliant light. *Telephones and covered wire*, and *A Magic lanthorn* were contrivances Page had himself already made. The more everyday provisions among this bizarre list would have been suggested long ago by letters from friends who had emigrated to South America, Australia and the colonies in Africa, in particular Sidney Jackson to whom he had in 1862 sent out, as requested, a gun and other supplies.

He had of course been deeply impressed by Chambers' *Vestiges of Creation*, by Huxley's lecture and by discussion all around about Darwin's *Origin of Species*, made vivid for him by the presence in the fields nearby of those fossilized prehistoric creatures among the coprolites. Talk of evolution had prompted speculation about the 'missing link' between ape and primitive man. And so in this tale Max and Jack find from their native guides that there are rumours of a lost tribe called Nephilimbo, or Nephilim. One exciting episode follows another, leading at last to the encounter with the 'dragon'; for, deep in a rocky gorge cleaving a high remote plateau, they find their way blocked by 'a most hideous creature with bat-like wings'. This turns out to be one of a whole 'rookery' of pterodactyls, large enough to catch and eat small antelopes. It is a bad moment, and there is great tension and excitement in observing and overcoming these beasts. But as with every sticky situation in this unlikely tale, the resourceful heroes make use of their provisions, using a fire balloon in the shape of an animal, inflated from 'a bottle of spirits of wine'. Seeing it float away, the male monster follows; and then, returning, the unfortunate pterodactyl lands on an improvised booby-trap which detonates the dynamite.

The explorers will need to convince scientists back at home of this phenomenon, and so measure the dead creature and cut off his head as a trophy. Passage through the rocky gorge, strewn with bones, is tortuous. As night comes, darkness does not – 'for the curious substance with which the ground was covered was of a similar nature to luminous paint, and as daylight faded it shone out with a dreadful phosphorescent glare, awful to behold'; indeed it was 'like looking through a negative photograph in which all the shades are reversed'. Emerging from the gorge they find a lush valley, rich in fruits. Here are antelopes so tame that one is killed with shameful ease; so that, after the butchery, 'I declared I would turn vegetarian while I remained in this wonderful valley'.

Now they encounter first one settlement and then another of the Nephilim, and find them a gentle white-skinned tribe, the major group living beside a lake and sleeping in caves in a high volcanic cliff. These innocent people feed only on fruit, and exercise by swimming, dancing and playing at competitive sports – the last a sort of 'natural selection' by which the fittest males won their mates. (Jack has the notion that the Nephilim are arrested in their development because they have 'no souls, but only the same kind of life as animals ... they have never found out they are naked, just the amount of knowledge, or instinct, they had given them at the first they have now...')

But later, when Charley Day, venturing into the forest beyond the valley, has been wounded by a gorilla, and the weather grows stormy, the explorers are obliged to arrange a cave dwelling for themselves in which to rest for a while. The Nephilim, who had tried to warn them of the danger, now show sympathy; and one comely young woman pays particular attention to Charley. 'Her eyes had that wistful look we often see in a favorite dog, who looking earnestly in your face, seems trying to understand what you are saying.' With the embarrassed chivalry true to their public-school upbringing the Englishmen withdraw, finding a way (by using one of their conjuring tricks) to do so in accordance with their resolve that 'nothing should be done in act, word or deed, to demoralise, vex, or injure this harmless race'. Many more pages follow, describing their final adventures in escaping through underground caverns as an earthquake brings down the gorge behind them, the torrent rises, and they emerge to safety while the tranquil Nephilim community is sealed off for ever.

One hopes the book sold well. It was a time when, as the blank spaces in the maps of the world were gradually filled in, there was a keen appetite for adventure stories. Readers of popularised accounts based on those of Livingstone and Speke, and of Stanley's dispatches, were forming their own impressions of the dark interior. Vivid descriptions of fact had become entwined with thrilling rumours. But only that perpetual schoolboy, Page Widnall, the 'capital contriver', could have spun this particular fantasy.

CHAPTER 24

Friends & Family

THERE WERE BOUND TO BE sad events as they grew older. Page's cousin Sarah Tofts, herself widowed not long before, died in March 1889. A Hanbury cousin of Lally's died. In the village, pretty Miss Fowke died. On a Sunday in February Mr Glasscock, whom they had relied upon for the hire of a fly whenever their own carriage was out of action, was found dead in his chair after the evening service. Then Mrs Banyard died, followed by her husband. James Nutter, the miller, died. In April Thomas Frederick Howard, elder brother of George, died at Gaudia, Spain. On 9th December 'Poor little Puck died'. And finally, two days later, the Rev. George Howard himself died.

On 14th December there was an impressive funeral at Grantchester. 'George Howard buried Mr Borissow and the Trin choir and many of his friends attended the Church nearly full'. It had been known that George was grievously ill with tuberculosis, and when, in June, their old friend Miss Johnstone had come to lunch, Page had driven her to 1 Harvey Road to see him; and Lally too had called at the house a week before his death. For the last months his role as Parish Clerk of Grantchester must have been carried on by his deputy, Mr Cresswell. And now, with the college choir directed by C.V. Stanford,* he was laid to rest in the family tomb beside the chancel. A year later, memorial stained glass depicting the 'Agony in the Garden' was set in the nearby window above the church's Easter sepulchre, recalling his final sermon as curate, on Easter Sunday 1875.

Less gloomy thoughts will have attended news of a more distant death: 'Mr Slim great uncle by marriage to Jane Lapworth died leaving her a legacy of £4000'.

*

During 1889 several new installations were made in the chancel of Grantchester Church, reflecting the tendency towards 'high' church. First, new oak seating replaced the old: where once the servant-class had sat in chilly discomfort, the choir were now moved from the gallery at

*Later Prof. Sir Charles Villiers Stanford

the back of the nave and had their choirstalls, with a pair of reading desks added for the clergy . Then the floor of the sanctuary was slightly raised, with a mosaic displaying a large roundel framing a 'pelican in her piety', the emblem of the church's patron, Corpus Christi College.

*

During the summer months that year a number of pleasant events are mentioned, and new names are constantly introduced. There was now a Mr Worthington at Merton Cottage. Lally was bitten by his little dog, but he was evidently forgiven, as 'Mr Worthington went with us for a drive to Haslingfield called on Mr Clements &c' two days later. There were a Mrs & Miss Stewart, Mr Herbert, Miss Calvert and her fiancé Mr Knight … all no doubt interesting acquaintances.

But it was still the old family connections who counted most. Mrs Clark, glad of company now that Miss Kelsey had become Mrs Beard, came to the Old Vicarage for a month's stay at midsummer. Together they went for 'a lovely drive to Abington … found Hemlock, Catmint and Wild Marjoram', happily gathering trophies for Lally's flower book and, for the cousins, sharing memories of the days when the Freeman family had farmed and been wheelwrights at Abington.

When Polly Greene came, in September, they went for a drive one day lurching and rattling along the old Roman road, high up and breezy. Two days later their horse, Blossom, took them through the fen villages to Wicken Fen. But a fortnight after that Polly discovered the perils of traffic: 'Grace Lumby and Polly Greene went for a drive came into a collision with a cart Polly thrown out'.

The Hill family were now installed in the Master's Lodge at Downing, and in August Page and Lally attended an 'At Home' there. Since the Hills' departure from Grantchester, Riversdale had been taken by the Venns, who did not stay for much more than a year – in October 'Dr & Mrs Venn left Riversdale although they have the house until next spring'. It must have been the completion of their own new house, in Chaucer Road, which took them away. There was certainly no ill-feeling, for Dr Venn, a distinguished logician, is likely to have been very agreeable company for Page. He, too, had a talent for invention and had devised 'a very successful bowling machine for cricket'; he was a keen botanist; and, to a greater extent than SPW could ever dream of, an archivist. His major scholarly writings being complete, he was at this time turning his attention to the history of the University. First he gathered material about his own college, Gonville and Caius. Then, with the assistance of his son (himself President of Queens' and the ninth generation of the Venns at Cambridge), he recorded details of every matriculated member of the University from early times. The first section was published at the end of his life as the invaluable *Alumni Cantabrigiensis*.

As with previous Widnall tenants, friendship with the Venns would continue; and that winter Page removed a collection of alpine plants, left by Dr Venn as a gift, from the Riversdale garden to a bed by the Roundhouse.

*

In October, Page and Lally went off once again for a series of family visits. First they stayed with Amy in her new home at West Kirby. While there, Page got himself some amusing employment, 'painting scenery for Mr Bolton's breaking-up party "Cinderella"'. (Very likely Humphrey was at Mr Bolton's school.) Then they moved on to Alice's home at Delfield, where Bertie came to dine. Lally had not seen her nephew for ten years. He was a busy man and an increasingly prosperous one, and his third child, endowed with ancestral names – Hamo Folville Smith Carington – had been born just a week before. For more than one reason it must have been a celebratory dinner, as another entry on that same day states 'Richard Smith Carington elected Mayor of Worcester'. Page and Lally ended their visit by going to a studio in Liverpool for portrait

photographs to be taken. The one of Page, looking kindly and distinguished, survives in one of the family albums.

The round of visits ended with a spell at Gunnersbury with Tom and Dolly and a typical mixture of entertainments, the Natural History Museum and Barnum's Magnificent Show. Before leaving, Lally went with Dolly to see Ethel Palmer at her school at Blackheath, and next day, with Page, called at 108 Harley Street to see her younger sister Maud. And then, arriving home, they 'found Polly's picture (the willows by the pond) awaiting [them]'.

Page had been so caught up in his scene-painting at West Kirby that he returned there in December to complete the task and see the performance ('All went off satisfactorily'). But it was while he was away that George Howard's funeral took place, attended by Lally only.

After his return, at what seems a late date (21st December), he 'printed some Xmas cards for Mr Burr of Bath'. – Perhaps at that time greetings were customarily exchanged after Christmas.

For Christmas dinner, 1889, they 'dined at Prof. Bensley's'.

CHAPTER 25

Into the 1890s

ON NEW YEAR'S DAY 1890 the village was entertained by a reading of *The Rose and the Ring*** in the schoolroom, 'illustrated by Lanthorn views'; and one may guess that Page Widnall had a hand in the slide-show, using his home-made magic lantern.

Mr Burr of Bath had evidently been pleased with his Christmas cards, and so in mid-January SPW, jobbing printer, began to set up type for his personal poetry book. Three weeks later, on the way to delivering the proofs, he and Lally made a detour to visit old friends.

They travelled down to Bournemouth to stay with Mrs Martin, widow of the former Vicar of Grantchester. While there, they called upon Mrs Venn, at Boscombe. And then, recalling earlier times, '14 Feb Went to the cemetery at Bournemouth with Annie Creeke and put some Arum Lillies on Laura's and Mr Creeke's graves'. (Lally would always grieve for Laura; but they were not to know that both Annie and Mrs Creeke themselves were to die a year later.) Yet the mood was not entirely melancholy that day: 'Went in the evening to the Shaftsbury Hall to see and hear the Phonograph'. This was another of those innovations well worth noting, the machine which could play recorded sounds from the revolving of a wax cylinder. It may possibly have been a demonstration of the even more recent Gramophone, using a shellac disc turned by a handle. This had been developed by Berliner from Edison's wax-cylinder invention just two years before.

On they went to Bath, where they stayed for a few days with Mr Burr; and it may have been while there that Page was asked to print 'Mrs Harrison's Book of Poems' as well.

Their kind friends M. & Mme Boquel came to see them in April, Monsieur now in a Bath chair. He had retired from his teaching work three months before, receiving 'a magnificent testimonial from University friends and £180', and though ailing must have enjoyed being wheeled about the Old Vicarage garden among its spring flowers.

---

*One of the Christmas Books by W. M. Thackeray written under the pseudonym 'Mr Michael Angelo Titmarsh', it is a long and convoluted fairytale.

Later that month Ethel and Maud Palmer came for the Easter holidays. They were soon joined by Tom Davis with Dolly, their two children, Harold and Dulcie, and the nurse. After a week at Grantchester, Maud returned home. But Ethel stayed, and

> 1 *May* Ethel made a statement in writing concerning Mrs Donkin which was signed by Mr Godfray [the Vicar] and Tom wrote to his solicitor and Mr Bezant [*sic*]

She was now seventeen, and this action seems to have released her to some extent from an oppressive relationship with her stepmother. From now on, she seems to have depended upon her uncle Tom and her great-aunt as guardians.

*

Lally herself was enjoying her many friendships with like-minded women. Although the Gaskells had now moved into Cambridge, she was still able, in May, to join Mrs Gaskell for lunch, followed by Gluck's opera *Orpheus & Eurydice*; and then, a few days later, dine, see *The Gondoliers* and afterwards sleep the night at their new home at Petersfield, a pleasant row of houses looking onto a green close to Parker's Piece.

A new family had succeeded the Banyards at Cedar Lodge, the Pearces. The father was a Latin scholar and school tutor, and also a keen amateur photographer. (Could his third name, Nigel Douglas Frith Pearce, indicate a family connection with the eminent Victorian photographer Francis Frith?) They were quickly accepted into the circle of close village friends. In June, Lally

> Went to afternoon tea at Mrs Pearce's and met Miss Fawcett who came out as Senior Wrangler a few days after

Philippa Fawcett, aged twenty-one, would come to be regarded as a notable pioneer in the efforts to convince hidebound senior members of the University that women should be taken seriously as intellectual equals. From Clapham High School she had gone to University College, London, and from there won a scholarship to Newnham. She had already proved herself outstanding in her first and second years; and in a few days time, when the Tripos results were announced, she would be placed 'above the Senior Wrangler'. This moment was described in *The Granta*, an undergraduate magazine normally given to ridiculing Newnham and Girton:

The Senate House was crowded in expectation of a sensation, which was certainly forthcoming. The sweet girl Graduates who filled the galleries were very excited over so great a triumph, and the men, when once they had recovered from their natural astonishment, cheered heartily. She looked pleased, but bore her blushing honours very meekly. She left the Senate House on Miss Clough's arm, escorted by a large and enthusiastic chorus of Undergraduates ... no one more fitting than the daughter of so thoroughly characteristic a Cambridge man as the late Professor Fawcett...

Although Lally had herself missed, by some fifty years, the opportunity for further education at this level, she was deeply interested in the new developments. Her bluestocking friend Miss Hickey came to stay in June, and Lally went to hear her lecture at the 'training college', where they took tea with Miss Hughes. Founded only five years earlier with the support of Miss Clough, Principal of Newnham, the Cambridge Women's Training College, which prepared young women for the teaching profession, was still in temporary accommodation.* Miss Hughes, a Newnham graduate, would see the college move into stately buildings a little later; and long after her death, in 1949, it would be renamed Hughes Hall.

Page, meanwhile, was engaged in more homely pursuits. His sparse diary entries note, in May, that at the village's Choir Supper he gave a reading of 'The Bishop and the Caterpillar'; later in the summer he 'went up the river to see some Cormorants catch fish'; and he was setting to work on his fourth doll's house.

Lally, without the benefit of formal teacher-training, had done so well with her pupils that a lasting attachment continued with most of them. Dr & Mrs Gaskell, that July, took her to see their son Jack at his preparatory school near Hitchin. He, after Marlborough and Caius, would become a distinguished physician. And Polly Greene, that most faithful of disciples, surprised her a few days later with another lovely gift – a box of flowers sent from Lucerne.

Ethel Palmer came to spend the whole of her summer holiday with them, more than six weeks, and shared their outings and tea parties.

The Greene family had by now left their spacious house at Bedford for a less expensive, tall, gaunt one with no garden in Hampstead, which

---

*First in Merton Street, Newnham (still within the parish of Grantchester); and at this time in Warkworth Street, Cambridge.

suited none of them. They hoped to be able to return to the Cambridge area. Finding that Mr Worthington was to be away for two months, they were able in August to rent Merton Cottage. Enterprising as ever, in September 'Mrs Greene gave a Pic-nic we all went to Audley End in a wagonette'; and presently Polly and her mother joined Page and Lally in watching tableaux put on by the Lumby family at Merton House: *Sequah* – and what manner of entertainment was that? The Lumbys, like the Greene family, could supply an entire cast: when Professor Lumby had arrived in Grantchester he had brought the five children of his first marriage, and now Luise, the second Mrs Lumby, had just produced the sixth of her own seven children.

At the end of November the Old Vicarage, too, became more animated. Amy Giles arrived with Phyllis and Humphrey, both with whooping cough, and their nurse Liza. Once the wretched coughing was over, there would be plenty of chatter and laughter. Uncle Page was now making a four-fold screen for the drawing room, and in the kitchen there would be puddings and mincemeat to mix in preparation for Christmas. For this year, on 25th December, they spent 'Our first Christmas at home since dear Lilly's death'. Kind friends and relatives had entertained them year after year; but now they 'Spent a happy day with Amy and the children Multitudes of cards and presents'.

Altogether, this was a real Grantchester Christmas. First, during Advent there had been the Choir Supper. Then, on the day itself, Page's sixty-fifth birthday, there must certainly have been fun and treats as well as presents – surely conjuring tricks from the great-uncle, and a piano accompaniment to carols and dances from the little great-aunt.

*

No theatricals are mentioned for the New Year 1891; but on 9th January there was an 'Evening party at Mr Walthams Charades (Snapdragon) &c Very cold Thermometer at zero'. This sounds like a typically late-Victorian evening, with its dressing-up, acting, flickering light from the fire and candles – and the extra excitement of 'snapdragon'. For after presenting that particular word as a charade, they would surely have enjoyed something with no connection to the antirrhinum flower: the offering of raisins soused in brandy and set alight. And terrified and delighted, the children would have snatched hot raisins from the glimmering flames. Then they all wrapped themselves up and hurried around the corner and down the frosty road – a mercifully short walk from Yew Garth to the Old Vicarage. It really *was* cold: zero Farenheit equals minus 17.8 degrees Centigrade.

Lingay Fen, a field lying between the main river and the millstream, was flooded to provide a vast ice rink, and there was skating for eight weeks that winter. The river itself froze hard, right down to Ely and beyond; and from the 'other place' it was reported that 'the river is frozen with ice about 10 inches thick almost all the way from Oxford to Abingdon'. The National Skating Association was able to hold its championships, and *The Granta*, an undergraduate magazine, mentioned a new craze on the Backs:

> Skating by electric light has been the novelty, and the services have been called in of "those celebrated Electricians, Messrs Baily and Grundy" (I quote from an advertisement).

One of those badly-faded outdoor photographs showing a couple skating on the Cam must date from this time.

There were indoor occupations for Phyllis and Humphrey. Phyllis, now twelve, had written some lines of verse entitled *My Robin*, and Humphrey printed the poem 'in his toy press'. This must have been rather better than most children's printing equipment (perhaps a combined gift for both his tenth birthday, on 23rd December, and Christmas), for the result was good. It was even good enough to join the examples of Uncle Page's own printing stuck into the end of *Uncle Page's Book*.

As the year advanced, the melancholy entries of the deaths of friends and relatives continued. George Dilley in the village, and later Mrs Lilley, widow of the Manor Farm tenant; Mrs Cresswell, and the Rev. John Martin, of Croft Lodge. Their gentle French friend Mme Boquel; Louisa Williams; and 'poor Pixie'. But far the worst of all was the death, in February, of Tom Davis's sweet wife Dolly after giving birth to her third child, a daughter. Tom's heart-broken announcement in the newspaper was cut out and pasted into *Uncle Page's Book*.

*

More cheering was the reappearance of Mrs Greene and her family, this time for a spell at Cedar Lodge during the Pearces' absence; and by now there was an exciting move in prospect. It is said that it was Edward Greene, home from Brazil for a while, who,

> ... when bicycling through the village of Harston near Cambridge ... noticed that a beautiful 'William & Mary' house of rosy-pink bricks

and stone mullioned windows, was for sale. It stood behind a wall in a garden with fine old trees, right in the middle of the village.*

Harston House was the fulfilment of their hopes, a place where they, like Page Widnall at his Old Vicarage, could enrich the garden endlessly, and provide pageants, plays and festivities for the village. Polly would design ornamental gates, made by their local blacksmith, for the entrances to different sections of the garden; and Edward later had an artesian well bored to supply a fountain similar to the Old Vicarage one. (The village of Harston was to benefit, too, from a drinking fountain and communal taps provided from the same source.) Sir Graham and his sisters would remain there until their deaths, fifty years in all.

*

For Page the spring was spent in characteristic tasks. In April he 'gave a lecture in the Schoolroom on the Great Pyramid'; and some weeks later 'Went to London to take some models to the Gen Post Office to try for the prize "for improved mail apparatus"' ... but apparently won no prize. In June he 'made new weathercock for the roundhouse' – something which has by chance survived, a three-dimensional metal figure once gilded but now rather sad-looking on its wobbly legs. Page's amateur metalwork was known to some of the poorer folk in Grantchester, who used to bring to the door their pans and kettles for mending.

In mid-June Page and Lally set off for a month of visits to her relatives. First they stayed with Amy at her home on the tip of the Wirral peninsula, and found that she had arranged a wonderful treat. Uncle Page's midwinter birthday had been a proper family Christmas; and now they celebrated Aunt Lally's midsummer seventieth birthday with a proper family picnic, taking a boat over to Hilbre Island, rich in wild flowers and shore birds. A few days later, Lally went with her nieces, Amy and Alice, to spend a day in Chester.

Then, leaving Amy and the children, they moved to Alice's own home, from where they were able to visit and admire the Manchester Ship Canal at its western end. This lower end was near to completion and would soon receive traffic, though the formal opening of the whole 35-mile length by Queen Victoria would not happen for another three years. The gadget-maker of Grantchester must have been thrilled by the bold-

---

*Quoted from the recollections of Mrs Eva Greene, Edward's widow. The house must have been first rented, for the actual purchase was completed in 1893.

ness of the scheme and the ingenious solutions to its problems. In the section he was seeing, from Eastham to Runcorn, the tide was controlled by a system of locks and sluices. Further up, the approach to Manchester docks presented many more complexities. And the man who was solving these problems was Sir Edward Leader Williams, brother of Richard Smith-Carington's second wife, Patty. His great *tour de force* was to be the swing aquaduct carrying the Bridgewater canal high across the ship canal, operated by hydraulic power (and still functioning more than a century later). Although the scale of these engineering works was awesome, the various mechanisms involved must have been quite comprehensible to a man like Widnall, especially when he had Alice's husband Arthur Holme to explain things.

When they moved on to visit Bertie, Page must have been brought further up to date about advances in Victorian engineering; for some of the boldest innovations of the age were represented in these three family connections. There were not just Leader Williams' majestic works, but Herbert Smith-Carrington's involvement in precision engineering, too. His firm was about to become 'Armstrong, Whitworth & Co. Ltd.',* famous for the production of guns; and the armed conflicts of the following decades would bring the Smith-Carington family greater wealth than could have been foreseen. In the meantime, Whitworth's own specialised components may have assisted in Leader Williams' great achievement. The third of these family links was with Col. Arthur Holme, civil engineer, whose design of the ingenious rack-and-pinion Snowdon mountain railway, opened in 1897, would keep his name, too, in the records.

Moving on to St Cloud, Richard and Patty's house near Worcester, Page and Lally were among their contemporaries; and this more relaxed spell included a day spent visiting the Conders at New Court, Hereford. Finally, on 16 July, they returned home to find their new servant Sarah Docwra installed and everything, one hopes, in good order

*

In the late summer old friends appeared: 'Saw Fred Lilley who has lately returned from America'; Mrs Southam and her newly-married daughter Violet Pontifex came to stay; Miss Lockhart visited; and Lally's old pupil Connop Perowne called for tea. During that time Page had an

---

*The death of Sir W. G. Armstrong brought an amalgamation of his firm with Whitworths, in 1892.

unwelcome experience:

> 13 *Aug*   Fainted for the first time in my life had been unwell for some
> days

But he was restored, and was able to enjoy a 'Picnic in Byron's Grove in honour of Helen Greene's 21st birthday, party of 18', and was soon engaged in a new project – his final major literary effort, bringing together more reminiscences.

Various events were noted during that period. First, Polly Greene began painting a portrait of Lally, a picture which shows the old lady, instantly recognisable with her lace bonnet and white ringlets, holding a small flower and comparing it with the botanical drawing in her Bentham & Hooker handbook.

In November they went to a delightful lunch with the Hills at Downing Master's Lodge. 'Then followed the children's play "The adventures of a Princess, or the Ghosts Warning". Characters – A Princess, a Ghost, afterwards a Prince, a witch, a gnome and a fairy!!!'

That winter, in good time, Page printed his own Christmas cards, with a graceful rhyme of greetings to his friends (an example of which is stuck among other memorabilia at the back of *Uncle Page's Book*). Later, on 13th December, he noted:

> A Furious gale part of the Vestry window blown in A wall in Cambridge was blown down falling on two Grantchester girls one Kate Foster was killed, the other much injured

The turn-of-the-year theatricals, *The Area Belle*, were performed in the schoolroom this year by the Walthams, the Worthingtons and Miss Frost as the highlight of the Choir and Mothers' Meeting. But the Vicar, Mr Godfray, 'was ill and not able to be present'.

*

Page Widnall also had to acknowledge frailty:

1892

2 *Jan*   My serious illness began had breakfast in bed for almost the first time in my life. When I came downstairs I fainted and in the evening sent for Dr Carver

24 *Jan*   I came down stairs for the first time since my illness

He, like the Vicar, was back in church for the first time on the 7th February. And Lally, who some weeks earlier had 'called at Miss Bowes 13 Park terrace and brought back a white kitten "Peggy"', found that their white Persian cat 'Queenie', given by Grace Lumby the previous June but lost two days later, was now found and restored to them. (At this point in the diary Humphrey Giles, many years after, added a pencil note: 'all animals were white – cats, pigeons, ducks, hens, pony')

A wonderful piece of village news was the engagement of Julia Lilley to Mr Waltham. This was the Julia whom they had known from her childhood as one of the Manor Farm family, and who had acted in their first theatricals. Now aged fifty, she was settling for marriage with a widower, one of the pleasant family recently established at Yew Garth.

There was news of another village man. '23 March Poor old John Benton died he was taken to the Workhouse on the 19th'. The Benton menfolk were mostly carpenters and joiners, and Page Widnall as a boy, ever eager to learn, had quite probably acquired some of his own skills from them. John Benton, who is likely to have been the man who in 1840 had married their servant Amelia, seems to have gone his own way, and for a while been landlord of the Green Man public house. Now old, widowed and impoverished, he had come to that fate always dreaded by the poor in Victorian days. But at least the Cambridge Workhouse in Mill Road, newly built and laid out in four courts, was less intimidating than most.

A burial in Grantchester churchyard took place that March – Anne Jemima Clough, first Principal of Newnham College, probably not known to many in the village besides Lally and her women friends.

CHAPTER 26

Autumn Days

————•◦•————

IN MARCH 1892 A DIARY ENTRY could announce: 'Finished printing the "Gossiping Stroll"'. The printing of Page's *Gossiping Stroll through the Streets of Cambridge* had taken six months, and its gestation must have been a good deal longer.

As he explains in its Preface, the gossip came 'partly from my own personal recollections and from what I have been told at various times through a long series of years from my youth upwards' and a good deal from 'my friend Mr Alderman Ellis' – the father of Henry Ellis, companion of those holidays back in the 1860s. Page was also acquainted with John Willis Clark,* the university antiquarian whose own more serious book had been published the year before. It was J.W. Clark who lent some old engravings for use as illustrations. Page says that his own little book 'does not profess to be a Cambridge Guide' and is likely to be of greater interest 'to one who knows the town in its present state than to a visitor or stranger'.

By stringing his anecdotes along a 'stroll', he takes the reader from Trumpington Road down to the colleges on the Backs, through to Magdalene and up Castle Hill (with mention of the University Observatory in one direction and the Gog Magog hills in the other); then back along Bridge Street with a diversion up Jesus Lane; twisting through Sidney Street to the marketplace; up Petty Cury and on past Christ's, Emmanuel and Downing Colleges, with chat on the way about old and interesting parts of the town and thence eventually back to the starting-point.

Some of his stories were already familiar to those who had read his *History of Grantchester* and his *Reminiscences of Trumpington*. But here there are plenty more, giving us an impression of earlier times. One example:

> As late as about the year 1800 members of the University, in wet weather, went to St Mary's Church in pattens, which they left in the vestibule until the service was over. Pattens and Clogs are now almost,

---

*J.W. Clark had married a Miss Buchanan, daughter of a diplomat. She may well have been the subject of one of SPW's portrait photographs of the 1860s; and Clark's activities in the A.D.C. may have been another link.

if not quite obsolete, and some may not know what they were like. Clogs were thick wooden soles with a leather toe-cap and ears on each side for strings to tie round the instep. Pattens were similar but were mounted on oval iron rings to raise the wearer some three inches from the ground...

Other examples are more strictly local – how the glovemakers of St John's Street, once famed for the fine suppleness of their product, had later produced mostly gloves 'of the roughest kind' intended for the handling of sedge. Dried sedge came up by boat from the fens. The colleges had sedge lofts, and the bedmakers wore 'sedge gloves' when they took what was needed of this rasping stuff for kindling fires.

Speaking of All Saints Church, he describes another obsolete custom:

The writer remembers when a boy, attending a place of worship where tallow [rather than wax] candles were used; and several times during the service a man went round with a pair of snuffers and a stool on which he stood to snuff them. This caused a little mild excitement among the boys, who watched each candle to see if it would be extinguished, which sometimes happened, though not often, the man being an experienced snuffer. 　　　　[This illustrates the use of the verb 'to snuff' meaning 'to trim'.]

In Sidney Street there was the Post Office: the office to which, at a time before pillar boxes, everyone, even from the neighbouring villages, had to bring or send their letters.

I remember that at Grantchester letters were only delivered two or three times a week, when an extra penny, beyond the eight pence or ten pence postage, had to be paid to the man for bringing them from Cambridge

(But that was before that glorious day in 1840 when Page's father had celebrated the first day of the Penny Post by despatching 193 letters.)

In writing his *Gossiping Stroll*, Page was preserving distant memories, such as the celebration dinner 'provided for fifteen thousand of the poorer inhabitants in 1838 for the coronation of our beloved Queen' on Parker's Piece. As time moves on, his record of such events grows in value.

*

An event at the end of April marked the end of an era for the village:

Tea and Entertainment in the Schoolroom as a farewell to Miss Snelling who has been our Village Schoolmistress for nearly 40 years a purse of £14 was presented to her also to welcome back Mr Godfray our Vicar who has been absent from illness almost ever since Xmas.

In spite of the dignity evident in her bearing and her elegant handwriting Miss Charlotte Snelling, the schoolmistress, seems always to have been left on the fringe of the middle-class society of the village. The Old Vicarage household had given their support to her efforts with the village school, and there were no doubt warm and gracious greetings in church. But to be the Headmistress of a National School with a hundred pupils at that time meant being rather isolated and hard-pressed.

Miss Snelling lived in the Schoolhouse next to the little thatched school building where she had first taught her noisy throng in 1853. From 1872 she had, as required by law, set down in the school's Log Book the difficulties and developments encountered term after term. (Some of those difficulties have already been quoted.) The children she was required to teach ranged in age from three to twelve years, and her one assistant was a Pupil Teacher aged about fifteen. In 1874 she had commented on her 'staff', Emily Darby and three monitors:

> 15 *May*   Monitors – Annie Searle works well in her class, and makes children do the same. C. Barton teaches very loudly. Clara Marshall painstaking. Teacher E.L. Darby is improving.

But her helpers, being so young, could be troublesome.

> 1878
> 11 *March* …Friday afternoon Alice R. (Monitor) aged 15 yrs rudely left her class, and walked out, in the most defiant way, on being told six times, to "guide the hand" of a child who could not hold her pencil properly whilst writing. She will not be again employed here. More help is very much wanted. Average attendance 110.9

And then, even worse, the following year, came that sequence of entries when Monitor Rose Benton died. Miss Snelling must often have felt close to despair. Her salary depended upon the good attendance of pupils and their success in achieving grades; yet the cottagers of Grantchester, like those in other rural villages, wanted to get their children out to work as soon as possible rather than needing pennies for school fees. In her earlier days as teacher a child as young as nine might be already a 'farmer's boy' or a 'nurse girl', and there had been many deserters in the late summer, when boys helped with the harvest and their sisters looked after younger children while the mothers went out into the fields.

Conditions inside the school were as difficult as could be: in 1875 the Inspector had reported

> The Tone, Discipline and Instruction of this School do great credit to Miss Snelling's conscientious work. The great need of this School is a class-room for the Infants, who are at present huddled together in a draughty corner in a most inconvenient way. They are carefully taught, but their position is a great drawback to their advancement.

When eventually the Infant Room was added, it had matched the main schoolroom in having its windows at an unfriendly height of eight feet from the floor. For the remainder of Miss Snelling's time, and beyond, the rooms were ill-lit and desperately cold in winter. A dark afternoon meant a singing-lesson in place of sewing – that grimly practical hemming of teatowels or stitching the seams of nightshirts 'for charity'. And the crowded rooms, barely warmed by one smoky fire, must have encouraged the winter epidemics. The worst had been in February 1881, when the school was closed, by order of the doctor, for nine weeks beyond the usual holiday; and in March 1888, when there was six weeks' closure while measles ran its course.

An introduction of fines for non-attendance in 1883 had brought in more pupils (including two boys aged six and seven, 'neither of them can tell a single letter of the Alphabet!'), and later a change to rewards of certificates and medals had become more effective in ensuring regular attendance. But the demands upon the Headmistress never relaxed: when she had complied with new regulations and taught grammar, H.M. Inspector found that 'the desirability of the addition is not quite clear, as arithmetic has somewhat declined'. Still, there was gradual progress. Copy books – in place, perhaps, of slates – arrived in 1884, and the Infants were shown pictures of animals for their Object Lessons. 'This is a very Good School approaching to excellent' said the Inspector in 1888.

Miss Snelling 'gave the boys their first Drawing lesson' in 1891, and next year 'used new Geographical Reader (much liked)'. But it had been a hard winter, and after Christmas illness kept the school closed until February 1st 1892. The Inspector this year reckoned that Drawing had still not been taught and recommended that a Savings Bank should be established. Grudgingly, allowing for the interruption of the epidemic, he announced that 'My Lords have paid the Grant' It was no wonder that the following entry states:

April 30   Had head charge of this School 38½ Years. I resign the Sole
             Charge of this School today.   Charlotte Snelling

followed by an account of the sums – Principal Grant, Discipline, Singing, Needlework – which together made up the school's Total Grant for the year of £50:4:0.

Even allowing for the enormous change in value, £14 (about the cost of a cow or a pony, much less than the £33 paid for Page's grey mare 'Blossom', or the £180 presented to M. Boquel on his retirement) seems a meagre reward for her long devotion to duty.

Miss Snelling was by this time sixty-nine. More than sixty years later she was still remembered in the village: 'She was a dear, but mind, if she caught you going in by the wrong gate you were for it. And once you were in there, you had got to work. Try to play round, and she'd be after you!' How she ended her days is not known. She may have had relatives still down in Somerset, her birthplace, and gone to join them.

Her successor, Mr Houlton, was very different. A family man, previously Headmaster at Barton, he moved into the newly-built School House next to the school. His style was more easy-going, and he was happy to extend the curriculum, since he had an enthusiasm for both Geography and Drawing; and, as always tends to happen, the authorities provided new books and materials, and better assistants, for the new Head.

*

It was time for Page and Lally to visit family members they had not seen for a while, and so in May they spent some days with Tom Davis – a stay during which they saw a performance by 'Buffalo Bill' (partly, perhaps, for the benefit of seven-year-old Harold). They made, too, their customary visit to the Royal Academy followed by lunch with Richard and Patty at the Grand Hotel. On their way home they were able to get off the train at Cheshunt and spend a couple of hours with the Sonstadts; then again at Bishop's Stortford for a call on Mrs Clark and Mrs Beard. Those last, Lally's cousin Mary Sonstadt and Page's cousin Elizabeth Clark, were in turn to make their own visits to the Old Vicarage a few weeks later.

At home, Lally as usual followed her own interests. In May Week she went with her friend Mrs Palmer* to *The Comedy of Errors*, that year's Pastoral Play at Downing. And in July she attended 'a Women's Politi-

*Wife of Carey L. Palmer, son of Jonathan Palmer and also a printer.

cal meeting at Mrs Flather's',* a symptom of the times. There were now stirrings of feminine activity not only in the academic world but more generally, for in the village many overworked women came out from their cramped cottages for the Women's Meetings encouraged by the church; and in the chapel folk a spirit of independence, regardless of gender, arose from the need to raise funds and organize events entirely by 'self-help'. While *Uncle Page's Book* is simply a series of brief entries and does not discuss beliefs or attitudes, hints may be found in it that both Page and Lally took a sympathetic interest in the Co-operative movement and in the wider spread of education.

It could have been at around this time, indeed, that the pair were photographed, standing in front of their front porch. It looks as though they had been called outside quite unprepared (and very likely the photographer was their friend Mr Pearce of Cedar Lodge), for it reveals them in characteristic everyday clothes. This is the benign Uncle Page as remembered fondly by Humphrey Giles long after, dressed in the parsonical 'wideawake' hat under which he would place a cabbage-leaf on hot days. And it was perhaps at this stage, recognizing their increasing age, that the two of them copied entries from their own diaries into the red leatherbound volume which became *Uncle Page's Book*.

*

Now they made another journey, this time into Leicestershire. '16 July 1892 Lally & I went to visit Bertie at Ashby Folville ret. Aug. 3rd'. That is all the diary tells; but the visit must have been full of interest. This was the place of Richard's Lordship of the Manor, a small village tucked into pastoral country, halfway between Leicester and Melton Mowbray. When Richard and his son had purchased that title and the estate, and later the manor house itself, it had been with the idea of restoring a dynasty. It was their rightful place, since they could claim descent from

*The Flathers had moved into Grove Cottage in April, on Mr Flather's appointment to the Examinations Syndicate.

the Smiths who lie grandly entombed in the mortuary chapel of Ashby Folville church. There they are: George Smith (*d.* 1607), son of Francis Smith of Wootten Wawen and his wife Mary Morton of Ashby Folville, and his eldest son Sir Francis (*d.* 1629). The Smith-Caringtons' own line came through the fourth son Thomas, and Thomas's third son Robert … Although not the strongest line for the inheritance of lands and property, the descent is continuous in the male line. Catholics for generations, royalists in the Civil Wars, when it came to William Smith (1699–1795) and his son Richard Smith (1748–1810), the family had become Baptists, working in Nottingham at the manufacture of lace. But their property had been largely lost in 1793, and so the next Richard Smith, father of Richard Smith-Carington, had moved to Worcester to start that quite different enterprise, the St John's Nursery. This, through hard work and well-judged marriages, had secured the family's recovery. And while Lilly Smith's husband S. P. Widnall had made no contribution to their rise in fortune, he had shared Richard's passion for genealogy and helped to trace the long Smith-Carington pedigree, printing a preliminary summary of it all in book form in 1884.

Now he and Lally could see for themselves what Richard and Bertie were doing at Ashby Folville – and it was a huge undertaking. The Jacobean manor house was mostly in ruins, having been largely burnt down at the beginning of the century, and one wing only had remained intact. Mr John Ely, a Manchester architect, had been engaged to design a restoration which would produce something larger than the original building but retain its style. The work was probably at an early stage, with stonemasons and joiners busy. There was still a great deal of sawing and chiselling and plastering to do.

For Page, this was far from the creation of his own Castle Ruin forty years before, yet something of the romance of that enterprise would be stirred again by Richard's great Manor – especially when he heard of the discovery, hidden behind some panelling in the surviving wing, of a portrait of Henry IV. Throughout their long relationship as brothers-in-law he had shared something of Richard's dream, a fantasy once given expression in *The Miller's Daughter*.

For Lally it was a time for closer intimacy with the young family. The nursery was full of toddlers: Frank (Francis) was four, Neville three, Hamo two; and Bertie's wife Lizzie was expecting a fourth child. (When the baby was born at Ashby Folville two months later she would be named, fittingly, Mary Morton.)

Returning to Grantchester, they next day received Amy Giles with her two children and servant Jane, who stayed for a month. And while Humphrey and Phyllis played with their friends in that leafy riverside garden which was like no other, visitors called. Bertie had come, bringing his architect with him, for a few hours' discussion. Evidently Uncle Page's comments on their building plans were valued.

Tom Davis was with them, too, when another visitor, Mr Buckham (first met long ago on one of Lally's trips abroad) came. So on that Sunday in August, Tom rowed him to Cambridge.

Other old friends came to see them, among them Henry Ellis and his wife, 'he was looking very ill'. One visitor, after her stay, thought of an appropriate thankyou gift – for when, some weeks later, Tom Davis came again he 'brought a pair of Fantail Pigeons a present from Gertrude Lapworth'. And that rather strange great-niece, Ethel Palmer, now aged twenty, came for her customary stay in November.

The year ended with – of course – 'theatricals'. The Greene family, now established at Harston, put on *She Stoops to Conquer* for two evenings. Alice Greene, home for two months from South Africa (where she was teaching and became Head of a girls' school), left for her return voyage next day.

*

For New Year 1893 a party was given at Mr Worthington's, 'a sort of farewell to Leonard W. who is leaving for Australia'. Others were setting forth, too: on 13th January 'Henry Ellis and his son Augustus started on a voyage to Sidney [*sic*]'. Two months later 'Mr & Mrs Phillips [neé Florence Greene] started for B. Columbia'.

A party launching another sort of enterprise was the 'At Home' given by Polly Greene on opening her Garden Studio in St Andrew's Street, Cambridge. Polly, now aged thirty-two, had become an established artist in both oils and watercolours, with occasional pictures accepted for the Academy's Summer Exhibition. Her studio, when it was later enlarged, would receive painting classes. In the meantime, 'Miss Mary Greene' visited some local families to give lessons, notably the Darwin tribe. Among the many young Darwin cousins, her outstanding pupil was Gwen, later to achieve her own high reputation as Gwen Raverat, painter and wood-engraver.

*

A lecture series in the schoolroom this year was given by Dr Kimmins, on 'the Chemistry of Life and health'. In place of Page's sometimes frivolous topics, there were real efforts being made to improve sanitation and general health.

In February they were invited to dine with their latest Riversdale tenants, Mr and Mrs (Julia) Waltham. It may be that this couple found it uncomfortable to set up home so close to their relatives, for after just over a year they were to leave Grantchester.

In March an alarming accident occurred: 'Dr Hardcastle thrown from his horse and died on the 14 of April'. Lally and Mary Nimmo were cautious in their choice of transport when they attended an At Home at Downing in May, for they took themselves there in Mrs Pearce's borrowed donkey-cart. It was not the most dignified conveyance in which to arrive at a Master's Lodge; but at that particular lodge it would have caused no offence. Neither Lally ('Miss Smith' to the end of her days rather than Smith-Carington) nor her hostess, Mrs Hill, were intimidated by the stuffiness

of some Heads of Houses. A few days after this Lally was taken by her friend Miss Hickey to dine at Girton College.

Alice Holme arrived at the Old Vicarage, seemingly anxious to make sure that her ageing aunt and uncle should have a restful summer holiday. She took Lally to Cromer in order to arrange suitable lodgings, but nothing could be found. As it turned out it was scarcely necessary, for Page and Lally were soon off on a jaunt: 'Took Mary, Dora and Walter Lumby to Haslingfield for a pic-nic had tea in the Chalk-pit'. These children, aged from eight to eleven, must have given them a lively time; and their mother, expecting her seventh child, could gratefully welcome home a tired trio covered in white dust.

A contrast came the following week, with one of those days packed with May Week events: lunch at Downing Lodge; the Pastoral Play at Jesus College; back to Downing for tea; then to a concert at Caius – 'but obliged to leave in the middle suffering from the intense heat at the Pas. Play almost Sunstroke'.

From university style they again settled back into their more rustic ways, noting that the Nimmos this year were providing entertainment to 'the Mothers of Granta' in the schoolroom.

At the end of June they 'went to dine with the Herrings at Fulbourn'. For some years this had become a regular summer excursion, in turn visiting the Herrings and receiving them at home. It made a very agreeable day out, taking the pony and trap through Trumpington, turning right by the windmill at the entrance to Long Road, then out and along the flank of the Gog Magogs, to descend past another windmill to the village of Fulbourn, in the expectation of seeing work in progress at The Poplars. For their host, John Frederick Herring,* was a successful and popular artist, painting wonderfully sympathetic pictures of farm animals. Whether Page felt able to afford an example for himself is not known, but the exchange of visits suggests a warm friendship.

*

That summer Haddow, on whom Page had relied for some years for the care of his animals and last remaining acres, had become ill. On 1st July the master took him to the station for his journey to Hunstanton for a three weeks' stay at the Convalescent Home there; and on the way back called at Downing and picked up Mrs Hill and young Elsie and Alex to have dinner at the Old Vicarage.

On the 6th there were great celebrations in Cambridge for the royal wedding – the future George V's marriage to Princess May of Teck – and Page and Lally went into the town to see the fireworks, and have tea with their friend Mr Carey Palmer. On the 12th they went to the Grantchester & Trumpington Flower Show at Anstey Hall – 'a beautiful rain the first for some months'. And the following week

> Miss Waltham's little swallow flew away today they had it for some weeks having fed it since it fell out of its nest it was perfectly tame and flew about the garden but came when called and sat on ones fingers and fed from the hand   [which is one of the longest entries in the entire diary!]

On 9th August they 'went to an Evening Party at Dr Gaskell's "The Uplands" Acting and Dancing'. Like the Clarks, the Venns and others, the Gaskells had chosen to build a house for themselves, although not in one of the close suburban areas like Chaucer Road favoured by many: they had chosen a situation on the hill above Great Shelford.

*

*J. F. Herring (1815–1907), always referred to as J. F. Herring jnr, since his father had been a well-known animal painter, depicting race-horses at Newmarket particularly. There were two brothers also engaged in animal painting.

Now it was time to get away; and it was to be a quite different sort of holiday from the one suggested by their solicitous niece back in May. This project, calling for rather more energy, must have been arranged when Tom Davis and Harold had paid a visit to the Old Vicarage in July.

First Page and Lally went to London, to Tom's house, and then, on 18th August, they 'left London for Exmouth with Harold, Dulcie and Servant'. Harold (remembered by a contemporary as 'an odious boy') had his eighth birthday during the holiday, and Dulcie was a year younger. Their baby sister must have stayed at home with her nurse and the widower Tom.

Exmouth was a good place for children – red sandstone cliffs at the eastern end, a long sweep of sand, and a variety of sailing boats and small ships passing by from the great Exe estuary on the western side. It seems that Amy came to share the stay, so probably Phyllis and Humphrey were there with buckets and spades, too. One day the grown-ups went to Exeter 'to see the city and Cathedral &c', and also called for tea with old Grantchester friends, Miss Hawkes and her brother. And another day

> Went for a lovely drive at Exmouth saw the house where Sir Walter
> Raleigh was born [Hayes Barton] over Woodbury Common and Black
> Hill returning through Budleigh Salterton

That would indeed have been a lovely drive. High on the heathery common they could see for miles, down to the coast and across westwards as far as Dartmoor. Hayes Barton had evoked thoughts of that hero of Elizabethan times, the explorer-courtier-poet who would again come to mind on the pebbly seashore of Budleigh Salterton, which had been the setting for a recent painting (almost certainly seen by them, either in the Academy or as an engraving), Millais' *The Boyhood of Raleigh*.

For Harold and Dulcie, the holiday ended on 8th September, when Page accompanied them and their maid to Exeter – no doubt providing a commentary on the wildfowl and the ships and small craft to be seen on the Exe as their train passed by. He and Lally left Exmouth three days later, going to Clevedon to visit a friend there. At Exeter, where they changed trains, 'Miss Hawkes's servant met us°.with a beautiful basket of fruit'.

And so they lingered a little in the south-west, going one day to Bath to call on Mr Burr, and the next, with their hostess Mrs Visgar, to Cheddar where they were:

delighted with the rocks and caverns Mrs V. then took a carriage and drove to Wells saw the Cathedral and curious clock and returned to Clevedon by Rail.

Their return journey to London was 'much delayed by a sad accident in the Box tunnel where we had to wait more than an hour' ° but they arrived nearly four hours late, stayed for two nights with Tom, and got safely home to Grantchester a month after their departure.

The rest of the year was spent at home, with old friends visiting them: Mrs Southam for three weeks, Mrs Bell (née Louisa Harding), and, inevitably, Ethel Palmer. An old acquaintance, Mr Fish, giving a series of lectures in the Schoolroom on 'Fruit Culture' was invited to tea: it was a subject in which Page had some experience.

But it turned out that their gardener/bailiff's trouble had not been cured; and on 1st November, Page 'took poor Haddow to the Fulbourn Lunatic Asylum'. A few days later Haddow's son Charles 'came to say goodbye he goes to his new situation as Station Master at Takeley near Bishop's Stortford', and after a few months Mrs Haddow went to join him. Haddow Snr was only fifty-one. One wonders whether his increasingly extravagant purchases had displayed a manic tendency? Or had too much been required of him, causing a mental breakdown? He does not seem to have felt ill-used, for, as Humphrey Giles remembered, he had presented a bible to Aunt Lally. Without Page's farm records one cannot tell just what the true situation was.

CHAPTER 27

Page's Final Year

———•·•———

FOR 1894 THE DIARY ENTRIES ARE almost all Lally's. The New Year as usual had its festivities:

9 *Jan*   Went with Grace Lumby to a delightful Xmas party at
             Downing, about 70 children. There was a Boar's Head!
12 *Jan*   The Tableaux of the 'Sleeping Beauty' at Merton House.
             So lovely.
13 *Jan*   My Wonderful present of 10 new sovereigns from some
             unknown friend!!

On 10th February Page wrote 'The Round House all down'. Its collapse did not mean the end to his gardening, though, for he was putting together pieces of discarded stonework ('Roman coffin-lids', they surmised) in a heap to create a new rockery.

*

The year started poorly for Richard Smith-Carington. At the end of January his second wife, Patty, died. On 1st March he suffered another blow: 'The House and offices at St John's burnt down'. It was not quite an end to the nursery which had been his life's work, though, for Car was to carry on the business for some while.

*

At Grantchester, a grateful Lally noted that 'dear Gissy finished printing the list of Wild Flowers for me'. She had by now found specimens and coloured-in the illustrations of nearly all the plants in the companion volume to her Bentham & Hooker botanical guide. The list of those still not discovered was printed and distributed among friends and family. By the time of her death a good number would be crossed out. The still surviving volume, with its distinctive wooden boards carved by SPW, has only thirteen illustrations (mostly grasses) out of the total 1306 remaining uncoloured. In many cases the date and origin of her specimens are noted.

The Pearces gave a party: 'Dancing at Cedar Lodge' – the house having been newly enlarged with a noble entrance hall and drawing-room. Even if her own dancing days were over, Lally must have enjoyed the sight of twirling figures and the music. Probably the three little Pearces were allowed to peep from the balcony at the top of the stairs.

Another gathering took place in April, seemingly of female friends chattering over samples of silk, '… to choose my dress'. One is left guessing: could this have been preparation for a very big occasion due to take place two months later? If so, the Lumby ladies would be involved. And in May 'Grace Lumby came to dust and wash the China' (all those pieces on inaccessible shelves which could only be reached by a tall friend). Soon after, Lally went with Mrs Lumby and Grace to a debate at Newnham College, and a few days later dined there.

And now came that special occasion, the Royal Agricultural Show of June 1894. It was reported by the *Cambridge Chronicle* in great detail, being the culmination of more than a year's preparation, during which the showground – Midsummer Common – had been thoroughly levelled and drained, and more sheds and stands erected than ever before. Comparisons are given between Cambridge's former show of 1840 and the present one: then 115 exhibits, now 6,031; then 330 head of livestock, now 1,684…

One man who could remember well that show in the grounds of Downing College fifty-four years earlier was Page Widnall, and the organisers had not forgotten his name.

27 *June*   Gissy had lunch in the King's Tent and dined in the Hall at King's by invitation. We met the Greenes at the Show.
Lovely Fireworks

This day was the climax of the show, the Wednesday which coincided with the presentation of Honorary Degrees in the Senate House, when a constellation of grand visitors proceeded after the ceremony to King's College for the luncheon: the Prince of Wales, Princess Alexandra and their party, the Duke of Devonshire (both University Chancellor and President of the Agricultural Society) and all the senior academics, including the Lumbys, the Hills and Dr E.C.Clark. To add to the excitement of this day, congratulations were offered to the Duke of York, who was present, on the birth of his son, the future Edward VIII, three days before. And the 'lovely fireworks' were (as advertised in the local newspaper) *Two Great Illuminated Fêtes, Water Carnivals & Fireworks*

Displays held in the grounds of Trinity and St John's, with two military bands, a Mandolin Band, a Military Tattoo and a *Grand Procession of Decorated & Illuminated Boats*. Victorian Cambridge was showing how it could celebrate, with 30,000 *Lamps and Lanterns, Hundreds of shells, thousands of rockets … water fireworks – The Sea Serpent, the River on Fire, &c*. General admission cost one shilling; but perhaps the group from Grantchester paid half-a-crown to be on the 'reserved lawn'.

*

A few days later, when they had Mrs Clark & Mrs Beard staying with them, they went over to Harston for the Flower Show there. The diary does not say whether the Greene family had any successes; but at the Trumpington & Grantchester Show which followed, Lally did well: 'Basket of Flowers 1st Prize'. And in mid-July there was one of those delectable days which so suited the two ageing botanists:

> Had such a pleasant time – Gissy & I – at Coe Fen found the Frog bit and 2 new Duckweeds

Twice in July, though, 'Gissy had Dr Carver'. This was worrying, yet not allowed to prevent their travelling to Ashby Folville for one of those wonderful family parties they both loved so much, to celebrate Richard's seventieth birthday.

They were met at the station (Melton Mowbray) by Bertie's brother-in-law, Leonard Stallard. 'Soon after the whole party arrived and had a most joyful meeting.'

> 1894
>
> 1 *Sept* The family gathering at Ashby Folville Manor – We were 20 at dinner. Richd, Bertie, Lizzie, Frank, Neville, Car, Alicie, Enid, Alice, Arthur, Amy, Phyllis, Humphrey, Lally, Myself, Tom, Leonard Stallard, Mr Ely (architect), Mr & Mrs Godson [Vicar and wife] completed the dinner party

Page's writing is a little creaky, but what satisfaction is expressed! And the event is recorded in a photograph of them all, assembled on the steps of the Manor.

Richard, having achieved so much by his own efforts, had now (with a little help from that odd brother-in-law Widnall) reached fulfilment. The rebuilding of the Manor House was complete. All his beloved family were there; and in a speech to the assembled tenantry he recalled how

seated l-r: Amy Giles; LizzieS-C with Hamo; Leonard Stallard; Arthur and Enid S-C; Herbert S-C; Alicie S-C. *behind*: Richard S-C with Lally Smith. *standing*: Humphrey Giles; Arthur Holme and Phyllis Giles; Tom Davies; Alice Holme; Page Widnall; ?Mr Eley; Francis S-C; Car S-C; Neville S-C.

it had been his life's dream to possess again the old hall of his ancestors:

> ... at first this hope had been indeed but a very shadowy and undefined sort of hope, but as time went on it formed itself more and more clearly into definite shape, and he greatly rejoiced and considered it a truly remarkable and most pleasant coincidence that the earnest desire, and he might say the constant dream, of at least fifty years of his life should receive such a perfect fulfilment, and this, too, just at the time when he attained his seventieth birthday.

This is just a fraction of the resumé of Richard's speech as given in the definitive *Smith-Carington Pedigree*, produced in two huge and heavy volumes a few years later. It makes a contrast with Lally's final entry in *Uncle Page's Book*:

2 *Sept* At Ashby Gissy ill in church (SS)

*

Page, as he watched the falling of the leaves during his final weeks, could look back on a life well spent. Of the land which had come to him through a great-aunt's connections with the Rev. Dr Sam Peck and the prosperous farmer Thomas Page, little remained in his care. The modest fortune built up by his father's successful nursery-gardening was mostly spent. But Page Widnall had not squandered his endowments, and his busy life had enriched many others'.

A small newspaper cutting is stuck into the back of the diary, saying that S. P. Widnall died on 16th December 1894 'of an affection of the heart... The deceased', it added, 'was of an ingenious and mechanical turn of mind.'

CHAPTER 28

Lally the Survivor

AUNT LALLY LIVED ON. Page's will, made a few weeks before his death, was proved at less than £350, so it is supposed that he had already made some provision for a small income to go to Lally from the properties intended to go ultimately to Tom Davis.

Alone in a secluded house, she was seldom allowed to be lonely. She had friends in abundance – old neighbours, old pupils, and though there were no members of her family living nearby, they still came to the Old Vicarage or invited her to stay with them. Scant as they are, the records* of her final years show the tiny old lady full of spirit still.

Back in March 1892 her brother Richard, trying to fill in the details of his family tree, had written to a Mr Lees, a first cousin once removed, asking for a full copy of everything in the old family Bible which might relate to the Smith connection. That led to contact with his correspondent's sister, Mary Sonstadt, who was already in touch with her Grantchester cousin. Mary Sonstadt, writing to her brother George in December 1894 says:

> …Look in your Pedigree papers for the name of Mr Widnall, husband of one of Mr Smith Carington's sisters. He lived at Grantchester, nr Cambridge, since his wife's death. Another sister Sarah – also in the P.Pages has kept house for him & they have been so happy together. On the 16th of this month he died suddenly – & the enclosed is from

---

*The Giles family continued to add very occasional notes in *Uncle Page's Book*; similarly Car S-C added a few entries to his copy of *Aunt Lally's Diary*, another transcript from Page & Lally's diaries.

Cousin Lally (Sarah). Isn't it a kind one – I should have liked to go – but they do not know our position, so I have been obliged to explain why we must decline, she is such a sweet old lady – exactly like Aunt Boot in the face, as she looked when we were children.

(To be described as looking 'exactly like Aunt Boot' seems unflattering. But that Mary, who had married a Nottingham lace-maker called Richard Boot, had stayed with the Smith family at Worcester in 1845 and cannot have been too frightful.)

Mary Sonstadt grew fond of her old cousin and visited her regularly, as did the Giles family and Tom Davis. Tom presently married again, his second wife being Lilian, daughter of the Rev. E. Robinson, one of the family distantly related to his own. Two more children were born, Vera (1897) and Edward (1898). Visits to Aunt Lally at the Old Vicarage continued to be part of their lives.

The Pearces of Cedar Lodge and the Greenes at Harston remained especially faithful friends. It was for Mrs Pearce that Lally wrote down a full description of the Old Vicarage garden, a thoroughly characteristic one, beginning

Such sweet memories connect my darling sister and her beloved husband with this garden, and they have done so much to make it what it is, that it seems impossible to say other than Our Garden, though both these dear ones have passed away – she, more than nine years ago, and he some few months.

Lally in 'Our Garden'

Her whole account is alive and interesting. The fountain, for instance – seen from the verandah, hung with blossoms, the Fountain in the early morning was a 'beautiful object':

...The water comes from an Artesian Well nearly 150 feet deep. It is strongly impregnated with iron which has clothed the Pedestal with a brown rust, giving it a nice old appearance. The pretty shallow vase is the favourite drinking place of the white Fantail Pigeons, and never does the Fountain look prettier than when several of these birds are standing on the edge, preening themselves, drinking or fluttering in the water...

The dark brown Pigeon House (given by Mrs Gaskell as her family were leaving the village) is, she says, mounted on a pole and has 'a croquet ball on the top' – surely one of Page's typical improvisations: if one feels the need for a finial in spherical form, why look further when the very thing can be found, perhaps, in the Swiss Cottage, 'in which in its palmy days, were kept bows, and arrows, and targets'?

> But I must not forget the Sundial, standing on the fair and mossy lawn, my dear Brother made it. It is a copy of one he saw in the island of Sark. He carved the stone book which looks as old as the Pedestal on which it stands, though that must date centuries back, as it is part of one of the old Crosses taken from the Chancel of the Church when the present crosses were erected. The open book marks the hours, and the shadows are formed by the curling leaves of the book. I well remember how my Brother used to rush out whenever the sun shone, to mark the spot where the shadow fell°.

She then quotes the six texts inscribed by her sister Lilly on the 'book', some in Latin. Working her way around the garden, she comes to 'a building which looks like an old ruin'.

> …Here is my Brother's workshop and a large room hung with Tapestry. In this room he once built a boat, and has made four Dolls' Houses, each one more elaborate than its predecessor. The last he made is still in the room, and represents a fine Elizabethan Mansion, with gables and a Clock Tower, and pretty stained glass windows. There are many wonderful surprises in this Dolls' House. After ringing the bell at the door, a Page appears standing in a noble Hall, with winding stair case, pictures and armour, and right opposite the door is a handsome fireplace in which a bright fire is burning. In the Dining room a gentleman is reading, and his wife is doing some fancy work; her arm moves up and down with the needle and thread. In the Drawing room a young lady is sitting at the Piano ready to play a tune. In the Kitchen the cook is grinding the coffee. The back kitchen contains a pump that gives forth real water, which may be pumped up to supply the bath. In the bathroom a young lady is seen in a Dressing gown. Shut the door, and on re-opening it you see the little lady dressed as before in her blue dressing gown. In the bedroom a little lady lies in bed, but she will sit up and open her eyes, closing them when she lies down again. It is indeed a very perfect Dolls' House.

There is a handsome carved oak fireplace in this Tapestry Room, and a pretty bow window, looking onto a little mound of rock work which my Brother built of great mossy stones, many of them portions of old Roman Coffins. He has planted many ferns and other things in it and about it. This may be called his last work in the garden, for he built it in the Spring of the year in which he passed away.

… so I must end my very in adequate description of Our Garden, admired by very many, and to me the sweetest garden the sun ever shone upon in all our dear Merry England.

'Roman coffins' sound improbable; but strange things had turned up around the churchyard and in the fields. And Stella Morland (née Pearce), writing 65 years later, commented that Lally had been 'away in Worcestershire when she wrote it staying with dear Tom (Mr Davis) and Amy, Mrs Giles. She was, you will see, a very sweet old lady, probably called terribly sentimental by the young folks of today°'

It was two years later that Lally wrote another description, this time of the five large tapestries which Page – who had an eye for antiques – had bought at a sale long ago and hung in what then became the Tapestry Room. This piece was concluded with the note: 'The Tapestry was sold and taken away on Saturday May 15th 1897'.

Someone who had missed the chance of buying the tapestries for himself was A. C. Benson*, a young man who knew the house. Humphrey, too, grieved over this sale for years afterwards, telling how a 'kind man' had come to the door and offered her £100 (in another version he says 'Ten golden sovereigns, my dear!'); and she, 'greatly pleased and astonished, never having seen so much hard cash', had accepted the offer. Amy Giles later heard of the sale of some similar-sounding Flemish tapestry in America for a very big sum. But perhaps the old lady had not been so very foolish: she may have been growing anxious about these fine hangings mouldering away in the damp and neglected Ruin.

*

Lally Smith was still playing a minor part in village affairs. When Queen Victoria's Diamond Jubilee was celebrated in 1897 with revelries and commemorative mugs (costing a penny each) presented to every child in the parish, she made her own gift: each child received a hand-embroidered bookmark.

*Later to become Master of Magdalene College

It was a village which had changed a good deal since her arrival in the 1850s.

Those 'labouring poor' now had a social life of their own. The new Headmaster and his wife, Mr & Mrs Houlton, as well as introducing a slightly more imaginative curriculum at the school, were running evening classes at which young men learned to mend boots or write business letters, and girls moved to more advanced sewing. These young people were even encouraged to speak in public.

Church and chapel vied with each other: the little Baptist chapel offered hearty congregational singing and temperance outings, while the Church Sunday School had their own 'treats' and the choir gave frequent concerts and went on great summer jaunts to Cromer (where, one year, a four-horse brake took them for a ride through the woods). The men of the village had regular entertainments, for the Reading Room was used for 'smoking concerts', with performances by their own String Band as well as comic readings given by the schoolmaster and others. The Mothers' Meetings (with music provided by Miss Smith and Mrs & Miss Pearce) supplied fun and friendship for the womenfolk. The cricket team were strong; and a photograph of (probably) the early 1890s shows young men with their bicycles – a means of escaping the confinement of village life. In August 1899 the Flower Show seems to have been combined with the usual village feast, for there were steam-horses, boat-swings, coconut shies and more. Altogether, the final years of the nineteenth century seem to have been rather more cheerful than the earlier ones.

The population of Grantchester had risen to more than a thousand, for terraces of houses were spreading along the streets around Newnham Croft. But that northern area of 'New Grantchester', which already had its own church, was to be severed from its parent and become the parish of Newnham in 1912.

In Old Grantchester, in the meantime, the church of SS. Andrew & Mary was receiving more improvements. The east window was given stained glass in May 1900, and the stonework of the tower was restored. Preaching at the service of thanksgiving after the completion of this work, the Archdeacon of Ely spoke of his own memories of the church over the past fifty years, and mentioned by name 'the saintly William Martin' and 'good Mr Widnall'.

Good Mr Widnall was to be recalled again later that year when the parish:

... received a valuable gift from Miss Smith in the shape of a plaster of Paris model of the Church and a portion of the Churchyard. It was made by the skilful hands of the late Mr Widnall.

This is the model, with all its detail ('including even such things as hassocks and books'), which Page had always intended to go to the church; and there for many years it was kept on display, with the roof taken off for visitors on payment of a few pence. Now, a century after its original presentation to the church, it is encased in a transparent showcase so that people may once again see exactly what the building was like before its enlargement in 1877.

*

Lally's brother Richard Smith-Carington enjoyed several happy years in his manor house at Ashby Folville where, as a newspaper obituary was to express it:

The pursuits of the ordinary country gentleman, farming and breeding of stock, leavened with the exercise of literary and antiquarian tastes, filled up much of [his time].

Lordship of the Manor entailed obligations, and both he and Bertie were eager to use their wealth in improvements to the village. The ancient church with the tombs of their ancestors was restored and given a full peal of bells, and would later be enriched with windows commemorating their own generations of the family.

A final portrait shows Richard, benign and bewhiskered, in scarlet uniform with sword and plumed helmet. He had become, in April 1900, High Sheriff of Leicestershire, the office held by his forebear Francis Smith of Wootten Wawen in 1565. It was the culmination of a great career. Patty was no longer there to share it, but Amy Giles, who had moved with her children to Ashby Folville in 1896, accompanied him on grand occasions and acted as hostess at the Manor.

On 4th January 1901 there was a particularly splendid event. Richard and his daughter 'went to Wedding of Miss Cassel and Mr Wilfred Ashley. Prince of Wales etc. at the reception at Sir Ernest Cassel's, 48 Grosvenor Square'.

But at home two days later, Richard's doctor found him 'very unwell'. Lally was staying at Ashby Folville at the time, and so travelled with him across to Manchester, where a celebrated surgeon, Mr Whitehead, was to operate. On the evening of the following day Queen Victoria died; and

25 *Jan*   Prince of Wales proclaimed King Edward VII. R.S.C. not out of Danger was represented by Under Sheriff at Leicester.

2 *Feb*   Humphrey went to London with his Volunteers and was in the funeral procession of Queen Victoria.

For Richard, unable to play a part in this drama, the glory of his office was cut short. It would have given him immense satisfaction to know that his son Herbert (Bertie), his grandson Francis and great-grandson John were also to serve as High Sheriffs.

A late example of Lally's writing, by now a little uneven but still strong and legible, is a letter written to 'My dearest Cousin' (Mary Sonstadt) on 24th January 1901 from Bertie's house in Manchester, telling about her brother's final illness. The tone of the letter and the details are typical. While knowing that Richard's condition was grave and an operation must be performed within a few days:

> In the meantime everything was done to cheer him, and as it were take him out of himself. We, by dear Lizzie's arrangement, went to the Pantomime, and to see a very pretty little play, and he also went to a Concert with Bertie, but the best thing of all was his own calm temperament & cheerful forbearance. Well, the dreaded day arrived...

And another letter, written by Mary Sonstadt to her brother George, takes up the story. She had joined the rest of the family at Manchester; but in three days Richard had died ('a great shock as the Dr considered the operation very successful'). She then went to Ashby Folville for the funeral and tells of the huge assembly of dignitaries from London, Worcester and Leicester, and the 'county gentlefolk'; and how 'the servants were always in tears. They said he was such a good Master'. It was a gathering of all the family with the exception of Alice, who was herself 'in a dangerously weak state'. Poor Mary felt, as only a distant relative, that she should creep away afterwards.

> They were all very kind to me. I wanted to leave when I found how

many were expected – (There were 19 bedrooms to prepare for those
who would stay the night)…

but Amy would not hear of it, and she stayed for several days.

＊

Lally, the last of her generation, returned to her rather humbler establishment at Grantchester. A glimpse of her is caught in a Parish Magazine report of a Mothers' Meeting that July:

> So warm was the weather that we ventured to have tea in the Vicarage
> garden, the tables when the repast was ended, giving place to the green
> sward for the accustomed games. These continued after dusk in the
> school, and all seemed much to enjoy the evening. Our pleasure was
> enhanced by Miss Vibert's presence accompanied by Miss Smith, whose
> piano accompaniment to 'Sir Roger de Coverley' has long been a feature
> of these gatherings.

So that small intrepid figure was still strumming her *rum te tum ti tiddely*…
at the age of eighty.

In this first year of the new century many changes were taking place in
Grantchester. Once in a while a new sound alerted those wandering in
the road to the arrival of a mechanical beast, a motor car, negotiating the
mill bridge and the successive bends uphill with gear-changing and
honks at each blind corner. And all the larger houses received new, and
interesting, occupants.

After the death of Professor Lumby in 1895 his wife and children left
the village, and in 1901 Merton House was bought by William Bateson.
He it was who, having recognized the importance of the experiments
recorded by Gregor Mendel many years before, developed the science of
genetics. This entailed making similar experiments of his own, which
were conducted in the Merton House garden, both with poultry in pens
and with 'row upon row of peas, poppies and lychnis'.

In the same year Riversdale was acquired by another scientist,
Richard Assheton, who also enlarged the building he had bought. Lally
may well have found this disturbing, for it resulted in a complete change
in the appearance of the house she had known all those years. Assheton
left none of the old square yellowish outer walls visible, enclosing them
in red brick and raising an extra storey with steep gables – producing an
altogether Edwardian-seeming house. There he incorporated his own
private laboratory; he kept rabbits in hutches outside the kitchen door;

and he also used Garner Cottage, down the road, for incubators – all for experiments in his own special subject, animal embryology.

After Mrs Nimmo's death the last of her family had left the Mill House, and were succeeded by the Rev. R. H. Kennett, a university lecturer in Hebrew. He soon transferred to Yew Garth, and in 1901 the Whitehead family settled into Mill House.

In the summer of 1903 'dear Tom' was at the Old Vicarage, having a holiday to build up his strength and dispel the 'rheumatism in [his] back' (probably a symptom of his tuberculosis). He was there on his own, and so wrote letters to 'My dearest little VERA', the elder child of his second marriage, now aged five. The first of these surviving letters was probably written in May, and is mostly about his delight in all the flowers and birds. He had found a bullfinch's nest with four eggs, 'the hen bird let me almost touch her before she went off'; there are goldfinches and larks and rabbits, 'I also watched a hare, a big one, hopping about among the barley'. He asks after his son Harold, now sixteen and no longer odious: 'several people have been asking after him and hope he is well. I miss the old boy when I am here, and wish he too could come with me after nests and things'. His other letter was written in August, when Harold was with him, enjoying the haunts of those earlier golden days with Uncle Page.

> We have got such a nice boat here on the river, it just holds three people, and we have a Canadian canoe for two but we all get in it and then it wobbles about and the water comes in sometimes if we wink our eyes° I think we have a John Otter in our garden but we never see him, he lives in his hole in the bank all day; we found a lovely otter's hole up the Brook – it was full of straw and warm leaves and was difficult to find or see until you were close under the willow tree...

He and Harold and Humphrey, now twenty-one, went a long way up the river, through yellow waterlilies, and caught fish. 'There are 8 white pigeons here and 12 white ducks... We have had honey to eat and gooseberries and apples...' An idyllic summer; but two years later Tom was dead.

After that, Vera herself was taken for a few visits to Aunt Lally. The impressions of a little girl, recollected in old age, are rather bizarre. She had slept 'in a four-post bed which was warmed with a warming-pan and got beastly cold'. Aunt Lally's doves 'used to walk on the dinner table and get in the gravy', and she remembered the rats (probably in the bathing-shed) – 'but Aunt L. said they were very clean eating animals'.

Poor Aunt L.! Things were not quite as they used to be. Her new neighbours at the Mill House were the Whiteheads;[*] and there, another child was fascinated by the eccentric old lady. In 1965 T. N. Whitehead recalled:

> She lived in a charming little house with a lovely garden separated from ours by a footpath. Her garden ran down to the river through a grove of horse-chestnut trees. This was the house subsequently occupied by the poet Rupert Brooke; but that was after our time. As young children my sister and I were occasionally invited to tea by Miss Smith, together with our governess. She – Miss Smith, not the governess – had yellowish white hair which hung down on each side of her face in old-fashioned ringlets like so many corkscrews. She was a great dear and very gentle with the young. Towards the end of her life she took to drinking her tea straight out of the teapot through the spout; everyone else was welcome to the tea too, poured out of the same pot…

A more pleasant impression, dated 1904, comes from a picture which turned up in a Cambridge auction room nearly a century later, when, after her death at ninety-three, some of Polly's – Mary C. Greene's – oils and watercolours were sold. This painting was of her own home, Harston House; and on the lawn in front a tea party is in progress. In the foreground a child moves eagerly towards a tiny old lady with white ringlets descending from her lace cap, instantly recognisable. Polly's own label to the picture confirms that this was Lally Smith, and from the date and the black dresses it is clear that the occasion was the family gathering after the death of Mrs Charlotte Greene.

Kind Mrs Pearce 'took a little responsibility for her – as she became rather childish towards the end and her maid, devoted in other ways – was rather a drinker and an anxiety' [Mrs Morland, née Pearce]. (Drinking, with beer at a penny a pint, was indulged too freely by many in the village, and the chapel folk were conspicuous by their abstention.)

---

[*]Alfred North Whitehead, philosopher and mathematician, later Professor at Harvard. It was during his years (c. 1901–9) in Grantchester that Bertrand Russell joined him in writing their *Principia Mathematica*.

Other neighbours, and the new Vicar, the Rev. M.J. Sutton, all kept a sympathetic eye on her.

It was in May 1906 that Lally had a slight stroke, and Amy Giles sent the nurse who was to stay with her. And it may have been that summer, or the next, that she was photographed in a Bath chair – a doll-like figure still delighting in Our Garden.

On 26 February 1908 the end came. Amy Giles was summoned by telegram but was too late to find her aunt conscious. Again it is the devoted Polly Greene who provides a final impression:

> She lived to be very old and yet was always cheery and ready to be pleased. When at the last her nurse took her up a few flowers she said – "How beautiful! How very beautiful!" and with beauty on her lips she died.

The long obituary in the Grantchester Parish Magazine makes clear her quite exceptional place in village life:

> Not a few, who in bygone years, had come under the influence of her considerable intellectual powers and accomplishments, and under the spell of her gentle nature, have themselves passed within the veil; but others survive who can bear testimony to what they owe to her influence and guidance in earlier years, the ever-ready sympathy and willingness to help as far as lay in her power in good works for God and for her fellow-men...

Relatives and friends, some coming from afar, gathered at the graveside together with 'a large attendance of parishioners of all classes' and the surpliced choir singing 'Peace, perfect Peace'. She was buried in the Widnall vault at the east end of the church. The large slate memorial panel on the wall above commemorating Samuel Widnall, his wife Elizabeth, his sister Hannah, Elizabeth 'beloved wife' and Samuel Page Widnall had barely two inches left at its base. There the name of Lally Smith was added.

[CHAPTER 29]

After

THE OLD VICARAGE and its contents had, through Page's will, been intended to go after Lally's death to Tom Davis. But Tom had already died, and so the property came to Amy Giles. She, living far away and already in failing health, could not undertake to move to Grantchester, and her son Humphrey's future was unsure. And so in September 1908 the Old Vicarage was let, furnished, to Mr & Mrs Neave.

The Neaves, as tenants, made little effort to smarten-up the place. When they took in a lodger, the young King's graduate Rupert Brooke, he found an enchantment in the neglected garden. He had at first been happy with the Stevensons at The Orchard next door; but, needing to concentrate on the dissertation on the playwright Webster which was to earn him his college fellowship, in May 1911 he took rooms – a bedroom and sittingroom connected by the staircase at the north end of the house – at the Old Vicarage. Here he wrote:

> This is a deserted, lonely, dank, ruined, overgrown, gloomy, lovely house: with a garden to match ... It is a fit place to write my kind of poetry in.

and here he absorbed the charmed atmosphere without, it seems, becoming aware that less than a generation before it had all been humming with creative activity. The decaying romantic Folly was by now scarcely visible through its shroud of ivy, so he never thought of it as Samuel Page Widnall's busy workplace, his Castle Ruin.

Similarly, when Humphrey Giles, on his honeymoon in July 1914, called with his bride to choose some furniture from the house, and 'found there was an undergrad [*sic*] named Rupert Brooke occupying my mother's bedroom as a bedsitter!' that name meant nothing to him.

Mrs Giles had put all her Grantchester property – the Old Vicarage, Yew Garth, Ivy Dene and The Orchard – up for sale in May 1914; but the Neaves stayed on. Humphrey and his bride took away a few pieces of furniture, and afterwards regretted not having claimed more. More than sixty years later he wrote:

> We have still here the Jacobean chest from the Drawing Room and the
> Mirror over the Mantlepiece and Buhl clock and 3 cushioned chairs,
> and Lamp standard from 4 post bed, and black leather seated Dining
> Room chairs, and a few other things°. I also have on the mantlepiece
> here a penknife which was always on the mantlepiece in the Drawing
> Room at the O.V.... Uncle Page used to collect the best goose feathers
> and make all pens with it.

But his honeymoon ended abruptly on 3rd August 1914 when he, a Volunteer, was called to service in the Army and was to be away for five years.

Rupert Brooke, too, enlisted; saw some brief, fierce fighting in Belgium; and then in April 1915, *en route* for Gallipoli, developed septicaemia and died. Fittingly for a classics scholar, he was buried on Skyros.

After the Great War the Old Vicarage was for sale once more. Mrs Brooke, who had lost two children before the war and now both remaining sons on active service, bought the house and, as she felt Rupert would have wished, gave it to his great friend Dudley Ward.

In the meantime the little boy who lived around the corner at Ivy Dene was peeping inside Page's old workrooms. In old age he, George Rogers, would recall:

> Round about 1918 I was, with permission of the then occupier – Mr
> H.R. Neave (a carpenter employed by Negus) playing with my friends
> – the Pedleys (whose father was foreman at Nutter's Mill) – in the "Old

Ruin" in the Old Vicarage garden. In a small room we found hundreds of photographic plates that were of little interest to us but I must confess I took away a brass plate (approx 12" x 8") inscribed "S. Widnall, Photographer" and which I kept for many years.

By the time Dudley Ward's family moved into the Old Vicarage and investigated, only shattered glass was left. The few printable photographic plates had survived by being taken by the gardener and stored in his own shed; which is where they lay neglected for another sixty years.

Mr Ward's unexpected acquisition presented problems. The house needed major renovation, and the Ruin was indeed a ruin, all overgrown – 'part had collapsed, the lower floors were frequently flooded from the river and the upper floors were unsafe' (George Rogers). Across the road, though, in a small house* converted from two old cottages, lived a young architect, H. C. Hughes. As it turned out, Hughes was just the right man to make sympathetic improvements to the Old Vicarage. Over the following years he was to restore a number of the village's old houses and design most of the new ones.

As the Wards settled into the village they heard stories about old Aunt Lally – accompanied by a twiddling of fingers beside the face to indicate her old-fashioned ringlets – and knew that it was her 'brother' who had made their sundial and fountain and the Ruin itself.

So in the 1950s Peter Ward, himself now married and in charge of the Old Vicarage, set about tracing those elderly people – Humphrey and Phyllis Giles, Mrs Morland and Miss Mary (Polly) Greene†, who might have memories and even photographs and journals. The resulting collection of 'Widnalliana' is not large but it contains riches: glimpses of life in a not-quite-conventional Victorian household in a more-than-usually-interesting village society.

Mrs Morland was to lament that after occupation by the Neaves and the alterations made by Mr Hughes, 'the Cranford or Jane Austen like character of the Old Vicarage as I remember it is lost for ever' But she (née Stella Pearce), having arrived so late on the scene – she was born c.1890 – could not realize that Aunt Lally, the sweet old lady with the shawl, the lace cap and ringlets, had in her time shown a good deal more spirit than the spinster ladies of *Cranford*. She too had been obliged to

---

*Garner Cottage

†referred to disparagingly by her nephew Graham Greene in his *A Sort of Life* as 'dear muddle-headed Polly who lived at Harston and painted bad pictures and taught Gwen Raverat to draw and wrote ambitious plays for the village institute...'

make do with 'elegant economy'. But compared with theirs, her experience throughout a long life had been wonderfully broad: this little person had climbed Snowdon, swum in the icy Cam and from the Ladies' Rocks of Jersey, celebrated her seventieth birthday by picnicking on an offshore island; had travelled on the Continent, seen the Duke of Wellington ride his horse in Rotten Row; was a keen botanist; had acted, sung, written lively journals; and had given generations of children a wonderfully full and painless schooling.

And as for Uncle Page, what had he *not* done?

POLLY'S POEM

Mary (Polly) Greene had been a pupil of Lally's, living in the house across the road from the Old Vicarage. She was the most constant of disciples. As a professional artist living at Harston, some three miles away from Grantchester, she continued to visit Page and Lally to the end of their lives. Her landscape paintings of the countryside around Cambridge were accomplished; more importantly, she – perhaps influenced by Page Widnall's enthusiasm for recording places undergoing dramatic change – set down in watercolour those tumbledown courtyards and streets of old Cambridge, now lost, and the disappearing cottages of her own village. These are preserved in the city's Folk Museum and the Cambridgeshire Collection.

She never married. When herself an old lady in the 1950s (by the end, in her nineties, both deaf and blind in one eye), she sent this poem to Peter Ward. It is modelled on Rupert Brooke's nostalgic The Old Vicarage, Grantchester, *and celebrates her happy memories of the place. The third section gives an authentic picture of the Widnall household in its golden years.*

GRANTCHESTER

All Grantchester is magic ground;
Bright spirits beat the parish bound.
Houses, trees, fields they overlook
From Barton Road to far Bourne brook.
The Manor is not theirs alone,
The farm and e'en the church they own.
Though fire has burnt the dear old Mill
They laugh around the mill stream still.
They get the British king to move
His mighty limbs and walk Ball's Grove.
They take a little elfin boat
And row all round Ball's dried up moat.
Alas! His ancient grove is felled,
By modern folk his dun is held.
If haunt he must he has to stalk
Along a flowery garden walk.

That Orchard there is Pixies' ground,
They dance the apple trees around.
Unseen by those who there partake
Of bread and butter, jam and cake.
Pass through yon gate and you will stand
Within the bounds of Fancy's land.
For in that garden some could tell
Of haunted dusk and moonlight spell
And know who props those ancient walls
"The falling house that never falls".
Hear Memory's voice which sweet and low
Can call back those who loved it so.

The moonlight forms from shrubs and boughs
The portly form and lofty brows
Broad and benign of that child-man
Who worked the garden to his plan.
With smile serene he seems to stand
Bidding Romance enflower his land.
Thatched arbours, sundial, mystic wells,
Castles half ruined, bridges, dells.
Fantastic art and craft he wrought
To make the wonderworld he sought.
A lady comes tall, grave and sweet
With moonlit peacocks at her feet,
They peck at shadowy grain then fly
To the long roof with echoing cry.
And see her sister, still she seems
The godmother of childrens' dreams.
She feeds white doves when moons are bright.
Her curls seem made of silver light,
That rainbow in the fountain's fall
Looks like her silken flowery shawl.
Who sits and writes beneath the pines?
'Tis Clifford making nonsense rhymes,
For Euclid's science here would seem
Unfitted for this home of dream.
Hark! From within those castle rooms

Phantom applause at evening comes;
Here is rehearsed on mimic sands
A part well played in desert lands.
Palmer! The spirits still have power
Thus to bring back your happiest hour.

What youth stands godlike 'gainst the shade
By the stone dial old hands have made?
Ah, Rupert Brooke, we miss your voice
Here in the village of your choice.
Speak! Speak once more! Throw one more spell
Over the place you loved so well.
Great lover turn! Sing us more lays
As once before in far off days.
You sigh as loath to go so soon
Yet fade as fades the setting moon.
The wind gets up, the branches stir,
You wave farewell to Grantchester.
Ah, not for long! Still are you dear.
Your very ghost is welcome here!

Mary Greene

1*st* *passage: The parish of Grantchester, with its Manor and Church, had recently lost two of its notable places: the 'dear old Mill' had burnt down in 1928, and a grove of trees on a slope bordering the Meadows had been cleared for the building of a large house. The house, Balls Grove, stands above a great lawn, beneath which willow trees rise from a deep ditch or moat. This area has ancient mysteries – fertile ground for legends about 'Ball'.*

2*nd* *passage: The Orchard was planted by Page Widnall, but after his death became a popular meeting-place for university people and other visitors as The Orchard Tearoom. Tea and other meals can still be taken there; and the association with Rupert Brooke and the Bloomsbury Group is celebrated still.*

3*rd* *passage: This is the best of all descriptions of 'that child-man' Widnall and his household, together with two figures who made a deep impression on the children who had their schooling there.*

W.K. Clifford was a brilliant young undergraduate, and later Fellow, at the time when he was frequently at the Old Vicarage – 'distinguished for his vivacity and quaint humour' as well as the profundity and clarity of mind which later took him to the Chair of Applied Mathematics at University

College, London. In spite of the early death from tuberculosis which cut short his advanced mathematical and philosophical insights, 'Clifford Algebra' remains the essential foundation to modern scientific developments such as computers and space exploration.

Edward Palmer was an even more colourful figure, a linguist, explorer, conjuror, acrobat, who became Lord Almoner's Professor of Arabic and married the Widnalls' niece Laura Davis. Polly Greene remembered his performance, dressed in oriental robes, in Page's Castle Theatre. Palmer's life ended tragically: shot by Bedouin in the desert in Egypt.

Final section: Rupert Brooke, who came to Grantchester as a lodger at The Orchard, and then settled to study in rooms in the Old Vicarage, acquired general fame in the early years of the Great War for his war sonnets and early death. Among his collected poems, the most popular is his nostalgic piece about the Old Vicarage.

Appendix I

A good deal of Sarah Page's earlier story is revealed in legal documents: wills, deeds of conveyance and a marriage by special licence. More is hinted at in Gunning's Reminiscences of Cambridge, *in his anecdotes about Samuel Peck. Henry Gunning, Fellow of Christ's and Esquire Bedell, who himself had lived for some years in Grantchester, tells how one of Peck's fellow dons at Trinity, Dr Scale, had a curious experience when returning from London to Cambridge by coach (the* Fly*).*

> When Scale arrived at Gray's Inn Lane, he found Peck and two ladies already seated, who appeared to be entire strangers to each other. At Epping Place the passengers stopped to breakfast, when Peck suggested that the ladies ought not to be allowed to pay any share, which Scale immediately agreed to. The coach then proceeded to Chesterford, where the expense of dinner was shared by the gentlemen, the ladies signifiying by their approving smiles that they had a due sense of the liberality of their companions. On arriving at Trumpington, the coachman pulled up, and Peck's man was in waiting to convey *the party* to Grantchester. These *ladies were, in fact,* Peck's housekeeper and housemaid, who had for some years lived with him in a very equivocal capacity.

Sarah Freeman was that housekeeper; and when Peck died in 1791 she received a generous legacy. Various documents reveal that later Benjamin Howard, himself one of the principal farmers, helped her to invest and consolidate her own holdings in Grantchester. He arranged the sale of Peck's land at East Barnet, and he took part in a double or triple transaction which resulted in the purchase of a large estate of freeland in 1792 by Sarah Freeman for £1,250. There were further transactions between them on the eve of her marriage in 1794; and that marriage took place by special licence, with Benjamin Howard one of the two witnesses. The bridegroom was Thomas Page of Madingley – very probably connected to Benjamin Howard, whose own wife was Ann Page.

In due course Sarah Page, dying childless, left her property to her brother John Freeman, a farmer. It soon passed on his death to his wife Elizabeth; and on her death in 1848 much of it came to her grandson Samuel Page Widnall. It must all have amounted to a very useful provision for the life he was to lead.

*

Appendix II

TERRIFIC THUNDER AND HAIL STORM,
At GRANTCHESTER NURSERY,
NEAR CAMBRIDGE

The ninth day of August, 1843, will be long remembered here for one of the most awful visitations of Providence recollected by the oldest person living.

In the afternoon of that memorable day, vivid flashes of Lightning were seen and distant peals of Thunder heard approaching for some time previous to half-past four o'clock, when an intense darkness came over; at about a quarter before five the storm commenced raging with impetuous fury, and the inhabitants were horror-stricken with the roaring of the descending Hail, or rather showers of Ice, equalling the loudness of the Thunder and resembling reports from the discharges of vollies [*sic*] of the largest artillery. The pieces of Ice that fell measured generally from four to six inches in circumference, and in some instances extended to double that size. It continued in this manner for upwards of a quarter of an hour, and as it became less furious and gradually died away, curiosity naturally drew the workmen from their shelter: then was seen the work of destruction, all those fine and beautiful specimens of choice and valuable Plants, that but a few minutes before shone in gaudy splendour, were now become a complete wreck; upwards of 5,000 square feet of glass were shivered to atoms; and the young and tender Plants of rare varieties in the stoves, hothouses, and frames were driven into the soil, mingling with the ruins of broken pots and glass: the greatest portion of them were totally destroyed. But here does not end the extensive loss of Mr. S. Widnall. The Crops on his Farm, which, previous to the above catastrophe were in excellent condition, are now in a ruinous state. His fields of Turnips and Mangel-Wurzel are stripped of their foliage and buried in the soil. The Wheat, Barley, and Oats are laid prostrate on the earth, and the greater half of the grain literally thrashed from the air. His individual loss is estimated to be not less than £1,000.

It may also be stated that on the 17th of May last, a flood of water inundated the lands of S.W., which caused the severe loss then of £150, by destroying a field of excellent potatoes, and the produce of meadows, pastures, &c.

*

Appendix III

From the Cambridge Chronicle, 23rd November 1844

INCENDIARY FIRE AT GRANTCHESTER

On Wednesday night, about half-past eleven o'clock, the inhabitants of this town were aroused by an alarm of fire, which was stated to have broken out on the premises of Mr. Frederick Lilley, farmer, of Grantchester. This report unfortunately proved true, and in a brief space of time, the Sun, the Phoenix, the Essex Economic, and Norwich engines were at the scene of the calamity, but even on their arrival the fire had attained such strength that nothing could be done except to attempt to preserve the property which the conflagration had not then reached. The fire was confined to the buildings in the farm-yard, from which the dwelling-house is separated by a garden, and is situated on the south-east side of the yard. This yard contained a large barn, in which were the produce of 15 acres of oats and 13 acres of peas, a patent horse-power chaff-cutting machine, a clod crusher, and a number of agricultural implements. A few yards from the barn stood a chaff-house and two stacks of corn. The eastern side was occupied by a long range of cattle shed, &c. It was in one of these sheds that the fire originated. A fact may here be stated with respect to the origin of the fire which allows some hope that it was accidental: - A cow which was sick occupied one of the sheds, and about 9 o'clock one of the farm servants went with a lantern to give the cow some physic. It is possible that during this operation some sparks might have dropped among the straw and caused the calamity we have to record. It is, however, affirmed by others that the fire originated in the roof of these sheds, and that it was communicated from the churchyard, on the wall of which the thatched roof of the sheds abutted. Shortly after twelve o'clock the fire had attained a fearful height, involving in complete destruction the whole of the property we have described in the farm-yard. At this time the scene presented was one of the most painful interest and excitement. The immense crowds which had congregated from Cambridge and the adjacent villages, surrounded the burning area, some on stacks extinguishing the fire which was blown from the burning property in flakes, others were amidst the crashing of beams and the fall of timbers, attempting to pull down the brick walls of the buildings. Hundreds were engaged in working the engines, among whom the undergraduates of the University, as usual, figured conspicuously.

They kept up a constant supply at the pumps, and worked in other ways with the greatest industry and earnestness. Fortunately the supply of water was very plentiful, there being large ponds in the yard. The wind blew due west, which was a most fortunate incident, for, had it been otherwise, nothing could have saved the whole range of stabling, and another very extensive barn on the road-side of the farm yard, and very probably Mr. S. Widnall's premises and Mr. Lilley's dwelling-house would have fallen a sacrifice to the flames. All the horses were happily saved: the sick cow before-mentioned, three or four calves, and several pigs were, however, burnt. The contents of the barns and other buildings were all destroyed, but, by the efforts of the people, the fire was prevented from extending further than we have described. Mr. Lilley's garden and premises suffered much damage from the crowds of people and the working of the engines. At one time the flames threatened to destroy the parish Church, but, fortunately, the fire was subdued before that edifice was injured. The picturesque church-yard, however, suffered materially; the shrubs being all either burnt or otherwise destroyed. By four o'clock all danger was over, and the engines had but to play on black smoking masses. On enquiry we learnt that Mr. Lilley estimated the damage at about £2,000, but this was but a very rough guess. We were told a tale of a man who had visited the farm in the course of the day with some books to sell, and who being refused assistance, threatened Mrs. Lilley "to make her remember it", and said she had no right to keep dogs which had barked at him. But little importance can, however, be attached to this incident as respects the origin of the fire. Mr. Lilley, we are happy to say, is well insured in the Sun and Phoenix offices. The premises are, we believe, only partly insured in the Norwich office; they are the property of King's College, and leased to Mr. Hamilton White, solicitor, of this town, Mr. Lilley being under-tenant.

*

Appendix IV

In September 1972, *judges making their assessment for the Best Kept Village competition were scathing in their criticism of Grantchester:* 'the world-renowned village is but a shadow of what it was'. *Their scorn for its* 'scruffiness' *was expressed, inevitably, in a parody of Rupert Brooke's poem.*

> In Grantchester, in Grantchester! –
> Some, it may be, can get in touch
> With unkempt gardens, graves and such;
> And village judges must have seen
> The weeds a-peeping through the green,
> And shabby, up-turned litter bins
> *And sconces made from old cake tins:*
> The "best kept" judges say this shows
> An English parish comatose.

*

Appendix V

Advertisement, 15*th June* 1867

The Grantchester Folding Form

THIS FORM or BENCH is admirably adapted for Concert, Lecture,
   or School-room, as they can be packed away when not required in
   such a small space that 20 of them (being sufficient to seat more
   than 100 persons), when folded and laid in a pile, are not more than
   4 feet high. It is a comfortable Seat with a Back; is strong, firm
   and light; 8 ft in length, stained and varnished. Price 20s each.
Agents for Cambridge: E. Headly and Son, corn Exchange Street, &
   Mr J. Piggott, 20 Sidney Street,
From whom further particulars may be obtained; also of the Inventor
   and Patentee,
   SAM. P. WIDNALL,
   GRANTCHESTER, CAMBRIDGE.

*

Appendix VI

In about 1980 *George Rogers, a builder, wrote the following piece describing the construction of a typical cottage in Grantchester, the village in which his long life had been spent.*

BUILDING A COUNTRY COTTAGE

Top or vegetable soil would have to be removed and shallow trenches dug for the walls and chimney foundations. To provide a solid bottom for these hardcore, stone, chalk, ballast or suitable old building material would be rammed in to a fairly level surface.

Bricks were generally made locally. Soft red ones were used for chimney stacks, harder for walls and well-burnt for paving bricks of varying sizes. Bricks were laid in sand and lime mortar.

The chimney stacks were built first with the fireplace opening over which a heavy hardwood lintel was built in. The foundation walls (2 or 3 courses) were built on the external foundations.

The main wall plates were of hardwood in straight lengths adzed or split to regular standard sections. Bedded on the brick walls and running through the doorways as thresholds, they were often morticed to receive the vertical studwork.

Timber for the studwork and braces was cut from suitable trees – rarely barked and only lightly adzed to give an outer surface for the laths. The roof plates at front and back were usually of lighter material.

Diagonal braces were fixed between the wall plates and the corner posts which could be of softwood about 6ins square. The vertical studs were fitted to the braces and fixed to the plates with blacksmith-made spikes. He also made brackets to secure wall plates and corner posts. Door and window openings were formed in the timber frame where required.

The "wattle" or laths consisted of trees or branches to be split for the purpose or from trimmings split from the constructional timbers. Lengths 4ft to 5ft, widths 1in to 4ins. Nailed to the outer woodwork spaced to form a plaster key.

The "daub" or plaster was made of clay and short straw mixed with shovel to a workable consistency. Applied with a wooden float to the outer face of the building, to an even surface probably in two coats. The amount passing through the spaces in the "wattle" would be smoothed off by a second man between the studs, etc, for interior finish.

Reasonably straight timbers were selected for the rafters though not usually barked or adzed. These were in pairs with the feet nailed or pinned with wood pegs to the roof plates on opposite sides of the building. The tops were fitted together and spaced with a ridge board. The thatch was supported by reeds, osiers or similar which was tied to the rafters with twine.

The roof was thatched with long straw or reeds. The overhanging eaves and gable ends protected the wall plaster. Extra thickness at the ridge tied both roofs together. The space between rafters was plastered as between studwork below.

Where an upper floor was required a heavy timber beam was built into the chimney above the fireplace lintel and the other end supported by the outer wall studs. Floor joists were fixed from the beam to the outer wall.

Tree trunks were sawn into boards over saw pits by vertical saws. Boards were sawn by hand to standard widths and planed where necessary. Timber for joinery was cut and planed to required sizes. Doors were in wide boards, ledged and braced and hung on gate-type hinges. Linings were used for both windows and doors with an architrave to cover between lining and plaster. Windows were made with two sashes, one fixed and one sliding. Panes were small as glass was expensive.

Wide boards were used for bedroom flooring. A staircase was provided in the corner of the ground floor, constructed of wide treads and risers housed into wall strings and a corner post to form a spiral staircase. A door was hung at the foot of the stairs and to a cupboard under stairs.

The ground floor was originally earth or clay, but later thin paving bricks were laid on sand, giving a sound but uneven surface.

The exterior wall surfaces were treated frequently to liberal coats of limewash (ground lime and water) which formed a weatherproof surface.

Doors, windows and other joinery were heavily painted but the bedroom supporting beam was generally stained.

Inside, housewives covered the timber framing and plaster between with coats of whitewash as part of the springcleaning (also the ceiling joists and underside of the bedroom floorboards). When cheap wallpaper became available this was used to cover timber and plaster.

Drainage was not provided but any nearby ditch could be a substitute. Household water and rubbish were thrown on the garden or on the "dungle" as it was known locally.

The lavatory was a small shed built at the bottom of the garden over a pit. A wooden box seat with cover and door were installed. The pit was covered with a slab at the back from where it had to be emptied with a long handled scoop. Bucket type lavatories were installed much later.

*

Appendix VII

From S. P. Widnall's *History of Grantchester*

There lived at Grantchester for some years during the latter part of the [18th] century, an eccentric person resided at Grantchester, the Rev. Samuel Peck, one of the senior Fellows of Trinity College.

... A photographic reproduction is here given of an old coloured print representing Mr. Peck, his Man, Pony, and Dog, entitled "The Triumphal entry of a PECK loaf into Grantchester."

The man who is riding on a pillion behind his master holding on tight by his coat, has a peck loaf on his head, and on his arm a basket, containing a couple of fowls, a bottle containing Trinity audit ale, (as appears from the lable) and a pair of stays for his housekeeper. At the back some one has written a curious and fanciful epitaph:

> Here lies a PECK as some Men say,
> Was first of all a PECK of Clay;
> This wrought with skill divine while fresh,
> Became a curious PECK of Flesh.
> Full sixty years PECK felt life's bubbles,
> Till Death relieved a PECK of troubles;
> And then he Died as all things must,
> And here he lies a PECK of Dust.

*

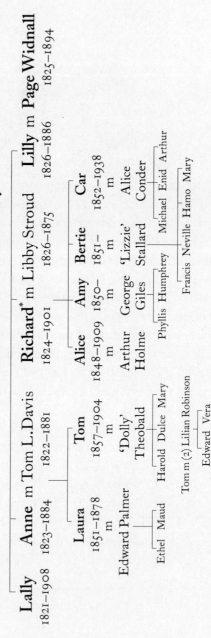

THE SMITH(-CARINGTON) FAMILY

Sir Thomas Smith of Charley, co. Leics
1578–1646

Robert Smith (3rd son of 2nd wife) – Nottingham

William Smith + 2nd wife
1699–1795

Richard Smith (3rd son) – Notts
1748–1810

Richard Smith m **Ann Hanbury**

Lally | **Anne** m Tom L. Davis | **Richard*** m **Libby Stroud** | **Lilly** m **Page Widnall**
1821–1908 | 1823–1884 | 1822–1881 | 1824–1901 | 1826–1875 | 1826–1886 | 1825–1894

Laura | **Tom**
1851–1878 | 1857–1904
m | m

Edward Palmer | 'Dolly' Theobald | Harold Dulce Mary
Ethel Maud

Tom m (2) Lilian Robinson
Edward Vera

Alice | **Amy** | **Bertie** | **Car**
1848–1909 | 1850– | 1851– | 1852–1938
m | m | m | m

Arthur George | 'Lizzie' | Alice
Holme Giles | Stallard | Conder

Phyllis Humphrey | Michael Enid Arthur

Francis Neville Hamo Mary

The principal figures in this book are marked by bold type, and given with their informal names, as they appear in Uncle Page's Book. Their proper names are: 'Lally' – Sarah; 'Lilly' – Elizabeth; 'Amy' – Emily; 'Bertie' – Herbert; 'Car' – Richard Carington.
**Richard's second marriage was to Patty Leader-Williams (1841–1894).*

THE WIDNALL-FREEMAN FAMILY

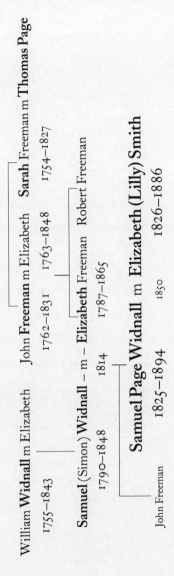

William **Widnall** m Elizabeth   John **Freeman** m Elizabeth   **Sarah** Freeman m **Thomas Page**
1755–1843   1762–1831   1763–1848   1754–1827

       Samuel (Simon) **Widnall** – m – **Elizabeth** Freeman   Robert Freeman
       1790–1848   1814   1787–1865

            Samuel Page Widnall m **Elizabeth (Lilly) Smith**
            1825–1894   1850   1826–1886

John Freeman

Samuel Widnall is recorded in the marriage register as 'Simon Widnall of Wellingore, Lincs'.
His sister Hannah (1793–1866) came to live in Grantchester; and there were five or more children of that family.

Although never mentioned in SPW's reminiscences, the baptism (11.11.1818) of an earlier child, John,
is recorded in the parish register of Wellingore. He must have died in infancy.

John and Sarah Freeman had several brothers and sisters.

Robert Freeman was a wheelwright in their native village of Little Abington.
Of his many children, only Sarah (Tofts) and Elizabeth (Clark) are named in Uncle Page's Book.

Index of Selected Names and Subjects

Bold type indicates illustrations